Women and War in the Middle East

Women and War in the Middle East

TRANSNATIONAL PERSPECTIVES

Edited by Nadje Al-Ali and Nicola Pratt

Zed Books

LONDON & NEW YORK

Women and War in the Middle East: Transnational Perspectives was first published in 2009 by Zed Books Ltd, 7 Cynthia Street, London N1 9JF, UK, and Room 400, 175 Fifth Avenue, New York, NY 10010, USA

www.zedbooks.co.uk

Designed and typeset in Monotype Joanna
by illuminati, Grosmont, www.illuminatibooks.co.uk
Cover design by Lucy Morton at illuminati
Cover photograph: 'To Eat Bread' by Sama Alshaibi
Index by John Barker
Printed and bound in Great Britain by the MPG Books Group

Distributed in the USA exclusively by Palgrave Macmillan, a division of St Martin's Press, LLC, 175 Fifth Avenue, New York, NY 10010, USA

A catalogue record for this book is available from the British Library
Library of Congress Cataloging in Publication Data available

ISBN 978 1 84813 185 9 Hb
ISBN 978 1 84813 186 6 Pb
ISBN 978 1 84813 187 3 Eb

Contents

Acknowledgements

We would like to take the opportunity to thank all those who made this book possible.

First of all, we thank the Mediterranean Programme of the Robert Schuman Centre for Advanced Studies at the European University Institute, which organized the Eighth Mediterranean Social and Political Research Meeting at Montecatini Terme, 21–25 March 2007, and hosted the workshop from which this book emerged. The workshop enabled us to invite scholars from a range of disciplines who are interested in the gendered and transnational dimensions of war, conflict, 'post'-conflict transitions, reconstruction and peace-building in the context of the Middle East. While we were unable to include all workshop participants in this volume, we would like to express our deep gratitude to everyone for their contributions, papers and the stimulating discussions throughout our workshop.

We are obviously very much indebted to all the contributors of this book, who trusted us to put together this volume and who generously and patiently worked on revisions to their chapters, often to tight deadlines.

In terms of our own contribution to this book, we would like to thank the British Academy who funded our project, 'Women, Gender and the Political Transition in Iraq', and enabled us to conduct research in Amman, Detroit, Erbil, Sulaimaniya, London, San Diego, and Washington DC, in the years between 2004 and 2007. We would like to thank all the Iraqi women and other interviewees who generously gave us their time and shared their insights.

We are also grateful to the feminist scholars who have inspired our work, many of whom are cited here. In particular, we thank Cynthia Cockburn, Cynthia Enloe, Deniz Kandiyoti, V. Spike Peterson and Nira Yuval-Davis, whose writings have helped us a lot to think through many of the issues addressed in this book and who have also provided crucial support and mentoring.

Finally, we would like to thank our publisher, Zed Books, for their support and faith in us and this project, as well as their patience. We are particularly grateful to our commissioning editors Ellen Hallsworth and Tamsine O'Riordan.

INTRODUCTION

Women and War in the Middle East:
Transnational Perspectives

Nadje Al-Ali and Nicola Pratt

For many people in Europe and North America, the Middle East represents an area of danger and disorder – popularly characterized as a site of wars, poverty, despotic governments and an absence of women's rights. It is seen as a source of migrants and violent extremist groups and, consequently, as a threat to the security and stability of the West. These fears, often echoing the European characterizations of the Orient that legitimized colonial domination (Said, 1978), have been amplified in the wake of 9/11 and the Madrid and London transport bombings. Security concerns, in addition to the region's huge oil and gas wealth, have made the Middle East a strategic priority for North American and European governments, paving the way for a number of interventions under the banner of 'peace and security' but with differential and often devastating impacts for the well-being of people in the region. These include support for the creation and continued existence of Israel; arming Western allies, such as the Gulf and Jordanian monarchies, the former Iranian Shah, Saddam Hussein during the 1980s and the Egyptian government since the 1970s; and, most recently, the US-led 'regime change' in

Iraq. Whilst Western interventions have contributed to creating and sustaining conflicts (Hinnebusch, 2003: 154), simultaneously Western diplomacy has also aimed at bringing peace and reconciliation – notably, by promoting peace negotiations between Israel and the Palestinians and post-conflict reconstruction in Iraq.

Whilst Middle East armed conflicts are often perceived by Western politicians as a threat to their own countries' security, it is people within the Middle East who have borne the major burden of war and conflict. In addition to decades of conflict between Israel and the Palestinians, as well as Iraq's numerous wars, brutal dictatorship and thirteen years of international sanctions, other Middle East conflicts include several wars between Israel and its neighbours (1948, 1956, 1967, 1973, 1982 and 2006), wars in Lebanon (1975–90), Algeria (1991–2000) and Yemen (1994), low-intensity conflict between the Egyptian government and armed Islamists, and state violence against ethnic minorities, such as Kurdish nationalists in Turkey, Iraq, Syria and Iran. The large Middle East diaspora around the world is an indicator of the instability caused by various wars, incidents of violence and political persecutions. Whilst the majority of those killed or injured are men, war and conflict have had a largely negative effect on women's lives, as they struggle to maintain households and keep families together in a context of limited basic services, lack of social safety nets, restricted income-generation activities and dismantling of social networks. More recently, and since the passage of UN Security Council Resolution 1325 on mainstreaming gender issues in conflict, the international community has given attention to the impact of war and conflict on women and the role of women in peace-building and conflict resolution, often providing funds for the empowerment of women in the context of wars, post-conflict reconstruction and migration.

Western interests and interventions in the Middle East, together with the increasing international recognition of women's particular experiences of war, post-conflict reconstruction and peace build-ing, demonstrate not only the links between the international and the personal but also the gendered dimensions of international security practices and agendas (among others, Enloe, 2001; Tickner 1992). In addition, such events and processes illustrate the transnational dimensions of wars, conflict, post-conflict reconstruction and peace-building, which link Western governments, Middle East governments, inter-governmental organizations, international NGOs, transnational social movements, migrant communities, Middle East NGOs and other public actors in different configurations that go beyond traditional inter-state dealings.

Against this background, this volume[1] represents a critical examination of the nature of the relationship between gender and transnationalism in the context of war, peace-building and post-conflict reconstruction with respect to the Middle East. We consider the ways in which a variety of actors, including women's movements, diaspora communities, national governments, non-governmental actors and multilateral bodies act transnationally to shape (either intentionally or unintentionally) the experiences of women in conflict situations, the possibilities for women's participation in peace-building and post-conflict reconstruction, as well as long-term prospects for peace and security. In particular, the volume pays attention to the ways in which gender roles, relations and identities are constructed, negotiated and employed within transnational social/political fields in the context of 'post'-conflict – with particular consequences for women. Contributions focus on the two countries with the longest experience of wars and conflict in the Middle East and that have experienced the most prominent international intervention: the Occupied Palestinian Territories and the military invasion and ongoing occupation of Iraq.

In particular, this volume seeks to answer the following questions:

• How do interventions by Western governments, multilateral bodies and non-governmental actors, among others, in the context of 'post'-conflict in the Middle East, influence gender roles/relations/identities?
• What is the impact of transnational feminism/women's solidarity

movements on women's empowerment within situations of 'post'-conflict?

• What is the implication of transnational interventions that mainstream gender in conflict, post-conflict reconstruction and peace-building for peace and security in the Middle East?

• What is the impact of transnational feminism/women's solidarity movements on conflict resolution, peace-building and post-conflict reconstruction processes?

• What alliances are forged and which strategies pursued by transnational actors?

• What sort of (transnational) feminist politics can/should be constructed in contexts of conflict and peace-building?

Rather than presenting a coherent theoretical framework, we use this introduction to highlight a number of theoretical, methodological, conceptual and political issues related to debates around conflict, post-conflict reconstruction, peace-building and the role of transnational actors. This book's major concern is to explore the significance of gender in understanding processes related to conflict, reconstruction and peace-building. It is our overall argument that we have to move beyond a simple 'add women and stir' approach, and to gender our perspectives and approaches to include power relationships and structures as well as shifting notions of femininity and masculinity.

Transnational feminisms

The original impetus for this book came from our experiences of involvement in the UK anti-war movements against the US-led invasion and occupation of Iraq and the Israeli occupation of Palestine, as well as participation in UK branches of transnational women's peace movements. The process of constructing transnational solidarity with people living under occupation, whilst ensuring that such solidarity is supportive of women, who are often particularly disadvantaged by conflict, is an exercise in applying our commitment to transnational feminism.

Transnational feminism is not a new phenomenon but it constitutes a contemporary paradigm. The term implicitly differentiates itself from international conceptions of feminism, or rather feminisms. International feminism has existed for a long time and links were established among women's movements in various countries in the early part of the twentieth century (Moghadam, 2005a). Examples are the International Women's Council, the Women's International League for Peace and Freedom, the Women's International Democratic Federation, and the International Federation of Business and Professional Women (Moghadam, 2005a). However, transnational feminism suggests a conscious crossing of national boundaries and implies a shift from the nationally oriented second-wave feminisms and the clashes between 'Western' and 'Third World feminists' characterizing many of the debates during the third wave in the 1970s and 1980s (e.g. Mohanty, 1991). It entails going beyond the false universalism of some Western feminisms to consider the particular experiences of those women on the margins of the global political economy, 'allow[ing] for a more concrete and expansive vision of universal justice' (Mohanty, 2002: 510). The emergence of transnational feminism may be linked to specific historical developments, as Moghadam (2005b) argues:

> During the decade of the 1980s, a shift began to take place. In the socio-demographic context of a worldwide growth in the population of educated, employed, mobile, and politically-aware women, feminist discourses and networking began to spread and to take on not only an inter-national but a transnational form. The new information technologies, along with the changing and increasingly harsh economic environment and the emergence of fundamentalist movements, broadened the horizons of women's organizations, resulting in considerable international networking and many joint initiatives. Feminists from the North came to appreciate the relevance of economic conditions and foreign policies to women's lives, while feminists from the South came to recognize the pertinence of 'body politics'. The Nairobi conference in 1985 seems to have been the turning point, and several transnational feminist networks were established around the time of the conference.

Transnational feminists not only work across borders but often pursue an 'intersectional analysis', recognizing that women's oppression and struggles are constituted by a wide array of structural inequalities linked to gender, race, class, sexual orientation, as well as nationality. As black, post-colonial and post-structuralist feminists have argued, 'woman' and 'gender' are not unitary categories and do not represent some 'essence' that is shared among women across time and space (Carby, 1982; Butler, 1990; Mohanty, 1991). Indeed, categories such as 'gender', 'sexuality', 'class', 'race', 'ethnicity', 'nationality' are always constructed, reproduced and resisted through intersections with one another and, as this volume illustrates, transnationally. The intersectionality of identities and its challenge to the unitary category of 'woman' has presented particular challenges to feminist solidarity – whether within or across national boundaries. We concur with Wenona Giles and Jennifer Hyndman, who state:

> By employing a transnational rather than an international approach, we aim to destabilize the centrality of the nation-state as the principal unit of inquiry into relations of conflict and to highlight dimensions of power that traverse an array of borders, including political boundaries, cultural or national identity markers, and class fractions. (2004b: 313–14)

It is useful to distinguish analytically between 'transnationalism from above' and 'transnationalism from below' when exploring feminist networks and campaigns. The United Nations, social-democratic governments in the North and wealthy private foundations have played an important role in facilitating interaction and cooperation between feminist organizations in different countries (Keck and Sikkink, 1998) – what may be considered 'transnationalism from above'. As Isis Nusair discusses in this volume, the policy of gender mainstreaming by the European Union and United Nations in the context of conflict and peace-building has opened up new opportunities for feminist organizing in the Middle East. In the South, many feminist/women's non-governmental organizations (NGOs) rely on external funding sources in order to maintain their activities at the grassroots as well as to participate in 'transnationalism from below'. However, as demonstrated by work on women's NGOs in the context of Egypt (Al-Ali, 2003) and Palestine and other Arab countries (Jad, 2004), and as Shahrzad Mojab and Sophie Richter-Devroe show in their contributions to this volume with respect to Iraqi-Kurdish and Palestinian women's organizations, respectively, external funding has contributed to the processes of professionalization and bureaucratization as well as producing new debates in Middle East countries over 'authenticity', 'independence', 'neocolonialism' and the social and political role of NGOs. Mojab argues that not only are many Iraqi-Kurdish women's NGOs, like their counterparts in other parts of the world, characterized by 'their short-term, piecemeal agenda; their failure to engage in long-term planning; their elite and non-grassroots leadership; their role as alternatives to women's movements and as agents of depoliticization and control' but they also fail to confront the national and colonial patriarchies that are inextricably linked in the context of the US occupation of Iraq. Similarly, Richter-Devroe argues that Palestinian women's NGOs funded by foreign donors are divorced from grassroots struggles against Israeli occupation and, therefore, are irrelevant to many Palestinian women.

Some theorists claim that a refusal to speak for or to offer solutions to women of the South is intrinsic to transnational feminism. We would argue that it is also necessary to emphasize that transnational feminist networks are not spaces devoid of power relations. Access to transnational networks represents an important resource in and of itself. In practice, the voices of some feminist activists in the South may become marginalized within transnational networks in favour of other activists – both North and South – due to unequal resources, political pressures, language, and so forth. This is particularly the case where countries are experiencing war and occupation, such as in Iraq and Palestine, and where indiscriminate violence, conservative gender ideologies, limits to personal freedoms under the banner of 'security' concerns and the political-strategic concerns of the most powerful actors may restrict the voices of women activists in conflict zones. Isis Nusair demonstrates in this volume how Arab women activists mobilize on the national and regional levels, rather than the transnational, due to structural obstacles. Moreover, transnational feminist solidarity may be severely hampered by cleavages among women activists in conflict zones on the basis of religious and/or ethnic associations, class origins and/or political affiliations.

Negotiating a transnational politics that challenges gender inequalities in the context of conflict is fraught with difficulties. As Sophie Richter-Devroe's chapter highlights, the feminist anti-national stance employed by certain externally funded conflict-resolution projects risks alienating the majority of Palestinian women who are supportive of the Palestinian national movement. Transnational feminism needs to be supportive of Palestinian national self-determination, first of all, if it is to have any relevance to the majority of Palestinian women. Another major challenge, as Isis Nusair explains, is the political dilemma of rescuing the positive dimensions of gender mainstreaming without falling into the trap of technocratic jargon that leaves intact neoliberal and neoconservative policies, military interventions and militarized peace processes.

Gendering violence, conflict and war

Gender is a structural feature that pervades all aspects of domestic and national lives; furthermore, as V. Spike Peterson has stressed: 'gender is a structural feature of the terrain we call world politics … [a] pervasive ordering principle' (1998: 42). Gender not only denotes the social and cultural construction of what it means to be a woman and a man; it also refers to relationships characterized by power differences. The concept of gender points to processes in which hierarchies are established, reproduced and challenged. Common to a wide range of feminist gender analyses is the view that the differentiation and relative positioning of women and men constitute an important ordering principle that 'is seen to shape the dynamics of every site of human interaction, from the household to the international arena' (Cockburn, 1999: 3).

Feminist scholars of international relations have problematized those concepts and categories that have previously been taken as self-evident in the mainstream study of war and conflict – including the state, sovereignty and security – in order to identify 'the complex ways in which gender is deeply implicated in the carving out of political spaces, the construction of identities and the demarcation of the boundaries of community in practices of "state-making"' (Steans 2006: 38), as well as discourses of national sovereignty and security (e.g. Enloe, 1983, 1990; Peterson, 1992). The 'gendering' of international relations enables us to consider interactions beyond those of statesmen and politicians, to include those of 'nonstate, antistate and trans-state actors' (Peterson and Runyan, 1993: 113) and the differential impact on women and men of global processes, such as economic restructuring, war and migration (among others, Enloe, 1990, Marchand and Runyan, 2000; Rai, 2002; Tickner, 1992; Peterson, 2003). V. Spike Peterson's contribution to this book, for example, illustrates how 'gendered divisions of authority, labour, and power structure [informal war economies in Iraq] and effectively reproduce a hierarchy that devalorizes women and feminized concerns'.

Instead of thinking about armed conflict and warfare as isolated instances of violence, feminist scholars and activists have alerted us to the 'continuum of violence':

> a gender analysis suggests that it is meaningless to make a sharp
> distinction between peace and war, prewar, and postwar. ...
> Gender is manifest in the violence that flows through all of them
> and in the peace processes that may be present at all moments too.
> To consider one moment in this flux in the absence of the next is
> arbitrary. (Cockburn, 2004: 43)

Similarly, Johan Galtung argues that conflict is much more than the outbreak of open hostilities and violence: 'There is also the violence frozen into structures, and the culture that legitimizes violence' (1996: viii). Violence exists whenever the potential development of an individual or group is held back by conditions of the nature of a relationship and, in particular, by the uneven distribution of power and resources (Kelly, 2000). As Cynthia Cockburn argues, Galtung's

concept of 'structural violence' has gendered dimensions and implications (Cockburn, 2004: 30). The concept of intersectionality discussed
above alerts us to how structural inequalities are (re)produced
through gender relations, roles and identities.

Men and women are positioned differently in societies prior to,
during and after conflict and are affected differently by war and conflict. According to some analysts, all such violence should be situated
within a 'sexual violence approach' (Jacobs et al. 2000: 2) even where
no overtly sexual act is involved. In this interpretation, a whole set
of violent acts is subsumed under a broad definition of male sexual
violence: 'Violence which takes place in the home or the workplace
and on the street corner; violence involving racism, homophobia,
xenophobia and other prejudices; violence on international and global
levels including trafficking in women and women's experiences of
war violence' (Corrin, 1996: 1).

However, we concur with the view of other authors that this
approach essentializes men and masculinities as well as women and
femininities, whilst glossing over the multiple causes of violence,
which are not simply rooted in male sexuality. Iraqi and Palestinian
men are not perpetrators of various forms of political, ethnic and
domestic violence because of their sexual drives or frustrations and
testosterone levels. Nor are they culturally hard-wired to be violent,
as many Islamophobic and racist commentators may like us to believe.
Rather, brutal occupations, states of lawlessness, economic crises, unemployment and political corruption, among other factors, may shape
the intersection of different identities, rooted in class, nationality,
religion, as well as gender, to give rise to various forms of violence
among men. This is not to deny the continuum of violence – that is,
the relationships between forms of violence within the home, on the
street and within society at large and the violence occurring during
pre-conflict, conflict and post-conflict situations (Cockburn, 2004).
But it is important to recognize the complex causes of violence, and
acknowledge that men and women can both be active agents in
perpetrating and resisting violence (Moser and Clark, 2001). In both
cases presented here, Iraq and Palestine, men are not only perpetra-

tors but also the main victims of the violence associated with the occupation, the various militias and tensions between communities and political parties. Nevertheless, women and men experience violence differentially because of the ways in which femininity and masculinity are constructed. The potential of violence against women may operate to push women back into the home whilst women who experience actual violence may be too scared to admit it due to the repercussions for their 'reputation', leading possibly to their killing at the hands of their own male relatives, who claim to be protecting 'family honour' (e.g. Human Rights Watch, 2003).

Sexual humiliation and mutilation, forced prostitution, rape and forced pregnancy are among the gender-specific violence that occurs during wars. Historically, rape has certainly been the most widespread form of gender-specific violence. It can occur as a random act within the context of general lawlessness, anarchy, chaos and aggression. However, rape has also been used systematically as a deliberate weapon of war and means of torture to inflict maximum harm (Seifert, 1994). Rape is not only used to attack and humiliate the 'enemy woman', but through her to attack her supposedly male protectors. As symbols of a nation's 'honour and pride', or ethnic markers in nationalist ideology (Meznaric, 1994), the act of raping a community's womenfolk traumatizes and violates women individually and also humiliates and attacks the whole community.

Yet when men are raped or sexually abused and humiliated, as also happens during wartime, these acts are also gendered. Aside from the individual abuse, it is the enemy's masculinity and ability to protect the nation that are under attack. These acts of aggression and humiliation are particularly devastating in societies where sexuality is strictly channelled through heterosexual marriage and all other forms of sexuality considered taboo and associated with shame. This is not specific to 'Muslim culture/religion': it is not only Iraqi men in Abu Ghraib prison who experienced severe humiliation and a sense of emasculation at the hands of US soldiers inflicting sexual abuse. Across 'cultures', men who experience rape and sexual abuse also suffer from trauma – although the symptoms may be expressed differently.

Moreover, as Ronit Lentin (1997) argues, women are not homo-geneously powerless and are not always victims. We need the political and analytical space to conceptualize women as benefactors, support-ers or even perpetrators of violence. As our chapter on Iraq describes, Iraqi women in the diaspora played an important role in lobbying for US military action against Iraq. In addition, women in various parts of the world have joined guerrilla armies, militias and militaries, and there have been several cases of women suicide bombers in the Israel/Palestine conflict as well as in Iraq since 2003. Simultaneously, we also need to theorize and explain women's and men's agency with respect to peace initiatives and resistance to patriarchal gender ideologies and relations (Cockburn, 1999).

When violence and conflict erupt, women and men tend to suffer in gender-specific ways. Men often continue to be the major decision-makers, politicians, generals, 'leaders' and the militia members/soldiers involved in 'making war'. As a result, certain types of men – namely, soldiers/members of militias – constitute the vast numbers of the casualties of war. However, increasingly, wars are fought on the home front (Giles and Hyndman, 2004a). In Iraq, Algeria, Israel/Palestine and Bosnia-Herzegovina, for example, marketplaces, bridges, water supplies, houses and shelters have been bombed. The casualties of these wars are predominantly civilians, among them women and children. Women and children often make up the majority of refugees and internally displaced who are fleeing the violence. Whether they stay under bombardment or flee the sites of violence, it is often left to women, almost universally viewed as the primary carers and nurturers, to ensure the day-to-day survival of their families.

Diaspora mobilization

As mentioned above, wars and conflicts in the Middle East have created diaspora communities around the globe.[2] Members of diasporas are not only victims of war. By engaging in economic, social, cultural and political activities that span national boundaries, members of diasporas might contribute to accelerating or prolonging war and conflict, as well as creating new possibilities and opportunities for peacemaking and reconstruction. For example, our chapter discusses the role played by Iraqi diaspora women in garnering US support for the toppling of Saddam Hussein. Simultaneously, many Iraqis in the UK and USA were part of the anti-war movement that opposed the invasion of Iraq. In the Palestinian context, diaspora business-men contribute to post-conflict reconstruction through establishing charitable foundations, such as the Welfare Association. Although transnational links between migrants and their countries of origin have always existed,[3] the nature and quality of these ties have under-gone significant changes in time, being shaped by the restructuring of the global economy and the transformation of processes of capital accumulation, as well as by the expansion and broader access to new technologies of travel and information (Al-Ali and Koser, 2002; Glick Schiller, 1999; Vertovec, 1999, 2001). However, limited attention has been paid to the various ways transnational fields and activities are gendered – that is, the various ways women and men in the diaspora are positioned differently in terms of prevailing gender ideologies and relations within the country of residence and the country of origin. In order to grasp the gender dimensions significant for the political mobilization of diasporas, it is important to explore predisposing conditions prior to the outbreak of armed conflict and war, during 'hot conflict' and in its aftermath.

Throughout the process of diaspora formation, from the moment of flight, including a possible stay in a refugee camp, through the journey to the 'host country' and until the process of settling within a new country, gender constitutes one of the factors structuring agency and mobilization. In the process of forced migration, social structures and institutions are unravelled or undergo significant changes. This might make women even more vulnerable to poverty and violence and increase their dependency on male refugees, or it might open up new spaces as women and men are forced to give up previously accepted norms, modes of behaviour, divisions of labour and responsibilities (Al-Ali, 2007b). Nevertheless, it is extremely difficult to generalize about the gendered dimensions of what happens in circumstances of war and migration. This is because different refugees have differential economic resources and access to power, encounter different conditions and are informed by varying cultural and social norms. The question of increased vulnerability or empowerment depends on access to legal and civil rights as well as available infrastructure in the place of settlement (Al-Ali, 2007b). The conditions for being involved in transnational social fields and activities or moving transnationally are not always available to women in particular diaspora contexts, or are limited or framed within a set of normative and cultural gendered rules in the place of residence.

The gendered concept of citizenship as well as gender norms in the country of origin may also impact upon diaspora mobilization in the country of residence. For example, as Riina Isotalo discusses in her contribution to this book, Palestinian women, predominantly through their kinship practices, play a crucial role in maintaining 'connectivity' between Palestinians, who are dispersed globally. Yet Palestinian citizenship is being conceived in a way that privileges expatriate capitalists, who are predominantly men.

The potential for political mobilization of women is greater in situations where livelihood and survival are not the predominant concern. This is often the case for members in diasporas who are settling in 'developed' countries where there is some basic provision of housing, health care, income support, and so forth. Countries with active and diverse women's movements might also be more conducive to the political mobilization of diaspora women than countries in which women-specific activism is marginalized or suppressed (Al-Ali, 2007b).

Gender ideologies and cultural norms might enable women in the diaspora to engage with women from different ethnic and/or religious backgrounds or political convictions with greater ease than their menfolk or than 'back home'. This has certainly been the case among the Iraqi diaspora women and men interviewed for our chapter. As women are often perceived to be less significant for

INTRODUCTION   15

political processes, their transgression of 'talking to the other side'
may appear less threatening than if men were to do it. Women may
be more willing to build bridges and mobilize as women, rather
than in terms of their ethnic and religious affiliation or political
parties. Partly, this may be the result of being physically removed
from the conflict and needing to build a new life. On the other
hand, divisions associated with a conflict may be reproduced even
more rigidly in the diaspora, particularly in countries such as the
USA, where ethnic and religious identity politics are prominent in
public life. Again, it is important to stress that gender is only one
among many differentiating factors within a diaspora, others being
class, ethnic and religious background, political affiliation, place of
origin and the specific experience of conflict.

   Those who have had traumatic experiences of violence might have
a very different emotional and political attitude towards conflict than
those who did not experience violence directly. And it could go in
both directions: experience of violence might radicalize a person
and create militant supporters of armed struggle, or it might create
people who abhor violence and promote peace. While this holds
true for men and women alike, there are certain indications and
possible predisposing conditions in societies prior to the outbreak
of conflict that might shape the way men and women react and act
during conflict and in the aftermath (Al-Ali, 2007b).

Gendering post-conflict

The gendered nature of nationalist ideologies and national and
state processes is key to understanding the gender-specific ways in
which violence and conflict impact upon women and men (Giles
and Hyndman, 2004) and shape their ability to participate in peace-
building, conflict resolution, post-conflict reconstruction and other
political processes. Gender roles may become 're-traditionalized' as
a result of conflict. As the biological and cultural reproducers of the
community, women's bodies and identities become the battlefields
for both sides of the conflict (Al-Ali, 2007b; Peteet, 1991; Sharoni,

1995; Yuval-Davis, 1997: 66–7). Meanwhile, men are frequently equated with the worlds of arms and glory, and are enjoined to be the 'protectors' of their 'womenandchildren' (Enloe, 1993: 166). The growth of such gender ideologies during conflict situations may pave the way for introducing new notions of citizenship, based on gender difference, in post-conflict contexts, as Martina Kamp illustrates here with regard to the Iraqi constitution of 2005.

On the other hand, war may open up opportunities for transforming gender roles and relations (Meintjes et al., 2001; Sharoni, 1995). Women may become workers, heads of households, community leaders and political activists in the absence of male relatives and/or exceptional circumstances, as Sophie Richter-Devroe and Riina Isotalo describe in the case of Palestine. Simultaneously, men may reject the 'hegemonic', militarized notions of masculinity, opening spaces for peace and reconciliation (Connell, 1995, 2002). However, in post-war contexts, women often experience a backlash as 'traditional' gender roles inside or outside the home are evoked by various political actors. It often seems as if the challenges posed to traditional gender ideologies and roles during times of war become too great for patriarchal societies to accept in peace. As a result, women often have less political space to secure their rights and to contribute to political processes in the aftermath of conflict. According to Pankhurst,

> The ideological rhetoric is often about 'restoring' or 'returning' to something associated with the *status quo* before the war, even if the change actually undermines women's rights and places women in a situation that is even more disadvantageous than it was in the past. This is often accompanied by imagery of the culturally specific equivalent of the woman as 'beautiful soul', strongly associating women with cultural notions of 'tradition', motherhood, and peace. (2004: 19)

This tendency is felt by Palestinian and Iraqi women who are experiencing selective, and often conservative, constructions of gender roles, relations and identities in the context of political and military competition among different actors and ongoing occupations and resistance, as Isis Nusair, Riina Isotalo and the editors demonstrate in our respective chapters here.

Peace for women does not mean the cessation of armed conflict. Women's security needs are not necessarily met in 'post-conflict' situations, as gender-based violence still remains rampant even after 'formal hostilities' have ended (Gervais, 2004). Cynthia Enloe's definition of peace is 'women's achievement of control over their lives' (Enloe, 1988: 538). Peace, as defined by Enloe, would require not just the absence of armed and gender conflict at home, locally and abroad, but also the absence of poverty and other 'structural inequalities' and the conditions which create these (Kelly, 2000: 48).

Yet, violence against women is often endemic in post-war situations, partly due to the general state of anarchy and chaos, but also as an element of heightened aggression and militarization, and of prevailing constructions of masculinity promoted during conflict. Both Palestine and Iraq are examples, par excellence, of the increase in violence on all levels as a result of the ongoing occupations and militarization of societies, lawlessness and significant role played by local and national militias. Indeed, in the Iraqi context, the level of everyday violence experienced is even greater now than during the period of formal military intervention. Meanwhile, Palestinians are suffering greater violence and deprivation than before the Oslo Peace Accords of 1993. These are clearly examples of countries experiencing acute conflict and war as opposed to post-conflict situations, despite their designation as such by international donors. Indeed, several of the contributions to this volume question the designation of Iraq and Palestine as 'post'-conflict.

Women and gender in formal reconstruction/peace-building processes

In many conflict and post-conflict settings, women have been sidelined or marginalized from formal peace initiatives, political transitions and reconstruction efforts. Historically, women rarely sustain wartime gains in peacetime. Societies neither defend the spaces women create during struggle nor acknowledge the ingenious ways in which women bear new and additional responsibilities. Formal peace negotiations among warring parties and their mediators serve to define basic power relations and to identify priorities for immediate post-war political activity (Sørensen, 1998). Traditional militarized gender regimes tend to endow men with the power in politics and locate women's importance within the family (Cockburn and Hubic, 2002). However, women within conflict-ridden societies as well as within diasporic communities find ways to work for peace and reconciliation through grassroots activism. Women from all walks of life participate in this informal peace-building work, but their activities are often disparaged as 'volunteer', 'charitable' or 'social', even when they have a political impact (Ferris, in Sørensen, 1998).

Despite UN Resolution 1325, passed in October 2000, stating the importance of the inclusion of women and mainstreaming gender into all aspects of post-conflict resolution and peace operations, the reality of post-conflict situations is often quite different. If at all, UN Resolution 1325 is frequently translated into adding a few women into governments and ministries. However, the mainstreaming of gender would not only involve the appointment of women to (interim) governments, ministries and various official bodies, and the allocation of resources to 'women's issues' and women's organizations, but also be a systematic attempt to eradicate the intersectionality of 'structural inequalities' at the national, regional and transnational levels, as Riina Isotalo and Isis Nusair argue in respect of the Palestinian context. In addition, as Sophie Richer-Devroe shows in her contribution, also focusing on Palestine, feminist transnational peace-building initiatives can only be successful if they incorporate the locally significant politics of opposing and resisting the occupation.

The cases of Iraq and Palestine draw attention to the need for reconstruction processes to ensure security for all individuals to live in dignity. This entails not necessarily the promotion of women's participation per se, as a means of peace-building and conflict resolution, but rather the redefining of security, away from the deployment of militaries and security services towards the fair distribution of resources to enable people's access to livelihoods and to ensure political and social justice, regardless of nationality, gender, class, ethnicity/race and religion. As feminist scholars and activists have observed, the fate of women is often indicative of the fate of whole societies. With regard to Iraq, war, occupation and political transition involved the establishment of new hierarchies of power along axes of gender, class, religion and ethnicity (Al-Ali and Pratt, Mojab and Peterson, in this volume). The emergence of new structural inequalities, alongside the reproduction of old inequalities, has fuelled the violence in Iraq and dramatically narrowed the spaces available for women's activism. This is despite the attempts of various women and men to establish a post-Saddam Hussein order based on peace and justice.

Indeed, UN Resolution 1325 may not only ignore the 'bigger picture' of reconstruction and political transition. It may provoke a backlash against the idea of women's rights and women's participation. In some post-conflict settings, the insistence by the UN, other international agencies and foreign governments on the inclusion of women may be perceived or presented by certain political actors as part of a 'Western plot' to undermine a society's 'traditional' culture and values. This is seen particularly in contexts of US-led military intervention, such as in Afghanistan and Iraq. In the Palestinian context, a depoliticized gender and conflict-resolution approach, as Richter-Devroe argues, is also seen by most Palestinians as a foreign ploy aiming to fragment and weaken resistance to the Israeli occupation. Paradoxically, people who might otherwise be sympathetic to issues pertaining to women's rights and women's equality could express strong opposition to women's inclusion in post-conflict reconstruction if this is presented as one of the aims of the occupying powers. Threats to sovereignty posed by foreign interventions may lead to intensified attempts among some actors to affirm an 'authentic' national identity that is different from the West (Pratt, 2007a: 201). Gender relations are central to processes of national differentiation, and local political actors often instrumentalize women by promoting conservative gender ideologies, relations and roles in their struggle to assert their authority within emerging political, economic and social institutions, as both Martina Kamp and the editors describe in relation to Iraq.

Gender mainstreaming in peace and security

The international community, including specific national govern-ments, have increasingly supported the idea of 'gender mainstream-ing' in post-conflict reconstruction and peace-building as stated in UN Resolution 1325/2000. However, a stated commitment to promoting women's participation does not guarantee that women are empowered to participate. Indeed, the case of Iraq demonstrates that gender concerns may be sacrificed to 'greater priorities' – namely, security and the political agendas of different actors, as we discuss in our chapter. It is necessary to examine how and when gender-sensitive policies are pursued in post-conflict situations and with what results for women and for men.

Just as women may be instrumentalized by political actors within 'post'-conflict countries, so they are by external actors. In previous times, the situation of women in colonized countries was held up as one of the justifications for colonial intervention. In India, the British abolished sati – the Hindu practice of widow-sacrifice. In North Africa, the French attempted to ban the veil. Indigenous practices were regarded as representative of the 'barbaric ways' in which colonized men treated their women. As the post-colonial critic Gayatri Spivak notes, colonial intervention was presented as a process of 'white men saving brown women from brown men' (Spivak, 1988: 93).

The US interventions in Afghanistan and Iraq have similarly identified the need to 'liberate' women from the barbaric practices of the Taliban and the regime of Saddam Hussein, respectively. Simultaneously, women have been promoted as the 'heroines' of the reconstruction of post-Taliban and post-Saddam Hussein societies. US concern for women implicitly justifies its military intervention in these countries. Moreover, the US administration utilizes the discourse of liberating 'brown women from brown men' to assert its global moral leadership and to differentiate 'the West' from 'the rest'. In this way, the USA co-opts its allies and defines its enemies in international relations (Pratt, 2007b). Yet, as we argue in our chapter, the degree to which this rhetorical support is translated into actual support for women's involvement in reconstruction is brought into question by the US pursuit of its 'national strategic interests' in these countries. In the case of Iraq, US support for its local political allies has operated to encourage the fragmentation of the state and political authority (Herring and Rangwala, 2006) in ways that undermine women's participation and women's rights (Al-Ali and Pratt, 2009). In this sense, the promotion of women's participation in peace-building and reconstruction may merely constitute a form of 'embedded feminism' that operates to camouflage the real and damaging consequences of larger international processes of empire-building (Hunt, 2007).

Most significantly in the context of the so-called war on terror, women's and human rights are being severely compromised by foreign military interventions, the 'internationalization' of reconstruction and state-building, as well as the instrumentalization of development and humanitarian aid as tools of global security (see Isotalo in this volume; Kandiyoti, 2007). Feminist activism within the UN framework has been discredited by the inability of the UN to uphold international law and even in some instances by its rubber-stamping of illegal operations. Women's rights and gender mainstreaming have become part of transferable packages driven not only by women's rights but by neoliberal international organizations and foreign government agendas (Kandiyoti, 2007).

'Post-conflict' political processes and reconstruction are severely curtailed by US occupation, escalating violence and increasing sectarian and/or ethnic conflicts in Afghanistan and Iraq (Kandiyoti, 2007; Al-Ali and Pratt, 2009) as well as continued Israeli occupation and the absence of a Palestinian sovereign state (Isotalo and Nusair in this volume). Due to the nature of intervention in these places, Islam has become one of the main markers of 'authentic identity' and resistance to foreign occupation. Democracy imposed from outside has inadvertently consolidated and possibly even legitimized social forces that oppose women's equal rights and participation in public life in Afghanistan and Iraq (Kandiyoti, 2007). The fact that neoliberal institutions as well as governments have adopted women's rights as part of their technocratic approaches to good governance presents a huge problem to transnational feminist activists in terms of alliances, funding and strategies.

Structure of the book

The chapters that follow are grouped into three sections: 'Gendering the Neoliberal Imperial Project'; 'Revisiting Transnational Women's Activism in the Context of Conflict, Post-conflict Reconstruction and Peace-building'; and 'Gender, Citizenship and Post-conflict Reconstruction'. Each of these three sections includes chapters that address a major area of findings with regards to the initial questions posed by our workshop and this volume: Part I, the role of global processes related to US empire-building and neoliberalism in restructuring gender relations and defining women's agency; Part II, the scope of women's agency in post/conflict contexts; and Part III, the reconfiguration of gender relations as part of 'post'-conflict reconstruction. Running through all of the contributions is the consideration of the transnational dimensions of these processes.

Following this introduction, Part I begins with V. Spike Peterson's 'Gendering Informal Economies in Iraq'. Her chapter focuses on the gendered informal economies produced in the context of war and reconstruction in Iraq. The increasing significance of informal economies is a function of the neoliberal project. This chapter pays particular attention to the 'coping economy' – in which individuals and families engage in order to ensure their everyday survival and where gender relations are especially visible. In addition, military objectives motivate individuals and groups to participate in 'combat economies' that fund and facilitate insurgent activities. As regulatory mechanisms break down, profit motives generate 'criminal economies' that are gendered and transnational. While these economies overlap and interact, they entail distinctive sets of actors, motivations and activities. Peterson's chapter offers a preliminary attempt to 'map' these economies and indicate how they are gendered.

Our own co-authored contribution, 'The United States, the Iraqi Women's Diaspora and Women's "Empowerment" in Iraq', examines the implications of the US occupation of Iraq and the US administration's promotion of women's 'empowerment' for gender identities inside Iraq, on the one hand, and for the transnational mobilization of Iraqi women in support of women's rights in Iraq, on the other. US rhetoric about the 'liberation of Iraqi women' created opportunities for some Iraqi women to become active in establishing NGOs and participating in political processes. In particular, diaspora women played an important role in both legitimizing the US invasion and in establishing initiatives in post-Saddam Hussein Iraq to empower women. However, US measures to reconstruct the Iraqi state have empowered ethnic and sectarian political leaders, and their associated militias, thereby hardening national/cultural differences within Iraq and between Iraq and the 'West'. The reconstruction of ethnic, religious and national identities has operated to marginalize women within the political process and to create often violent contestations over gender identities. These notions of gender identities impose new restrictions on women's mobility and are sometimes reproduced within the women's movement, both inside Iraq and transnationally, consequently presenting new obstacles to women's participation in the 'new' Iraq.

The last chapter in Part I, '"Post-war Reconstruction", Imperialism and Kurdish Women's NGOs', is written by Shahrzad Mojab. She critically explores the reconstruction projects in Iraqi Kurdistan, prior to and after the invasion of 2003, focusing on the activities of women's NGOs as helping the USA and its allies in furthering the new imperialist project in the region. Since the end of the Gulf War of 1991, Kurdish women have participated in a state-building project initiated within the 'Safe Haven' region of northern Iraq. Challenging neoliberal approaches to reconstruction, Mojab explores the significance of foreign funding of women's NGOs in creating a new economic and political elite, depoliticizing the women's movement and further marginalizing the poor.

Isis Nusair's assessment of the role of feminist and women's groups in local, regional and transnational advocacy and organizing in the Middle East introduces Part II. Nusair examines the strategies used and the challenges faced by feminist and women's groups in the Middle East. On the one hand, the gender mainstreaming agendas of the United Nations and European Union have opened up new spaces for feminist and women's groups to lobby for their rights. On the other hand, Nusair argues, the local remains the site for action for women's and feminist groups as a result of structural conditions and limitations imposed on their work through the intersection of local, regional and transnational economic and political structures of power that keep women absent from decision-making processes. This contribution demonstrates the need for effective networking between women's groups in order to make the links between the budgetary and gendered socio-political implications of the Iraq and Israel–Palestine conflicts, on the one hand, and gender hierarchies within Middle East countries, on the other.

In Chapter 5, Sophie Richter-Devroe provides an in-depth examination of post-Oslo (particularly post-2000) Palestinian women's activism. She compares, on the one hand, participation in joint Palestinian–Israeli women's dialogical conflict resolution – what is mostly referred to as 'people-to-people' or 'conflict resolution' projects among Palestinians – to, on the other hand, participation in non-violent resistance to Israeli occupation. The former is often supported through foreign funding to Palestinian NGOs, whilst the latter is mainly based on grassroots activism and informal networks. She argues that certain women's people-to-people dialogue projects risk working with an 'upside-down' version of the feminist slogan 'the personal is political', starting from the personal and risking ignoring wider structural and political root causes of the conflict. In contrast, women's non-violent resistance activism recognizes the significance of the political for determining material conditions

on the ground, thus targeting the political reality of the occupation directly. The author concludes that international concerns to
promote strategic gender interests as part of conflict resolution
processes are largely irrelevant to grassroots Palestinian women's
mobilization, for they fail to address the political agenda of resisting
the occupation.

In Part III of the book, Martina Kamp's chapter on 'Fragmented
Citizenship: Communalism, Ethnicity and Gender in Iraq' examines
the reconstruction of Iraqi citizenship since the collapse of the Ba'th
regime in 2003, focusing on the drafting of the constitution in 2005.
This chapter explores the policies of the internal and external actors
involved in the constitution-drafting process and demonstrates how
relationships between state power and the subject have been defined
in terms of the intersection of ethnic, religious and/or communal
affiliation and gender. Taking up the notion that gender relations
are a vital field for conflict and compromise in power bargains
(Kandiyoti, 1991; Thompson 2000), Kamp analyses how questions of
ethnic autonomy and the role of religious and communal ideologies
are intertwined with a redefinition of gender relations in the context
of internationalized reconstruction processes. She argues that, in
spite of gender equality policies laid down in the constitution, the
emerging Iraqi citizenship strengthens the patriarchal privileges of
ethnic, religious and social communities. This patriarchal privilege is
established not only between different communal leaders within the
nation-state but also transnationally in relation to the United States,
as the major occupying power.

In Chapter 7, 'Gendered Palestinian Citizenship: Women, Legal
Pluralism and Post-conflict Aid', Riina Isotalo examines gendered
contestations over Palestinian citizenship. While the Palestinian
women's movement lobbied to add a gender perspective into the
legal system, international donors introduced 'gender mainstreaming'
selectively into Palestinian legal spaces focusing on aid and security
concerns. Meanwhile, Isotalo shows how the circumstances related to
the occupation and the geopolitical fragmentation of Palestinian communities have encouraged certain 'alternative' and often traditional

legal practices. Palestinian women's connective transborder practices create community cohesion despite the increasing legal pluralism and diverse legal statuses of communities. Isotalo concludes that 'it is not sufficient to simply analyse legal systems or citizenship as autonomous institutions (as legal scholars tend to do) or to limit attention to specific problems (as is characteristic of development thinking or human rights organisations)' in addressing the contradictions between women's rights and legal pluralism in a transitional context.

Finally, we conclude this book with a joint chapter that not only brings together the findings of each of the chapters but also reflects on the issues and questions raised in this introduction. In this Conclusion, we attempt to present new ways of theorizing and problematizing the links between gender and transnationalism in the context of war, peace-building and post-conflict reconstruction in the context of the Middle East more generally.

Notes

We thank the other contributors to this volume for their comments and feedback on an earlier draft of this Introduction. However, we alone take responsibility for the final outcome.

1. This volume is based on a workshop, entitled 'Gendering the Transnational in Conflict, Migration and Post-conflict Reconstruction: From the Middle East to Europe', organized by Nadje Al-Ali and Nicola Pratt and held in March 2007 as part of the Eighth Mediterranean Social and Political Research Meeting hosted by the European Institute University and the Robert Schuman Centre for Advanced Studies in Montecatini, Italy. The twelve participants of our workshop included well-established as well as up-and-coming scholars in the field of feminist international political economy, feminist international relations, anthropology, sociology and political science. The volume consists of articles based on papers delivered at this workshop that focus on the two country case studies.

2. In the context of post-modern and post-colonial approaches and the increasing appeal of cultural studies, the terms 'diaspora' and 'diasporic communities' havee gained new meanings and dimensions. Diaspora denotes experiences of movement and displacement, and the social, cultural and political formations emerging out of this displacement. Increasingly, it has been used in a metaphorical sense, referring to hybrid identity formations,

arguing against reifications of ethnicity and culture and explaining cultural shifts. For the purpose of this chapter, the term 'diaspora' is defined much more narrowly as we are specifically focusing on diasporas generated by conflict and/or forced migration. Unlike the view of some authors, we argue, however, that 'forced migration' cannot simply be contrasted with voluntary or economic migration. Rather, there exists a continuum between flight in a situation of acute danger and hot conflict and migration in a pre-conflict yet tension-ridden period. Economic necessities and crises force people to migrate, as do armed conflict and violence.

3. See, for example, Glick-Schiller, 1999; Vertovec, 2001.

References

Al-Ali, Nadje (2002) 'Transnational or a-National: Bosnian Refugees in the UK and the Netherlands', in Nadje Al-Ali and Khalid Koser, eds, *New Approaches to Migration: Transnational Communities and the Transformation of Home*, pp. 96–117. London: Routledge.

Al-Ali, Nadje (2003) 'Losses in Status or New Opportunities? Gender Relations and Transnational Ties among Bosnian Refugees', in Deborah Bryceson, ed., *Forging New Frontiers in Europe: Transnational Families and their Global Networks*, pp. 83–102. Oxford and New York: Berg.

Al-Ali, Nadje (2007a) *Iraqi Women: Untold Stories from 1948 to the Present*. London: Zed Books.

Al-Ali, Nadje (2007b) 'Gender, Diasporas and Post-Cold War Conflict', in Hazel Hammond, ed., The *Political Mobilization of Post-Cold War Diasporas*, pp. 39–62. New York: United Nations University Press.

Al-Ali, Nadje, Richard Black and Khalid Koser (2001) 'Refugees and Trans-nationalism: The Experience of Bosnians and Eritreans in Europe', *Journal of Ethnic and Migration Studies* 27(4): 615–34.

Al-Ali, Nadje, and Nicola Pratt (2009) *What Kind of Liberation? Women and the Occupation of Iraq*. Berkeley, University of California Press.

Al-Ali, Nadje, and Nicola Pratt (2008) 'Women's Organizing and the Conflict in Iraq since 2003', *Feminist Review* 88: 74–85.

Butler, Judith (1990) *Gender Trouble*. London and New York: Routledge.

Carby, Hazel (1982) 'White Woman Listen! Black Feminism and the Boundaries of Sisterhood', in The *Empire Strikes Back: Race and Racism in Seventies Britain*, pp. 212–35, pp. 212–35. London: Hutchinson, in association with the Centre for Contemporary Cultural Studies, University of Birmingham.

Cockburn, Cynthia (1999) *Background Paper: Gender, Armed Conflict and Political Violence*. World Bank Conference on Gender, Armed Conflict and Political Development, Washington DC.

Cockburn, Cynthia (2004) 'The Continuum of Violence: A Gender Perspective on War and Peace', in Wenona Giles and Jennifer Hyndman, eds, *Sites of Violence: Gender and Conflict Zones*, pp. 24–44. Berkeley: University of California Press.

Cockburn, Cynthia (2007) From Where We Stand: War, Women's Activism and Feminist Analysis. London: Zed Books.

Cockburn, Cynthia, and Meliha Hubic (2002) 'Gender and the Peacekeeping Military: A View from Bosnian Women's Organizations', in Cynthia Cockburn and Dubravka Žarkov, eds, The Postwar Moment: Militaries, Masculinities and International Peacekeeping, pp. 68–84. London: Lawrence & Wishart.

Cockburn, Cynthia, and Lynette Hunter (1999) 'Transversal Politics and Translating Practices', Soundings: A Journal of Politics and Culture 12, Summer: 88–162.

Cockburn, Cynthia, and Dubravka Zarkov, eds (2002) The Postwar Moment: Militaries, Masculinities and International Peacekeeping. London: Lawrence & Wishart.

Connell, Robert (1995) Masculinities. Berkeley: University of California Press.

Connell, Robert (2002) Gender. Cambridge: Polity Press.

Corrin, Chris (1996) Women in a Violent World: Feminist Analyses and Resistance across 'Europe'. Edinburgh: Edinburgh University Press.

Enloe, Cynthia (1983) Does Khaki Become You? London: Pandora.

Enloe, Cynthia (1990) Bananas, Beaches and Bases: Making Feminist Sense of International Politics. London: Pandora.

Enloe, Cynthia (1993) The Morning After: Sexual Politics at the End of the Cold War. Berkeley: University of California Press.

Enloe, Cynthia (2000) Maneuvers: The International Politics of Militarizing Women's Lives. Berkeley: University of California Press.

Enloe, Cynthia (2001) Bananas, Beaches and Bases: Making Feminist Sense of International Politics. Berkeley, University of California Press.

Enloe, Cynthia (2004) The Curious Feminist: Searching for Women in a New Age of Empire. Berkeley: University of California Press.

Enloe, Cynthia (2005) 'What if Patriarchy is "the Big Picture"? An Afterword', in Dyan Mazurana, Angela Raven-Roberts and Jane Parpart, eds, Gender, Conflict and Peacekeeping, pp. 280–83. Lanham MD: Rowman & Littlefield.

Galtung, Johann (1996) Peace by Peaceful Means: Peace and Conflict, Development and Civilization. Thousand Oaks CA: Sage.

Gervais, Myriam (2004) 'Human Security and Reconstruction Efforts in Rwanda: Impact on the Lives of Women', in Haleh Afshar and Deborah Eade, eds, Development, Women, and War: Feminist Perspectives, pp. 301–14. Oxford: Oxfam.

Giles, Wenona, and Jennifer Hyndman, eds (2004a) Sites of Violence: Gender and Conflict Zones. Berkeley: University of California Press.

Giles, Wenona, and Jennifer Hyndman (2004b) 'New Directions for Feminist Research and Politics', in W. Giles and J. Hyndman, eds, Sites of Violence: Gender and Conflict Zones, pp. 301–16. Berkeley: University of California Press.

Giles, Wenona, Malathi de Alwis, Edith Klein and Neluka Silva, eds (2003) Feminists under Fire: Exchanges Across War Zones. Toronto: Between the Lines.

Glick Schiller, Nina (1999) 'Transmigrants and Nation-States: Something Old and Something New in U.S. Immigrant Experience', in C. Hirschman, Josh DeWind and P. Kasinitz, eds, Handbook of International Migration: The American Experience, pp. 94–119. New York: Russell Sage.

Glick Schiller, Nina, Linda Basch and Christina Szanton-Blanc (1992) *Towards a Transnational Perspective on Migration*. New York: New York Academy of Sciences.

Herring, Eric, and Glen Rangwala (2006), *Iraq in Fragments*, London: Hurst.

Hinnebusch, R. (2003) *The International Politics of the Middle East*. Manchester, Manchester University Press.

Human Rights Watch (2003) Climate of Fear: Sexual Violence and Abduction of Women and Girls in Baghdad. New York: Human Rights Watch.

Hunt, K. (2007) '"Embedded Feminism" and the War on Terror', in K. Hunt and K. Rygiel, eds, *(En)gendering the War on Terror*, pp. 51–72. Aldershot: Ashgate.

Jacobs, Susie, Ruth Jacobson and Jennifer Marchbank, eds (2000) *States of Conflict: Gender, Violence and Resistance*. London: Zed Books.

Jad, I. (2004) 'The NGOization of Arab Women's Movements', *IDS Bulletin* 35(4): 34–42.

Kandiyoti, Deniz (2007) 'Between the Hammer and the Anvil: Post-conflict Reconstruction, Islam and Women's Rights', *Third World Quarterly* 28(3): 503–17.

Kandiyoti, Deniz (1991) 'Introduction', in D. Kandiyoti, ed., *Women, Islam and the State*, pp. 1–21. London: Macmillan.

Keck, M., and K. Sikkink (1998) *Activists beyond Borders: Advocacy Networks in International Politics*. Ithaca, Cornell University Press.

Kelly, Liz (1988) *Surviving Sexual Violence*. Cambridge: Polity Press.

Kelly, Liz (2000) 'Wars against Women: Sexual Violence, Sexual Politics and the Militarized State', in Susie Jacobs et al., eds, *States of Conflict: Gender, Violence and Resistance*, pp. 45–65. London: Zed Books.

Korac, Maja (1998) *Linking Arms: Women and War in Post-Yugoslav States*. Uppsala: Life and Peace Institute.

Lentin, Ronit (1997) *Gender and Catastrophe*. London: Zed Books.

Lorentzen, Lois Ann, and Jennifer Turpin, eds (1998) *The Women and War Reader*. New York: New York University Press.

Marchand, Marianne, and Ann Sisson Runyan (2000), *Gender and Global Restructuring*. London: Routledge.

Meintjes, Sheila, Anu Pillay and Meredith Turshen, eds (2001) *The Aftermath: Women in Post-Conflict Transformation*. London: Zed Books.

Meznaric, Silva (1994) 'Gender as an Ethno-Marker: Rape, War, and Identity Politics in the Former Yugoslavia', in Valentine M. Moghadam, ed., *Identity Politics and Women: Cultural Reassertions and Feminisms in International Perspective*, pp. 76–97. Boulder CO: Westview Press.

Moghadam, Valentine (2005a) *Globalizing Women: Transnational Feminist Networks*. Baltimore and London: Johns Hopkins University Press.

Moghadam, Valentine (2005b) 'Globalizing the Local: Transnational Feminism and Afghan Women's Rights'. www.peuplesmonde.com/article.php3?id_article=20; accessed 3 January 2007.

Mohanty, Chandra Talpade (1991) 'Under Western Eyes: Feminist Scholarship and Colonial Discourses', in C.T. Mohanty, A. Russo and L. Torres, eds. *Third World*

Women and the Politics of Feminism, pp. 51–80. Bloomington and Indianapolis: Indiana University Press.

Mohanty, Chandra Talpade (2002) 'Under Western Eyes Revisited: Feminist Solidarity through Anticapitalist Struggles', *Signs: Journal of Women in Culture and Society* 28(2): 499–535.

Moser, C., and F. Clark, eds (2001). *Victims, Perpetrators or Actors? Gender, Armed Conflict and Political Violence*. London, Zed Books.

Ong, Aiwha (1999) *Flexible Citizenship: The Cultural Logics of Transnationality*. Durham NC: Duke University Press.

Pankhurst, Donna (2004) 'The "Sex War" and Other Wars: Towards a Feminist Approach to Peace Building', in H. Afshar and D. Eade, eds, *Development, Women, and War: Feminist Perspectives*, pp. 8–42. Oxford: Oxfam.

Peteet, Julie (1991) *Gender in Crisis: Women and the Palestinian Resistance Movement*. New York: Columbia University Press.

Peterson, V. Spike (1998) 'Gendered Nationalism: Reproducing "Us" versus "Them"', in Lois Ann Lorentzen and Jennifer Turpin, eds, *The Women and War Reader*, pp. 41–9. New York and London: New York University Press.

Peterson, V. Spike (2003) *A Critical Rewriting of Global Political Economy: Reproductive, Productive and Virtual Economies*. London: Routledge.

Peterson, V. Spike, ed. (1992) *Gendered States: Feminist (Re)visions of International Relations Theory*. Boulder CO: Lynne Rienner.

Peterson, V. Spike, and Runyan Anne Sisson (1993) *Global Gender Issues*. Boulder CO: Westview Press.

Pratt, Nicola (2007a) *Democracy and Authoritarianism in the Arab World*, Boulder CO: Lynne Rienner.

Pratt, Nicola (2007b) 'Gender-mainstreaming in International Security: The Case of the Middle East'. Paper presented at the British International Studies Association annual conference, University of Cambridge.

Rai, Shirin (2002) *Gender and the Political Economy of Development*. Cambridge: Polity Press.

Said, Edward (1978) *Orientalism*. London, Penguin Books.

Seifert, R. (1994) 'War and Rape: A Preliminary Analysis', in A. Stiglmayer, ed., *Mass Rape: The War against Women in Bosnia-Herzegovina*, pp. 54–73. Lincoln: University of Nebraska Press.

Sharoni, S. (1995) *Gender and the Israeli–Palestinian Conflict*. New York: Syracuse University Press.

Smith, Michael P., and Luiz Guarnizo, eds (1998) *Transnationalism from Below*. New Brunswick NY: Transaction Publishers.

Sørensen, Brigitte (1998) *Women and Post-conflict Reconstruction: Issues and Sources*. Geneva: UNRSID.

Spivak, Gayatri (1988) 'Can the Subaltern Speak?', in C. Nelson and L. Grossberg, eds, *Marxism and the Interpretation of Culture*. London: Macmillan; reprinted in P. Williams and L. Chrisman, eds, *Colonial Discourse and Post-colonial Theory*, New York: Columbia University Press, 1994, pp. 66–111.

Steans, Jill (2006) *Gender and International Relations*. Cambridge: Polity Press.

Thompson, E. (2000). *Colonial Citizens: Republican Rights, Paternal Privilege, and Gender in French Syria and Lebanon*. New York: Columbia University Press.

Tickner, J. Ann (1992), *Gender in International Relations: Feminist Perspectives on Achieving Global Security*. New York: Columbia University Press.

Turshen, Meredith and Clotilde Twagiramariya, eds (1998) *What Women Do in Wartime: Gender and Conflict in Africa*. London: Zed Books.

Vertovec, Stephen (2001) 'Transnationalism and Identity', *Journal of Ethnic and Migration Studies* 27(4): 573–82.

Vertovec, Stephen (1999) 'Conceiving and Researching Transnationalism', *Ethnic and Racial Studies* 22(2): 447–62.

Yuval-Davis, Nira (1997) *Gender and Nation*. London: Sage.

PART I

Gendering the Neoliberal Imperial Project

ONE

Gendering Informal Economies in Iraq

V. Spike Peterson

Processes associated with neoliberal globalization have had many dramatic effects. Particularly striking is the unexpected and phenomenal growth of informal-sector activities – 'work', licit or illicit, that is outside of formal market transactions. How to define, document and measure informalization is controversial, and how to secure reliable data is problematic. Moreover, while scholars agree that women do the majority of informal work, current research largely ignores gender and its hierarchical politics.

Ironically, data on informalization are becoming relatively more visible in contexts of conflict and war. A growing scholarship indicates the emergence of three economies: (1) sheer survival needs motivate individuals and families to engage in 'coping economies' that facilitate social reproduction; (2) military objectives motivate individuals and groups to participate in 'combat economies' that fund and facilitate insurgent activities; and (3) as regulatory mechanisms break down, profit motives generate 'criminal economies' that are gendered and transnational.

While these economies overlap and interact, they entail distinctive sets of actors, motivations and activities. They are variously marked by hierarchies of culture, ethnicity/race, class, gender, sexuality and geopolitics. My larger research agenda is to develop a theoretical framing that enables us to describe and 'map' these economies and, in particular, illuminate how structural hierarchies (of culture, ethnicity/race, class, gender, sexuality and geopolitics) shape, and are shaped by, the specificities of these economies. The present chapter constitutes a portion of that project, narrowed to focus on gendering these economies in the context of war in Iraq, and especially the coping economy where issues of social reproduction are paramount.

Theoretical framing for the larger project draws on my book *A Critical Rewriting of Global Political Economy: Integrating Reproductive, Productive and Virtual Economies* (2003). This book attempts to demonstrate the interdependence (co-constitution) of the three (reproductive, productive and virtual) economies and to advance critical theory by illuminating the intersection of race, gender and economic inequalities (within and among states) as structural features of global political economy (GPE). For present purposes, I first draw on the book's theoretical framing and empirical data to clarify gender as an analytical category and to 'situate' informalization in the context of economic globalization. I then introduce three modes of informal activity – coping, combat and criminal economies – found especially in the context of war zones. The bulk of the chapter attempts to build a picture of their operation in the particular case of Iraq. This involves a discussion of historical developments as well as contemporary dilemmas.

The analytics of a critical project

A Critical Rewriting of Global Political Economy moves beyond a narrow definition of economics to develop an alternative analytical framing of reproductive, productive and virtual (RPV) economies as interactive and mutually constituted.[1] I argue that a more expansive 'RPV framing' is necessary to address two globalization trends that affect everyday lives worldwide. The first is explosive growth in financial markets that shapes business decision-making and public policymaking. The second is dramatic growth in informal and flexible work arrangements that shapes income-generation and family well-being. While these developments are widely recognized, they are rarely analysed in relation. In contrast, the RPV framing provides a way to see licit and illicit informal activities, global production, migration flows and capital movements as interacting dimensions of transnational processes. In short, the RPV framing permits me to examine how local informal activities are connected to transnational financial flows, including the circulation of funds that affect coping, combat and criminal economies.

With other feminists I argue (1992, 2005) that gender is not merely an empirical category of male–female sex difference, but an analytical category of masculine–feminine difference and hierarchy that constitutes a governing code. The claim here is that gender pervades language and meaning systems, 'ordering' how we think (and hence shaping how we act) by privileging that which is associated with masculinity over that which is associated with femininity. Stated differently, devalorization of the feminine pervades language and culture, with systemic effects on how we 'take for granted' (normalize and effectively naturalize) the devaluation of all feminized bodies, identities and activities (Peterson, 2007). In short, and notwithstanding romanticism, feminization constitutes devalorization. In particular, feminization is a 'way of thinking' that devalorizes not only women but also racially, culturally and economically marginalized men, as well as work that is deemed unskilled, menial and 'merely' reproductive. This devaluation is simultaneously manifested in cultural and economic terms; for example, no matter what skills are involved, feminized jobs have little status and are poorly paid. The key point is that multiple hierarchies are linked and ideologically 'naturalized' in so far as whatever is denigrated in each hierarchy is characterized as feminine. The feminist orientation I advocate, then, is neither simply about male–female relations nor limited to promoting the status of 'women'. Its transformative potential lies in subverting all hierarchies that rely on devalorization of 'the feminine' to naturalize exploitation and domination.[2]

While the RPV framing is more specific to rewriting global political economy, a second analytical innovation – 'triad analytics'

– is applicable to social relations more generally. To facilitate a shift from the binary tendencies of conventional framing, triad analytics posits identities (subjectivity, self-formation, desires), meaning systems (symbols, discourse, ideologies) and social practices/institutions (actions, social structures) as *co-constituting* dimensions of social reality. These are of course inseparable in practice, but analytically specifying their interaction affords additional 'order' for systematic investigation of social relations.

Stated simply, the triad insists on integrating 'who we are', 'how we think' and 'what we do.' It rejects oppositional framing in favour of understanding the symbolic (concepts/discourse/'thinking') and concrete (action/practice/'doing') relationally, and insists that these are equally inextricable from emotional/affective/psychological dimensions, processes of subject-formation, and the complex politics these entail. It is especially important to take identities – and our investments in them – seriously when we are analysing conditions of conflict and war. I deploy the triad throughout this chapter to draw attention to the interaction of identities, ways of thinking and activities.

Economic globalization is shaped by the dominance of neoliberal policies promoted primarily by geopolitical elites in the interest of powerful states and the inter- and transnational institutions they effectively control. Deregulation has permitted the hyper-mobility of ('foot-loose') capital, induced phenomenal growth in licit and illicit financial transactions, and increased the power of private capital interests. Liberalization is selectively implemented: powerful states engage in protectionism while imposing 'free trade' on less powerful economies. Privatization has entailed loss of nationalized industries in developing economies and a decrease in public-sector employment and provision of social services worldwide. The results of restructuring are complex, uneven and controversial. While economic growth is the objective and has been realized in some areas and sectors, evidence increasingly suggests expanding inequalities, indeed a polarization, of resources within and between countries. Of particular relevance to this chapter, neoliberal policies are linked to explosive growth in informal activities and unregulated global financial transactions. This growth affects social reproduction and gender relations worldwide, as well as illicit activities and their transnational criminal networks.

The reproductive economy of the RPV framing is typically neglected in conventional accounts that remain preoccupied with waged/commodified labour, formal market exchange and public-sphere activities.[3] This economy involves essential social reproduction and informal economic activities; the latter merge with flexibilization that is so prominent a feature of economic restructuring. I include the reproductive economy in my analytical framing because the productive and virtual economies depend on it in non-trivial ways (e.g. to produce appropriately socialized workers and desiring consumers; to provide socially necessary but not socialized welfare and caretaking) and the extent and value of its informal feminized labour are staggering in scale and increasing worldwide. This growth and its ambiguous relationship to the formal economy raise important theoretical and practical/political issues.

Informal activities and international developments

Defining informal activities is controversial, but at a minimum we can distinguish them from 'formal' activities that are the focus of conventional economic accounts, where not only exchanges of money but also labour regulation and regulatory institutions are presupposed (e.g. waged labour, industrialized production, corporate business). In contrast, informal activities range from domestic/socially necessary and voluntary 'work', where cash is rarely exchanged and 'regulatory authorities' are absent (e.g. child-rearing, housekeeping, neighbourhood projects), to secondary, 'shadow' and 'irregular' activities where some form of enterprise and payment is expected but regulation is either difficult to enforce or intentionally avoided/evaded (e.g. petty trade, home-based production, street vending, sex work, drug dealing, arms trading).

Informal activities span a wide range of activities and blur conventional boundaries separating public and private, licit and illicit, production and reproduction, national and international. This heterogeneity complicates the already significant challenge of identifying and measuring what by definition escapes documentation and in practice involves hard-to-quantify activities and effects.

Analysts note that global restructuring has dramatically increased the volume, value, extent and socio-political significance of informalization. Recent measures indicate that informal activities constitute more than one-half of all economic output and equal 75 per cent of the gross domestic product of some countries. Hence, informal activities have tremendous *economic impact*. They also *matter politically* due to the quandaries of documentation, measurement and policy-making they pose.

In sum, phenomenal growth in informalization profoundly complicates conventional ways of understanding economics, the legal status of various economic transactions, and the societal implications of reducing formal regulation of economic activities. A general observation is that the power of governments, presumably serving public/societal interests, is being ceded to the power of market authorities, presumably serving the interests of private capital. Informalization is not simply and wholly 'negative'; as indicated below, it may afford the only means of survival in desperate conditions. But there are undeniable social *costs* of informalization: society loses when unregulated activities thwart tax collection and decrease public revenues; when inaccurate accounts of work and production generate misguided policies; when unregulated work practices pose safety, health and environmental risks; and when criminal activities threaten the security and stability of social order. We clearly need adequate analyses of informalization and, especially, how it affects social reproduction, upon which all else – daily survival, production, consumption, war-making and peace-building – depends.

An emerging literature facilitates research in two ways. First, it suggests new questions and concerns regarding linkages between informalization and its social and economic effects (e.g. linking illicit trade in drugs or arms with military strategies and outcomes). Second, it provides crucial empirical data regarding informal activities: who are the key players (e.g. traffickers, conflict entrepreneurs); what are the motivations for, practices of, and profits generated by informal activities (e.g. from family survival to business gains, street vending to transnational smuggling, meagre earnings to corporate windfalls); and how are these activities enabled and/or constrained by national and transnational policies and laws (e.g. regulating flows of information, people, arms or currencies)?

In so far as today's wars are more often intra- than inter-national, the acquisition of resources for conflict is not simply a matter of governmental authorization and its presumably 'legal' funding. Many combatants finance their activities through informal sectors, licit and illicit, and especially partnerships with armed groups, arms suppliers, organized crime, corrupt governments and corporations, many of which operate transnationally. Hence, analysts are attempting to track licit and illicit economic activities and resource flows to make better sense of the causes, conduct and consequences of conflicts, and to identify more effectively regulatory and legal policies that will promote societal well-being.

In sum, the emerging literature argues for closer attention to 'shadow' or underground economies because they provide supplies and financing for conflict activities (Kaldor, 2001; Ballentine and Sherman, 2003; Jung, 2003; Arnson and Zartman, 2005); to the blurring of licit–illicit boundaries in so far as criminal, corporate and corrupt governmental interests converge (Ruggiero, 2000; Duffield, 2001; Naylor, 2002; Andreas, 2005); and to regional and systemic conditions that shape local conflicts and longer-term prospects for social stability (Le Billon et al., 2002; Pugh and Cooper, 2004). The last point is especially salient in terms of transnational actors and processes in the context of the Middle East.

This literature also illuminates a disturbing development in global dynamics: how neoliberal policies guiding *economic* globalization are having deleterious, indeed disastrous, *political* effects in the form of expanding forms of corruption and militarization. In brief, as the centralized power, regulatory capacity and public accountability of states is eroded in favour of unaccountable decentralized markets, international agencies and private interest networks, both informalization and transnational financial flows increase; in conflict zones there are powerful incentives for seeking, and multiple opportunities for securing, resources and profits through both licit and illicit informal activities and unregulated financial transfers. States weakened by neoliberal policies and/or protracted conflict are less able – and sometimes insufficiently motivated – to impose and maintain law and order, even when peace is proclaimed. Without effective public control and authority, post-conflict reconstruction may be continually undermined by established and effective networks of private – and often illicit – resource provision. In short, this disturbing trend reveals a convergence in studies of international political economy and international security that warrants much closer attention.

In this chapter, however, I turn to more specific insights regarding war economies. From the literature on IPE, and especially Pugh and Cooper (2004), three subgroupings of informalization can be identified as operating in many of today's war zones. These coping, combat and criminal economies[4] are overlapping and interdependent, but it is worth distinguishing for each subgroup a triad of what motivates the agents, who these agents tend to be, and what the primary activities are. I first offer general characterizations of each economy as they might operate in various conflict zones; I then begin to sketch how these economies operate, and what their effects are, in the context of Iraq's current conflict.

First, 'coping economies' emerge that facilitate individual survival and the social reproduction of families/households. Agents are primarily motivated by survival needs as conflict conditions undermine social stability, erode the formal economy and disrupt traditional livelihoods. Agents may include individuals, families/households, kin networks, neighbourhood communities or social solidarity groups. As economic conditions deteriorate, family/household coping strategies may include 'selling' organs for transplant, infants for adoption, or children for sex work; early marriage of daughters; debt bondage; and participating in potentially lucrative but high-risk criminal activities. Agents in this economy presumably have a greater stake in ending conflicts than perpetuating them, as they are structurally the most vulnerable when conditions are unstable and do not command sufficient resources to prosper from societal disruption. This will depend, however, on post-conflict conditions, including the actual level of security and availability of resources and employment through the 'regular'/formal economy.

Second, 'combat economies' emerge that directly supply and fund fighters and insurgent activities. Agents are primarily motivated by military objectives and include armed groups and their political supporters, as well as 'conflict entrepreneurs' who facilitate acquisition to war resources. Activities blur traditional licit–illicit boundaries as combatants in civil wars turn to a variety of sources, some of which are more accessible in so far as central authority and regulatory institutions are weakened. Movement of supplies and financial arrangements are typically transnational and implicate larger regional linkages. Insofar as operations are clandestine they often involve organized crime networks. Activities may include looting, theft, kidnapping, smuggling and other black-market activities, private fund-raising, aid manipulation, expropriation of natural resources, and economic blockages of dissenting areas. In support of military objectives, geographical areas and/or natural resources controlled by opponents may be targeted to cripple their economic power. In the combat economy, agents may resist peace if they anticipate a loss of status and/or power, or seek peace if they anticipate post-conflict benefits, including alternative livelihoods.

Third, 'criminal economies' emerge that directly and indirectly supply and fund conflict activities. Agents are primarily motivated by profit-seeking, opportunities for which are enhanced in conflict zones as regulatory mechanisms break down or are suspended, and centralized control is weakened by war, fractured by political divisions, and/or disabled by extensive corruption. Agents may include petty criminals, conflict entrepreneurs, war profiteers, traffickers, money launderers, and those who produce and/or transport trafficked goods. Obviously, the agents of this and the combat economy may overlap, especially as conflict continues and profit-making parallels or displaces military objectives – whether for personal gain or in pursuit of a solidarity group's political agenda. Agents are also likely to overlap with the coping economy as individuals and households pursue, or feel forced to engage in, illicit activities as a survival strategy. Activities in this economy fall outside of state regulation and documentation and may include smuggling, trafficking, predatory lending, aid manipulation, natural resource expropriation, fraud, tax evasion and money laundering. This economy also tends to be transnational and involve larger regional activities in support of smuggling, trafficking and supplying arms. Given its illicit status, financial arrangements involve money-laundering and banking activities outside of the country. Agents may resist peace if it represents loss of income, or seek peace if they will benefit from long-term investment and legitimate businesses. However, in the absence of strong central authority and reliable law enforcement, 'there are few incentives for entrepreneurs to make the shift toward longer-term productive activities' (Goodhand, 2004: 65).

Informal economies in Iraq

This chapter only begins to sketch how coping, combat and criminal economies are gendered in the particular case of Iraq.[5] Some brief history is essential for understanding national and regional dynamics and their effect on the development of informal economies. In particular, Iraq's war with Iran from 1980 to 1988, its invasion and annexation of Kuwait in 1990, the subsequent UN embargo and then first Gulf War against Iraq in 1991, and continued sanctions until the second invasion and war in 2003 had devastating and long-term effects. From a relatively prosperous, literate and 'modernizing' country under a strong (indeed, dictatorial) centralized government, Iraq deteriorated dramatically as a result of wars and international sanctions.

Ways of thinking and acting were most obviously affected, but identities changed as well. For example, one consequence of the prolonged war with Iran was to promote women's formal employment in support of war efforts as well as to stand in for absent men. Militarization of society involved promoting particular identities as well:

> a glorification of certain types of masculinity, i.e., the fighter, the defender of his nation and the martyr. Women were simultaneously encouraged by the state to replace male workers and civil servants, who were fighting at the front, and to 'produce' more Iraqi citizens and future soldiers. The glorification of a militarised masculinity coincided with the glorification of the Iraqi mother. (Al-Ali, 2005: 745)

In 1990, Iraq invaded Kuwait, which was followed by the United States waging war against Iraq in 1991. As a result of almost uninterrupted military hostilities for more than a decade, the number of widows and female-headed households in Iraq is very high,[6] and domestic work for many includes caring for war-damaged family members.

As sanctions and security threats continued in the 1990s, economic conditions deteriorated precipitously, especially in regard to health, education and employment. Research shows that Iraq experienced

> one of the most rapid declines in living conditions ever recorded. Iraq fell from 96/160 in 1991 to 126/174 in 2000 on the UNDP Human Development Index ... The impact of this decline on women included increased mortality rates; a significant increase in malnutrition among women and children; and an added burden of responsibility as women had to care for children traumatized by war, disease, and malnutrition. (UNIFEM, 2006)

In addition to war-torn families, what stands out for purposes of this chapter is how the long period of sanctions cultivated informal activities and Saddam Hussein constructed 'clandestine trade agreements and a vast international bribery network' (Andreas, 2005: 353). A class of newly rich black-marketeers emerged throughout the region. In important ways, class dynamics were restructured in Iraq with the emergence of new elite members, the continued decline of an educated middle class, and a rapidly expanding underclass of the poor. What observers note is how the sanctions era pushed economic activities underground, established criminal networks, and inflated the profitability of illicit trade.

Changes were socio-cultural as well. The overall literacy rate was cut 'from 80 per cent in 1987 to 40 per cent, ... and school attendance percentages sank, especially for rural girls' (Women for Women International, 2005: 13). Al-Ali (2005: 743–4) describes 'a massive deterioration in basic infrastructure (water, sanitation, sewerage, electricity) that severely reduced the quality of life of Iraqi families.' All Iraqis were affected, but not homogeneously. When basic infrastructure and services collapse, women bear a disproportionate share of the burden because they are held responsible, and typically hold themselves responsible, for family well-being and household management (e.g. Beneria, 2003; Peterson, 2003).

In sum, informal economies were expanding in Iraq *before* the military invasion of 2003. Individuals, families and solidarity groups were struggling to survive in the face of a crumbling infrastructure, the collapse of state services, and very constrained options. Smugglers and black-marketeers were active in a criminal economy that was both highly profitable and, in the context of sanctions and shortages, generally 'functional' for the Iraqi population. In the absence of alternatives, people make do with what is available, including contraband goods and illicit transactions. The effects are ongoing, both in terms of 'what people are doing' in the criminal and combat economies currently operating in Iraq, and in terms of 'how people think' about informal and illicit activities. In the face of devastating physical conditions, many Iraqis developed a 'rational' tolerance for informal and often illicit activities.[7]

Post-invasion informal economies

On 19 March 2003 the United States and a 'coalition of the willing' invaded Iraq. Within weeks the offensive had toppled Saddam Hussein's government, but he was not himself captured. On 1 May President Bush effectively declared victory from the deck of a US aircraft carrier, and the post-invasion period of occupation began. As the regime collapsed and disorder ensued, there was extensive looting that included government buildings and official residences, military facilities, museums and banks. Looted weapons and ammunition fuelled combat and criminal economies by constituting significant resources for subsequent insurgent attacks. While resistance was initially concentrated in groups supportive of Saddam Hussein and/or the Ba'th Party, resentment of the invasion quickly drew various other groups into attacks on US and coalition forces.

Coalition forces claimed they were committed to establishing a secure and stable democratic state in Iraq. In reality, they have failed to do so. While the location and extent of violence has varied, coalition forces have not been able to secure peace and ensure lawfulness; indeed the occupying forces are often considered a source of violence themselves.[8] Extensive surveys conducted in 2003 by both Physicians for Human Rights (2003) and Women for Women International (2005) document the absolute priority of security for the majority of the population. While security was the most significant problem people faced in their daily lives, meeting basic needs was also of tremendous concern. Years after the invasion, occupying forces have failed to ensure safe water, adequate electricity and reliable communications (Oxfam International, 2007). Obviously, the absence of security complicates the reconstruction of infrastructure and delivery of basic services. These issues are deeply gendered and the effects on women's lives cannot be overstated, though they are often overlooked in official accounts. Some of the effects are described in the Women for Women International report of conditions for women in the year following the war:

> women across social classes have seen their activities restricted. Older, educated, professional women who had created small businesses in their homes after losing public sector jobs could not continue these activities due to the electricity shortages following the invasion. Poor women who occupied much of the informal sector jobs in markets and in the streets lost their economic lifeline as they were forced to stop working out of constant fear of violence and

attack. The somewhat predictable violence that was the hallmark of the Hussein regime was transformed in this post-invasion period into general violence erupting from many different directions. Fear of abduction, rape, and murder has kept women confined to their homes. (Women for Women International, 2005: 14)[9]

The coping economy is about survival: how to guarantee social reproduction and meet basic needs even as conflict conditions undermine social stability, erode the formal economy, and disrupt traditional livelihoods. Patriarchal domination has institutionalized, indeed 'normalized', gendered roles that are especially prominent in the context of family and household life.[10] The point here is that coping economies more generally involve expectations that women will keep households functioning, and in crisis conditions these expectations compel women to engage in a variety of informal activities. These typically include communal sharing, redistribution through family networks, volunteer work, subsistence agriculture, petty trade, street vending, farm labour, home-based businesses, waged work, labour migration and remittances.

Lack of safe drinking water, compromised medical facilities, and inadequate, unreliable electricity are debilitating conditions for all Iraqis, but again not homogeneously. Women are frequently the managers of water treatment plants in Iraq, and the inability to get safely to work has exacerbated the breakdown of safe water delivery (UNIFEM, 2006). And women face tremendous challenges trying to fulfil their responsibility for family well-being when they cannot count on safe water, adequate food provision and access to healthcare. Here we can observe practices of gendered violence – domestic violence, unwanted pregnancies, and so on – interacting with infrastructural crises – unsafe drinking water, resurgence of epidemic diseases – with particularly devastating consequences for women and children.

We do observe Iraqi women engaging – or at least attempting to engage – in a number of the coping strategies indicated above. Individuals valiantly attempt to continue practices of communal, kinship and neighbourhood sharing. Act Together (2006) estimates that 16 per cent of working women are farmers. These women struggle to continue agricultural production in spite of unstable conditions, lack of fertilizers and cessation of subsidies. Zangana (2005) reported that '16 million Iraqis rely on monthly food rations for survival', but it had been three months since rations were distributed. Petty trade is extremely difficult when conditions are so insecure and even the simplest systems of communication and transportation are disrupted. When streets are not safe, all waged workers take risks getting to work, but the risks are greater for women in Iraq. Moreover, the war's destruction of public-sector employment disproportionately hurt women, 72 per cent of whom relied on that sector for waged work (Act Together, 2006).

One coping strategy Iraqis increasingly adopted was that of migration and remittances. Men's temporary emigration for work is a familiar aspect of the region's economy. As security deteriorates, growing numbers of women – and men – who have family abroad and resources to leave often do. One general effect is a further depletion of the middle-class presence in Iraq, with a growing underclass more visible and without support from families overseas.[11] Of course, specific forms of economic coping activity depend a great deal on local circumstances as well as class and gender. But for purposes of this chapter, what distinguishes the coping economy in Iraq is both the level of systemic insecurity more generally – affecting the work options and mobility of all Iraqis – and the religious conservatism that imposes particular constraints on women.

Coping economies shape and are shaped by combat conditions, and the gender-differentiated effects of the latter are widely noted. Most obviously, men and boys are at greatest direct risk of combat-related fatalities and injuries. As of November 2005 more than 200 foreigners had been abducted since the invasion (New York Times, 30 November 2005), and it is predominately men who have been killed. Yet it is also reported that more than 2,000 women have gone missing between March 2003 and spring 2006 (Jamail and Al-Fadhily, 2006). In addition, the dangers posed by unexploded ordnance, landmines and munitions storage containers are exceptionally high in Iraq. While these threaten entire communities, men and boys are at greater risk of mine-related injuries. Women then face increased responsibilities that include taking over for absent men and caring for physically and emotionally injured family members.

The actual number of deaths has been hotly contested throughout the war. The Project on Defence Alternatives estimated between 11,000 and 15,000 people killed during the 2003 war, with perhaps 3,000 of these being non-combatants (Conetta, 2003). Additional sources indicate that significant numbers of women and children were killed both directly and indirectly. As an example of indirect deaths, UNIFEM reports a number of women 'who died due to complications during home births when they could not reach a hospital' (UNIFEM, 2006). Ensuing years have entailed spiralling numbers. Hallinan (2007) cites the study published in *The Lancet* estimating 650,000 war deaths through September 2006, as well as a more recent Opinion Research Business poll indicating that 'the war may have killed more than one million people.'

Various forms of gendered violence occur within and as an effect of the combat economy. In the chaotic period following the overthrow of Saddam Hussein's government, Human Rights Watch reported 'at least 400 women and girls as young as eight years old being raped' (2003). The actual numbers are presumed to be higher but victims fear stigmatization and even 'honour killings' that reporting abuses might entail. The exclusively male police forces typically responded with indifference or hostility and medical attention was rarely available (UNIFEM, 2006). Reports of gendered violence have continued since 2003 and are variously documented. Lawlessness and deteriorating economic conditions have led to increases of prostitution, continued abductions, exploitation of homeless children, and human trafficking.[12] There are also numerous reports of increases in unwanted pregnancies (with their corollary: unsafe abortion attempts), and upsurges in domestic violence and divorce.[13]

While men have been the most frequent direct targets of coalition forces, women have suffered a variety of abuses as well. There are reports of women being sexually abused by coalition soldiers and, along with larger numbers of men, subjected to torture. The offences at Abu Ghraib involved both men and women prisoners and were often explicitly sexual in nature (ICRC, 2004; Rosen, 2006; Susskind, 2007). The United States has additionally admitted detaining Iraqi women as a tactic to pressure male relatives, which constitutes a violation of international law (UNIFEM, 2006). Women working for US agencies were also targeted as a 'warning' against those perceived to be supporting 'infidel' forces (UNIFEM, 2006, citing *New York Times*, 11 March 2004).

The gender-differentiated effects of insecurity are compounded in Iraq by the second factor noted above: religious conservatism that is gender-coded and affects the autonomy, rights, mobility, health and livelihoods of women. Prior to the 2003 war women in Iraq enjoyed considerable freedom of movement and faced no systemic threats regarding their mobility. Since the war the situation is aptly characterized as an intensified 'climate of fear' (Human Rights Watch, 2003) that prevents women and girls from exercising even the limited mobility available to men. Armed groups have targeted women's organizations and family-planning facilities, and threatened and killed women political leaders and women's rights activists (Pratt, 2005; UNIFEM, 2006; Al-Ali, 2007a). Women are increasingly the victims of kidnapping, street violence and 'honour killings' (Jamail and Al-Fadhily, 2006; IRIN, 2007; Susskind, 2007; Pollitt, 2007). The situation for women has continued to deteriorate as centralized government and occupying forces have failed to provide security and sectarian violence has grown. Power is increasingly exercised by local forces and especially 'clan leaders, militias, armed groups, religious parties and political strongmen' who rarely favour the empowerment of women (Act Together, 2006).

Threats and violence against women are clearly intimidating in the extreme. Attacks on and murders of women leaders not only send a powerful signal to all women but eliminate individual women who have much-needed leadership experience and intellectual resources. The intimidation not only institutionalizes a return to domesticity for women but reinscribes patriarchal ideologies and identities. Young women are especially affected and some argue that a generation gap has emerged between older women who were educated and often enjoyed a role in public life and younger women who have had fewer educational opportunities and who may 'willingly' adopt more conservative dress codes as well as reduced public-sphere aspirations.

It is this compounded reality that renders the coping economy in Iraq on the one hand so constrained, in terms of what activities can be undertaken, and on the other hand so impoverished, in terms of income-generating effects and sustaining social reproduction. In short, *systemic* conditions of insecurity in Iraq are exacerbated for women, due to their facing the *particular* insecurities posed by extreme religious conservatism and the climate of fear this has generated.

The extent to which the climate of fear affects particular individuals and households obviously varies according to location, class and other factors. But the general and key point here is the extent to which gendered ideologies, identities and practices in pre-war and post-invasion Iraq severely compromise women's abilities to contribute to even the coping economy. In so far as this economy is crucial for social reproduction and household survival, the constraints on women's mobility and activities have extreme and enduring consequences for all Iraqis.

I conclude by briefly focusing on combat and criminal informal economies. A broad historical context and some features of these economies have already been presented. And, as noted in the overview, the agents and activities of these economies often overlap. This is especially the case as lines between licit and illicit activities blur, not only in war zones but also as an effect of neoliberal globalization. Closely related is the blurring of boundaries between civilian and military activities, as the use of private-sector companies increases in combat zones and in support of military objectives.

Concerned primarily with military objectives, the *combat economy* centres on conflict-related funding, supplies of a wide variety for combat purposes, and related war-fighting activities. In Iraq the dynamics of this economy are shaped by Sunni and Shi'i identifications as these weave through combatant allegiances both within and outside of Iraq, as well as more specific divisions among ethno-religious groups and their supporters struggling for power on Iraqi soil.[14] In the post-invasion period, unemployment remains high for men and women, but men are much more likely to turn to combat activities. Feminist studies indicate that many men respond to perceptions of 'failed manhood' – exemplified by unemployment, inability to provide for the household, impotence in the face of occupying forces, and so on – by displaying aggressive behaviours, including participation in activities deemed 'out of bounds' in less conflictual times.

As noted above, the extensive years of war-making and sanctions-surviving had as one effect the elaboration of licit and illicit economic networks then available in 2003 for generating funds and moving supplies in and around Iraq.[15] These networks exist alongside traditions of clientelism in which men are the primary actors. Clientelistic and informal networking ties enable a variety of licit and illicit activities. The looting that marked the beginning of the war enabled some groups to gain access to military supplies (New York Times, 8 October 2003, 25 October 2004), and other resources that could be converted into war funding (e.g. antiquities; New York Times, 14 February 2005). As centralized authority and state power are weakened or destroyed, incentives increase for more predatory behaviours, typically in the form of looting, smuggling, theft, abductions and extortion (Goodhand, 2004: 63). We observe these activities in Iraq, with initial looting and subsequent use of kidnapping to make financial and political demands.[16] For example, Ariabi (2006) claims that more than 200 Iraqi doctors have been kidnapped for ransom, and the Brookings Institution reported 30–40 Iraqis kidnapped daily in 2006 (Jamail and Al-Fadhily, 2006). Women, perhaps thousands of them, have been abducted for ransom and for sectarian reasons (Jamail and Al-Fadhily, 2006), and Rosen (2006) reports Iraqi police testifying that 'some gangs specialize in kidnapping girls, they sell them to Gulf countries' (Rosen, 2006).

Without question, however, smuggling is at the heart of illicit funding and supplies in support of insurgent forces. The *New York Times* reported on regional smuggling in March 2005:

> So goes life these days along the 2,268 miles of border that separate Iraq from its six neighbors.... The list of items seized by the border police last year reads like a catalog of the riches of the region – 3,350 pieces of antiquities, 2,200 tons of oil and fuel products and 23 tons of minerals. (*New York Times*, 27 March 2005; see also 23 June 2003)

Most lucrative and extensive is smuggling of oil, which involves both small and large players,[17] both insurgents and criminal gangs, and, more than any other activity, reveals the difficulty of distinguishing between combat and criminal economies in Iraq. Drawing lines between these is additionally complicated by the increasing role of private enterprise in war, which blurs public/government and private/business distinctions.

This is starkly revealed in Iraq, where the *criminal economy* is also extensive, especially in so far as the combat economy relies on it for funding and supplies. The principal objective in this economy, however, is less military success than profit-seeking, which shifts who the dominant players are (in terms of ideologies and identities) and what the primary activities involve. Here, the actors – who are predominantly male – include 'less scrupulous conflict entrepreneurs' and others seeking to take financial advantage of the absence of centralized authority and hence less regulated conditions that prevail during war (Looney, 2005: 288). In Iraq key players include the 'new elites' that gained power during prior war conditions and the long period of sanctions, and that have networks in place for undertaking, and hiding, illicit activities (Andreas, 2005). But practices of war-profiteering extend into the larger region and include individuals[18] and businesses associated with occupying forces.

Indeed, concerns emerged early on regarding how the US government was handling preparations for the invasion and awarding contracts to private businesses in support of military activities. There is abundant evidence of profiting from the Iraqi war, as indicated by numerous reports of 'irregularities' and lack of oversight in contracts as well as auditing scandals. Early suspicions have been confirmed in more recent reports, though prosecutions and convictions continue to be minimal.[19] In May 2003 a *Mother Jones* article described the growth in private military companies, how they are altering the operations of war, their suspect financing arrangements and costs to the public, and their dangerous implications for civilians and official military combatants in war zones. In December 2004, a UN audit reported that during the fifteen months of US-led occupation 'there was widespread mismanagement, including financial irregularities, a failure to curb smuggling and overdependence on no-bid contracts' (*New York Times*, 15 December 2004). In 2005, George Monbiot drew on US and other sources to suggest the variety and extent of abuses:

> In just 14 months [under CPA rule], $8.8 billion went absent without leave.... [O]fficials in the CPA were demanding bribes of up to $300,000 in return for awarding contracts. Iraqi money seized by US forces simply disappeared. Some $800 million was handed out to US commandeers without being counted or even weighed. (Monbiot, 2005)

The corruption and profiteering displayed by occupying forces is matched by conditions in Iraq. For example, 'Oil smuggling is only one part of a broader corruption problem that ranges from small-scale kickbacks to major fraud of the kind that took place in Iraq's Defence Ministry, where investigators last August said they had identified more than $1.3 billion in misspent military contracts' (*New York Times*, 5 February 2006). Most of the prominent criminal activities have been noted as aspects of the combat economy: smuggling, kidnapping, extortion and extensive black-market operations. Illicit activities in Iraq are more difficult to track in the English-language media, because of both their clandestine nature and US reticence to acknowledge the extent of problems complicating military efforts in Iraq. Given the scale of oil smuggling, and the estimate that 'insurgents reap 40 to 50 percent of all oil-smuggling profits' (*New*

York Times, 5 February 2006), there remains an enormous discrepancy that presumably goes into the pockets of those seeking profits more than military advantage. As a related issue, the money-laundering involved is notoriously difficult to investigate, though reports suggest it is considerable and highly lucrative (e.g. O'Brien, 2004; New York Times, 5 February 2006).

Given the illicit nature of the criminal economy it is difficult to discern the gendered dynamics. It seems safe, however, to assume that the majority of agents are male. One dimension of the economy, however, that visibly reflects gender is trafficking for the purposes of prostitution. This is predominantly, though not exclusively, about masculinist and heteronormative desires that specifically position women and girls at risk. And in a dismal reflection of how the coping, combat and criminal economies intersect, an upsurge in prostitution subjects increasing numbers of women and girls to adverse conditions that impede their role in social reproduction, while it simultaneously 'satisfies' male desire for access to women's bodies in the combat economy (occupying forces as well as Iraqis), and provides illicit profits for pimps and traffickers in the criminal economy.[20]

Conclusion

Feminists note that, for the most part, the now extensive scholarship on conflict, war and terrorism continues to ignore or marginalize the politics of gendered ideologies, identities and activities. This is no less true of the war in Iraq. In this chapter I have attempted to illuminate some of the most pertinent gender dynamics at play in contexts of conflict and war generally, and in Iraq specifically. Drawing on earlier work that analysed gender in relation to neoliberal globalization, I have expanded the analysis of informalization to investigate how (informal) coping, combat and criminal economies emerge in, and affect the practices of, war contexts. What surfaces through this investigation is primarily the extent to which gendered divisions of authority, labour and power structure these economies and effectively reproduce a hierarchy that devalorizes women and feminized concerns (social reproduction, caring labour). It is not only that men and women are positioned differently in relation to accessing symbolic and material resources, but how masculinized and feminized identities and ideologies shape individual and group expectations, regulatory practices and conflict-related activities.

While this chapter has emphasized the constraints on and costs to women, its point is not that women are 'merely' victims. In spite of the daunting challenges posed by decades of war and deprivation, Iraqi women have shown tremendous courage, fortitude, ingenuity and political leadership (Al-Ali, 2007b; Al-Ali and Pratt, 2008). And the turbulent conditions of Iraq offer 'windows of opportunity' (Women for Women International, 2005) as well as sombre realities. But as Pratt and other feminists observe, structural inequalities tend to perpetuate conflict and impede post-conflict reconstruction (Pratt, 2005: 4). Inequalities have featured extensively in this chapter, especially in the form of gender hierarchy in Iraq. To realize systemic security and an enduring peace in Iraq, as elsewhere, involves recognizing and addressing how gendered ideologies, identities and activities affect operations of power. I hope this chapter contributes to that project.

Notes

1. The subjective, conceptual and cultural dimensions of these economies are understood as inextricable from material conditions, social practices and institutional structures. Thus, my alternative framing enables us to move beyond disciplinary boundaries and to map identities and culture in relation to conventional material and 'structural' phenomena. For argumentation, empirical data and extensive citations in support of claims made in this chapter regarding GPE, see Peterson, 2003.

2. To forestall misunderstanding, I am specifically not arguing for the primacy of 'women's oppression' or the reduction of culture, race/ethnicity and class to sex/gender relations. Rather, I am insisting that gender is a historically contingent structural feature of social relations, that the subordination of women is not reducible to other structural oppressions (or vice versa), and that the dichotomy of gender underpins – as the devalorization of the feminine naturalizes – hierarchies of culture, race/ethnicity, class and geopolitical 'difference'.

3. Feminist economists have produced a wealth of literature on social reproduction, some of which is cited in this chapter and more extensively in Peterson, 2003; Bakker and Gill (2003) offer perhaps the most comprehensive account of social reproduction in crisis as an effect of neoliberal globalization.

4. The Pugh and Cooper volume refers to 'combat, shadow and coping economies' (2004: 8), which I have modified in two ways. I use 'criminal' rather than 'shadow' to distinguish more explicitly the illicit character of that economy; and my reference to the 'coping' economy is more inclusive, encompassing social reproduction activities neglected by most authors.

5. Research for this chapter is drawn entirely from secondary reports produced by a variety of agencies, as well as journalistic and scholarly accounts. I have avoided US governmental sources because the veracity of statements, claims and characterizations of the war in Iraq by the Bush administration is much contested. I note here that this chapter makes no attempt to address, much less resolve, the fraught questions of US policy and responsibility in Iraq.

6. The Ministry of Women's Affairs in 2006 estimated at least 300,000 widows in Baghdad and 8 million throughout the country (IRIN, 2006).

7. Conditions in Iraq prior to military intervention in 2003 are reviewed in numerous studies and reports. For example, UN and World Bank, 2003; Center for Economic and Social Rights, 2003; Women Waging Peace, 2003; Physicians for Human Rights, 2003; Women For Women Interntional, 2005; Al-Ali, 2005; Amnesty International, 2005; and especially UNIFEM, 2006.

8. As widely reported, from the torture at Abu Ghraib to the rape and murder of civilians, occupying forces have repeatedly demonstrated a disregard for human rights and international conventions regarding war.

9. Accounts noting the gendering of insecurity include Human Rights Watch, 2003; Seymour, 2005; Hunt and Rygiel, 2006; Zangana, 2006; Susskind, 2007.

10. A long tradition of patriarchal households and male-dominated social institutions worldwide – including cultural, religious, educational, economic, legal and political institutions – presents us with formidable obstacles to realizing sex/gender equality. It is important to note that patriarchy is neither ahistorical nor monolithic; like all institutions and ideologies it assumes a diversity of forms and is continually undergoing change. How to characterize 'patriarchy' is itself contested, as there are tremendous socio-political issues at stake. Here I simply note that one of the more widespread patterns associated with patriarchy is a division of labour, authority and responsibility between women and men that is particularly visible in relation to activities of social reproduction.

11. UNHCR estimates more than 2 million Iraqi refugees and almost 2 million internally displaced; 'thousands of doctors, teachers and other professionals have been murdered. Many of the rest have fled' (2007: 2). Hallinan (2007) states that 'some 75 per cent of the country's doctors and pharmacists have

fled' and draws on various reports to argue that 'at least 20 per cent of Iraqi's pre-war population of 26 million has been killed, wounded, exiled, or displaced.'

12. Numerous sources document gender-based abuses. See Human Rights Watch, 2003; IRIN, 2003; Sandler, 2003; Amnesty International, 2005; Pratt, 2005; Women For Women Interntional, 2003; Rosen, 2006; CODEPINK, 2006; UNIFEM, 2006; McEwan, 2006; Jamail and Al-Fadhily, 2006; Susskind, 2007; Pollitt, 2007.

13. For example, Telegraph, 2003; IRIN, 2003; Ariabi, 2006; UNIFEM, 2006.

14. Holland (2006) makes this observation, indicating that 'there are at least 23 independent militias operating in Baghdad alone.' Also, a US report confirmed 'that ethnic and religious schisms have become entrenched across much of the country, … show that Iraq is undergoing a de facto partitioning along ethnic and sectarian lines, with clashes – sometimes political, sometimes violent – taking place in those mixed areas where different groups meet' (New York Times, 9 April 2006).

15. The New York Times reported (5 July 2004) that a 'network of Saddam Hussein's cousins operating in part from Syria and Jordan is actively involved in smuggling of guns, people and money into Iraq to support anti-American insurgency'; and (22 October 2004) that there were many more rebels and much more funding than anticipated, and regional dynamics are at play: 'American officials in Iraq and Washington say Iraqi insurgency draws on 'unlimited money' from underground financial networks run by former Baath party leaders and Saddam Hussein's relatives … [and] wealthy Saudi donors and Islamic charities funnel large sums of cash through Syria.'

16. The New York Times obtained a US government report estimating that 'groups responsible for many insurgent and terrorist attacks are raising $70 million to $200 million a year from illegal activities. It says $25 million to $100 million of that comes from oil smuggling.… As much as $36 million a year comes from ransoms paid for hundreds of kidnap victims' (26 November 2006).

17. Oil smuggling 'is also lucrative for the smallest of businesses. Bakers, brick makers and even fishing boat operators find it more profitable to sell fuel, which they receive at subsidized prices, to illicit traders rather than operate their businesses' (New York Times, 4 June 2006).

18. Working on his own, a Middle East scholar, Joseph Braude, confessed to smuggling stolen antiquities from Iraq in 2003 (New York Times, 4 August 2004). In November 2005, a US Army officer was charged with smuggling hundreds of thousands of dollars in stolen cash from Iraq, and others were expected to be charged in what was considered 'an extensive bribery, kickback and smuggling scheme based in an office of the Coalition Provisional Authority' (New York Times, 2 December 2005).

19. Coverage of war profiteering in Iraq can be accessed at AlterNet, a series in Mother Jones, and Iraq Revenue Watch.

20. A US State Department report in 2005 states: 'Iraq is a country of origin for women and girls trafficked to Yemen, Syria, Jordan, and Gulf countries for the purposes of sexual and labor exploitation. Some Iraqi women and underage girls are reportedly trafficked from rural areas to cities within Iraq itself. According to diplomatic and international organization sources in Syria and Yemen, there are thousands of Iraqi women working in prostitution in the two countries under conditions that constitute severe forms of trafficking in persons' (2005; also Bennett, 2006; McEwan, 2006; Human Rights Watch, 2003).

References

Act Together (2006) The Current Situation of Women in Iraq. www.acttogether. org/whoandwhy.htm#struggle; accessed 26 November 2007.

Al-Ali, Nadje (2005) 'Reconstructing Gender: Iraqi Women between Dictatorship, War, Sanctions, and Occupation', Third World Quarterly 26(4–5): 739–58.

Al-Ali, Nadje (2007a) 'Iraqi Women – Four Years after the Invasion', Foreign Policy in Focus, 14 March. www.whrnet.org/fundamentalisms/docs/issue-iraq-0703. html; accessed 9 April 2007.

Al-Ali, Nadje (2007b) Iraqi Women: Untold Stories from 1948 to the Present. London: Zed Books.

Al-Ali, Nadje, and Nicola Pratt (2008) 'Women's Organizing and the Conflict in Iraq since 2003', Feminist Review 88(1): 74–85.

AlterNet. 'Coverage on War Profiteering in Iraq'. http://alternet.org/module/ printversion/41320; accessed 16 December 2006.

Amnesty International (2005) Country Reports: Iraq: Women, Violence and Health. www. amnestyusa.org/countries/iraq/reports.do.

Andreas, Peter (2005) 'Criminalizing Consequences of Sanctions: Embargo Busting and Its Legacy', International Studies Quarterly 49: 335–60.

Ariabi, Entesar Mohammad (2006) 'Welcome to Liberated Iraq', 20 March. AlterNet. www.alternet.org/story/33771; accessed 15 December 2006.

Arnson, C., and I.W. Zartman, eds (2005) Rethinking the Economics of War. Baltimore MD: Johns Hopkins University Press.

Bakker, Isabella, and Stephen Gill, eds (2003) Power, Production and Social Reproduction: Human In/security in the Global Political Economy. London: Palgrave Macmillan.

Ballentine, Karen, and Jake Sherman, eds (2003) The Political Economy of Armed Conflict: Beyond Greed and Grievance. Boulder CO: Lynne Rienner.

Benería, Lourdes (2003) Gender, Development and Globalization: Economics as if People Mattered. New York: Routledge.

Bennett, Brian (2006) 'The Missing Girls of Iraq', Time, 22 April.

Center for Economic and Social Rights (2003) 'The Human Costs of War in Iraq', March. www.reliefweb.int/library/documents/2003/cesr-irq-07mar. pdf; accessed 11 December 2006.

CODEPINK (2006) Iraqi Women under Siege, A Report by CODEPINK: Women for

Peace and Global Exchange. www.codepinkalert.org/downloads/IraqiWom-enReport.pdf; accessed 8 December 2006.

Conetta, Carl (2003) *The Wages of War: Iraqi Combatant and Noncombatant Fatalities in the 2003 Conflict*, Project on Defense Alternatives Research Monograph 8. www.comw.org/pda/0310rm8; accessed 21 December 2006.

Duffield, Mark (2001) *Global Governance and New Wars*. London: Zed Books.

Goodhand, Jonathan (2004) 'Afghanistan in Central Asia', in Michael Pugh and Neil Cooper, eds, *War Economies in a Regional Context: Challenges of Transformation*, pp. 45–89. Boulder CO: Lynne Rienner.

Hallinan, Conn (2007) 'Iraq's Bloody Toll: History Repeats Itself', *Foreign Policy in Focus*, 19 October. www.alternet.org/story/65634/; accessed 27 November 2007.

Hayes, Christopher (2006) 'Were Sanctions Worth the Price?', *In These Times*, 6 March.

Holland, Joshua (2006) 'Iraq Is Coming Apart at the Seams', AlterNet, 21 October. www.alternet.org/story/43278; accessed 15 December 2006.

Human Rights Watch (2003) *Climate of Fear: Sexual Violence and Abduction of Women and Girls in Baghdad*. www.hrw.org/reports/2003/iraq0703; accessed 16 December 2006.

Hunt, Krista, and Kim Rygiel, eds (2006) *(En)gendering the War on Terror: War Stories and Camouflaged Politics*. Burlington VT: Ashgate.

ICRC (2004) *Report on the Treatment by the Coalition Forces of Prisoners of War and Other Protected Persons … in Iraq*. www.globalsecurity.org/military/library/report/2004/icrc_report_iraq_feb2004.htm; accessed 20 December 2006.

Iraq Revenue Watch. www.iraqrevenuewatch.org/index.shtml; accessed 16 December 2006.

IRIN (Integrated Regional Information Networks) (2003) 'Iraq: Focus on Increasing Domestic Violence', UN Office for the Coordination of Humanitarian Affairs, 14 October.

IRIN (Integrated Regional Information Networks) (2006) 'Iraq: Widow Numbers Rise in Wake of Violence', UN Office for the Coordination of Humanitarian Affairs, 20 December.

IRIN (Integrated Regional Information Networks) (2007) 'Iraq: Extremists Fuel Anti-women Violence in Basra', 20 November. www.irinnews.org/report.aspx?ReportID=75396; accessed 8 December 2007.

Jamail, Dahr, and Ali Al-Fadhily (2006) 'No Safety for Women in Iraq', AlterNet, 15 December. www.alternet.org/story/45476; accessed 15 December 2006.

Jung, Dietrich, ed. (2003) *Shadow Globalization, Ethnic Conflicts and New Wars: A Political Economy of Intra-State War*. London: Routledge.

Kaldor, Mary (2001) *New and Old Wars: Organized Violence in a Global Era*. Stanford CA: Stanford University Press.

Le Billon, Philippe, Jake Sherman and Marcia Hartwell (2002) *Controlling Resource Flows to Civil Wars: A Review and Analysis of Current Policies and Legal Instruments*. Rockefeller Foundation Conference Report. Bellagio, Italy.

Looney, Robert (2005) 'The Economics of Coping: The Plight of Women in Iraq's Informal Economy', *Journal of Social, Political and Economic Issues* 30(3), Fall: 285–304.

McEwan, Melissa (2006) 'Sex Trafficking in Iraq', AlterNet, 24 October. www.alternet.org/bloggers/mcewan/43434; accessed 26 December 2006.

Monbiot, George (2005) 'Where Has Iraq's Money Gone?', AlterNet, 10 February. www.alternet.org/waroniraq/21227; accessed 18 December 2006.

Mother Jones (2006) 'Iraq for Sale', 6 September. www.motherjones.com/news/special_reports/2006/09/iraq_for_sale.html; accessed 15 December 2006.

Naylor, R.T. (2002) *Wages of Crime: Black Markets, Illegal Finance, and the Underground Economy*. Ithaca: Cornell University Press.

New York Times (2003) 'After the War: Economy', 23 June.

New York Times (2003) 'The Struggle for Iraq: Missing Weapons', 8 October.

New York Times (2004) 'Two More Iraqis Working for Americans Are Slain', 11 March.

New York Times (2004) 'US Aides Say Kin of Hussein Aid Insurgency', 5 July.

New York Times (2004) Scholar in Smuggling Trial Switches to Guilty Plea', 4 August.

New York Times (2004) 'Abstract of: Estimates by US See More Rebels with More Funds', 22 October.

New York Times (2004) 'Huge Cache of Explosives Vanished from Site in Iraq', 25 October.

New York Times (2004) 'UN Criticizes Iraq Occupation Oil Sales', 15 December.

New York Times (2005) 'Picking Up the Stolen Pieces of Iraq's Cultural Heritage', 14 February.

New York Times (2005) 'Boats, Cows, Tasty Lamb: Iraq Battles Smuggling', 27 March.

New York Times (2005) 'Iraq is Struck by New Wave of Abductions', 30 November.

New York Times (2005) 'Army Officer Charged in Iraqi Investigation', 2 December.

New York Times (2006) 'Oil Graft Fuels the Insurgency, Iraq and US Say', 5 February.

New York Times (2006) 'US Study Paints Somber Portrait of Iraqi Discord', 9 April.

New York Times (2006) 'Attacks on Oil Industry in Iraq Aid a Vast Smuggling Network', 4 June.

New York Times (2006) 'Iraq Insurgency Has Fund to Sustain Itself, US Finds', 26 November.

O'Brien, Timothy L. (2004) 'Lockboxes, Iraqi Loot and a Trail to the Fed', *New York Times*, 6 June.

Oxfam International (2007) 'Rising to the Humanitarian Challenge in Iraq', briefing paper, 30 July. www.oxfam.org/en/news/2007/pr070730_iraq_humanitarian_crisis; accessed 7 December 2007.

Peterson, V. Spike (1992) 'Transgressing Boundaries: Theories of Knowledge, Gender, and International Relations', *Millennium* 21(2), Summer: 183–206.

Peterson, V. Spike (2003) *A Critical Rewriting of Global Political Economy: Integrating Reproductive, Productive, and Virtual Economies*. London and New York: Routledge.

Peterson, V. Spike (2005) 'How (the Meaning of) Gender Matters in Political Economy', *New Political Economy* 10(4), December: 499–521.

Peterson, V. Spike (2007) 'Thinking Through Intersectionality and War', *Race, Gender and Class* 14: 3–4.

Peterson, V. Spike (2008) '"New Wars" and Gendered Economies', *Feminist Review* 88(1): 7–20.

Physicians for Human Rights (2003) 'Southern Iraq: Reports of Human Rights Abuses and Views on Justice, Reconstruction and Government', 18 September. www.physiciansforhumanrights.org/library/documents/reports/southern-iraq-reports-of.pdf; accessed 12 December 2006.

Pollitt, Katha (2007) 'You Can Come Upon Women's Bodies Anywhere', *Guardian*, 18 May; accessed 27 November 2007.

Pratt, Nicola (2005) 'Gendering Political Reconstruction in Iraq', UEA Working Papers in European and International Studies. www.uea.ac.uk/psi/papers/papers/Nicola%20Pratt.pdf.

Pugh, Michael, and Neil Cooper with Jonathan Goodhand (2004) *War Economies in a Regional Context: Challenges of Transformation*. Boulder CO: Lynne Rienner.

Rosen, Ruth (2006) 'A Wave of Sexual Terrorism in Iraq', *AlterNet*, 14 July. www.alternet.org/story/38932; accessed 15 December 2006.

Ruggiero, Vincenzo (2000) *Crime and Markets*. Oxford and New York: Oxford University Press.

Sandler, Lauren (2003) 'So This is Liberation', AlterNet, 17 December. www.alternet.org/story/17410; accessed 15 December 2006.

Seymour, Richard (2005) 'Stepping Backwards into the Future?' *The Middle East* 354, March: 18–20.

Susskind, Yifat (2007) 'Promising Democracy, Imposing Theocracy: Gender-Based Violence and the US War on Iraq', New York: MADRE. www.madre.org/articles/me/iraqreport.pdf; accessed 20 November 2007.

Telegraph (2003) 'Home Abortions Soar in Iraq as Unwanted Pregnancies Rise', 26 October.

UN and World Bank (2003) 'Joint Iraq Needs Assessment', October. http://lnweb18.worldbank.org/mna/mena.nsf/Attachments/Iraq+Joint+Needs+Assessment/$File/Joint+Needs+Assessment.pdf.

UNHCR (2007) 'Iraq Bleeds', *Refugees* 146: 2.

UNIFEM (2006) 'Gender Profile of the Conflict in Iraq', WomenWarPeace.org; accessed 15 December 2006.

US State Department (2005) *Trafficking in Persons Report; Special Cases: Iraq*. www.state.gov/g/tip/rls/tiprpt/2005/46617.htm; accessed 20 December 2006.

Women for Women International (2005) 'Windows of Opportunity: The Pursuit of Gender Equality in Post-War Iraq', Women for Women International Briefing Paper, Washington DC, January.

Women Waging Peace (2003) 'Winning the Peace Conference Report: Women's Role in Post-Conflict Iraq', April. www.huntalternatives.org/download/60_winning_the_peace_conference_report_women_s_role_in_post_conflict_iraq.pdf; accessed 20 December 2006.

Zangana, Haifa (2006) 'All Iraq is Abu Ghraib', *Guardian*, 5 July. http://commentisfree.guardian.co.uk/haifa_zangana/2006/07/the_personality_disorder_of_th.html; accessed 26 November 2007.

TWO

The United States, the Iraqi Women's Diaspora and Women's 'Empowerment' in Iraq

Nadje Al-Ali and Nicola Pratt

This chapter examines the implications of the US occupation of Iraq for Iraqi women and gender relations, as well as for transnational feminist activism within the Iraqi diaspora. We provide a critique of the US administration's promotion of women's 'empowerment', which has been one of the main pillars of the democracy and human rights rhetoric. We find that the US invasion of Iraq initially opened up new, albeit circumscribed, spaces for Iraqi women's activism. However, the limits of US commitment to women's empowerment is demonstrated by the administration's support for the construction of a political system in which communally defined political interests erode women's rights and women's participation. Moreover, in the context of a foreign occupation and a political system in which ethnic and religious identities are salient, gender identities are being reformulated by various actors in order to mark national, religious and ethnic differences within Iraq, as well as between Iraq and the 'West'. Consequently, Iraqi women activists find themselves under increasing pressure and forced to negotiate a difficult situation.

Iraqi women's diaspora activism and the invasion

Prior to the invasion of Iraq in 2003, Iraqi women activists in the diaspora, particularly those based in the UK and the USA, tried to raise consciousness about the human and women's rights atrocities of the Ba'th regime, as well as the devastating impact of wars and economic sanctions on women and Iraqi society more generally. Many of the women activists linked to political opposition parties put emphasis on the atrocities committed by the regime. They often did not feel comfortable with local (US and British) anti-war and anti-sanctions activists, whose critique of imperialist policies by their own governments sometimes failed to take position adequately against the regime of Saddam Hussein in terms of its human rights abuses. In the context of anti-sanctions activism, political spaces opened up for Iraqi activists with an increased coming together of international and national organizations and activists. Yet only a few organizations, such as the Iraqi Women's League, the Organization for Women's Freedom in Iraq, and Act Together: Women's Action for Iraq, combined their fierce critique of the international sanctions regime with a campaign against the former regime.

In the run-up to the invasion, the Iraqi diaspora was divided in terms of its support or opposition to the war. Many were sceptical and even cynical of American and British motivations, mentioning, for example, oil and business interests or the support of Israel and Zionism. Other women, usually those who were in favour of military intervention by American and British forces, talked about democracy, human rights and liberation. We met a number of women linked to the former Iraqi opposition in exile who were united in their support for the invasion on the basis of their hatred for the Ba'th regime – despite differences in ethnic and religious backgrounds and whether they were secular or Islamist.

However, within the exiled groups and parties that supported the war, women were marginalized, as Nadia S., a women's rights activist living in Washington DC, who had been part of the Kurdish opposition in exile, explained to Nicola:

Before the war, I became involved in establishing Women for a Free Iraq. This was primarily a media campaign highlighting human rights abuses under Saddam Hussein. We were a multi-ethnic and multi-religious group. We felt that women's voices were lacking in the discussions about Iraq before the war. We wanted our voices to be heard. ... The Iraqi opposition didn't take us seriously. They thought our campaign was useful for their objectives. But they didn't give us any real support. Our campaign was not a priority for them. (Al-Ali and Pratt, 2009: 89)

Similarly, at a conference of the Iraqi opposition in exile, held in London in 2002 to unite in preparation for a political takeover in Baghdad (Cockburn, 2002a, 2002b), apparently only 5 women out of 300 delegates were invited, and only 3 out of 65 were members of the follow-up committee (Al-Ali and Pratt, 2009: 89). Yet, despite their marginalization within the former opposition, some of the staunchest supporters of the US-led invasion were Iraqi diaspora women. About a year after the invasion, Mona N., a fervent supporter of President Bush, was having lunch with several other Iraqi women of similar political persuasion in an Italian restaurant in Detroit, and told Nadje:

I have been waiting for this moment for years. We have been lobbying this government so hard, trying to get them to recognize the crimes of Saddam Hussein. Finally, they started to understand that he is a big danger because he works with terrorists. The brave soldiers of this country will make sure that we finally have democracy and human rights in Iraq. (Al-Ali, 2007b: 216)

Mona is involved in a US-based women's organization – Women's Alliance for a Democratic Iraq – whose activities have been supported by the US government.

Overall, only a few of the women with whom we spoke actively promoted the invasion. A greater number of women expressed mixed feelings. They were not convinced by the rhetoric coming from the White House, yet they felt that a US-led invasion was the only way to get rid of Saddam Hussein. This was the case with Widad G., for example, a housewife and mother of three teenage children, who had divorced her husband about ten years ago after they had settled in London. Unlike her husband, who had been an opposition political activist since his youth, Widad had not been involved in politics. Yet, during the sanctions period, she collected money, clothes and medicine to send back to her family and friends in Iraq. Sitting in her modest but impeccably clean and lovingly decorated council flat in North London, early in 2004, Nadje asked her what she thought about the invasion. She smiled sadly, lit herself another cigarette and said:

> I am under no illusion that the Americans did this for us, for Iraqis. They want our oil and they want to control the region. I don't trust them. But at the time I felt we had no other choice. I reluctantly supported the war because I saw no way out of the horrible situation: people being caught between Saddam and sanctions. This could not go on anymore. No one wants to be occupied, but this is our chance. Things have been bad but now people have hope. It will take a bit of time, but, insha'allah, the situation will improve in a little while. (Al-Ali, 2007b: 217)

Her feelings of scepticism about US and UK motivations intermingled with feelings of there being no alternative, but also a sense of hope, were shared by many other Iraqi women with whom we spoke in 2003 and 2004. By 2005, as the security situation had deteriorated beyond imagination and violence escalated continuously, any sign of hope and cautious optimism had turned into despair, anger and a great sense of helplessness.

It is important to stress that we came across a great range of views and opinions – some clear-cut and others more nuanced and/or ambivalent – among women who live in the diaspora, as well as women who live inside Iraq. Rather than ethnic and religious affiliation, differences in opinions had more to do with political affiliations, as well as specific experiences with the previous regime. Overall, the Kurdish women with whom we talked were more positive and supportive of the invasion, describing it as a 'liberation'. This reflects the position of the two main Kurdish national parties (the Kurdistan Democratic Party, KDP, and the Patriotic Union of

Kurdistan, PUK), which considered the end of the Ba'th regime as an essential step towards ensuring Kurdish rights. However, we also spoke to several Kurdish women activists – particularly those who are not allied to the two major Kurdish parties – who opposed the war and the occupation. These included women active in women-only groups, such as Women in Black, as well as women part of mixed groups, such as the Iraqi Workers' Party. Members or sympathizers of former opposition-in-exile parties such as the Shi'i Islamist Dawa' Party and the Supreme Council of the Islamic Revolution in Iraq (SCIRI), now renamed the Supreme Islamic Iraqi Council (SIIC), or the secular-oriented Iraqi National Congress (INC), led by Ahmed Chalabi, and Iyad Allawi's Iraqi National Accord (INA), were supportive of the war and occupation, yet their attitudes towards US and UK motivations were also wide-ranging, as were their dealings with the US and UK governments.

The US administration and gendered war talk

Official discourse in the run-up to the US-led invasion and occupation of Iraq clearly illustrates the way in which Iraqi women have been instrumentalized as a means for the US administration to justify and advance its political interests in Iraq. Echoing the discourse of colonial powers in the first half of the twentieth century, US officials have implicitly linked the invasion and occupation of Iraq to a mission to 'save' Iraqi women. The rescue scenario of 'white men saving brown women from brown men' (Spivak, 1988: 93) is not only about the plight of women in faraway lands, but more significantly about the 'remasculinization' of the USA in the wake of the attacks of 9/11 (Shepherd, 2006; Wadley, 2006).

From February 2003, Women for a Free Iraq met with various high-level US government officials, including President Bush, Vice President Dick Cheney, then Secretary of State Colin Powell, then National Security Advisor Condoleezza Rice and then Deputy Secretary of Defense Paul Wolfowitz, as well as giving congressional briefings and interviews to the media.[1] The media campaign was seen as a success by those involved. As Nadia S., one of those who organized the campaign, told Nicola in the spring of 2005:

> We personalized the atrocities. We demonstrated how the biggest losers under Saddam Hussein were women. Women were targeted as women.... Women relatives of political prisoners were taken and raped to shame the family.

Their aim was to demonstrate the need for the US invasion in order to usurp the Ba'th regime and to bring an end to these atrocities. Their representation of Iraqi women as victims of Saddam Hussein coincided with US objectives of regime change in Baghdad. On 20 March 2003, the Office of International Women's Issues (within the State Department) posted a 'fact sheet on Iraqi women in order to educate people about the horrors that women experienced under Saddam – torture, repression, illiteracy', the Coordinator for International Women's Issues told Nicola in spring 2005; 'Iraqi women have been through a lot. Their story is heroic.'

Interestingly, this state department official compares women in Iraq to women in Afghanistan – another country that was the target of US military intervention. Indeed, she suggested that a fact sheet was necessary for the Iraqi context because 'there was more awareness about Afghan women than Iraqi women'. There were no images of burqa-clad women to display in the media to illustrate the 'clash of civilizations' that underpinned the justification for the bombing of Afghanistan (Cloud, 2004). Whilst women in Iraq had been the victims of the brutal policies of Saddam Hussein, they also went out to work, went to school and, in urban areas, dressed quite similarly to women in the USA and Europe. There were women engineers, scientists and university lecturers. Despite growing religious conservatism under sanctions, from 1991 onwards, women regularly went out in public. In general, Iraqi women were not subject to the extreme social conservatism of their Afghan counterparts under the Taliban.[2]

Iraqi women were not only presented as victims who needed saving. Simultaneously, they were represented by the US administration as heroines, who, due to their long years of suffering, had a vested interest in being 'liberated' from Saddam and helping to build a 'new Iraq'. Indeed, some women involved in Women for a Free Iraq used their experience of suffering to give them an active stake in the future of Iraq (Zangana, 2006). At a press conference with Women for a Free Iraq, on 6 March 2003 (two weeks before the invasion of Iraq), Paula Dobriansky, undersecretary of state for global affairs, said:

> We are at a critical point in dealing with Saddam Hussein. However this turns out, it is clear that the women of Iraq have a critical role to play in the future revival of their society. (US Department of State, 2003)

Following the invasion of Iraq, the US administration continued to reaffirm its vision of the role of Iraqi women in the construction of the 'new Iraq'. Paul Wolfowitz, a central figure in US foreign policymaking, was one of several high-level administration figures promoting the inclusion of Iraqi women. According to Linda M. of Women Waging Peace, a US NGO dedicated to supporting women's involvement in post-conflict reconstruction, 'After meeting with the Iraqi women that we brought over [to the US for a workshop], he [Wolfowitz] said that he felt that the women "really got it" in terms of supporting democratization.' In an op-ed piece written about his second visit to post-invasion Iraq, Wolfowitz described Rajaa Khuzai, an obstetrician by profession and one of three women members of the Iraqi Governing Council, as 'helping to give birth to freedom in a country that was abused for more than three decades by a regime of murderers and torturers' (Wolfowitz, 2004). During the 2005 State of the Union address, Safia al-Suhail, an Iraqi woman activist who had been prominent in the former opposition in exile as well as in the Women for a Free Iraq campaign, stood in the gallery with Laura Bush as the president honoured her as one of Iraq's 'leading democracy and human rights advocates' (Bush, 2005). For supporters of the administration, such as Eleana Gordon of the neoconservative Foundation for the Defense of Democracies,

Safia al-Suhail represents 'the courage and determination of Middle Easterners, and in particular Middle Eastern women, to build free and just societies' (Gordan, 2005).

The US discourse that sees Iraqi women as victims of dictatorship and builders of freedom and democracy overlaps with the concerns of UN Security Resolution 1325 on women, peace and security (passed in 2000). This resolution, the first time the UN Security Council had considered gender in conjunction with war and conflict, was the product of years of lobbying by women activists and international NGOs to recognize the gendered impact of war on women and to promote the role of women in conflict resolution and peace-building processes (Cockburn, 2007). The text of UNSCR 1325 has been criticized for essentializing women as an embodiment of peace-making and reducing women's interests to their sex, which is not necessarily empowering for women (Shepherd, 2008). The voices of those whose objectives do not conform to liberal discourses on gender equality are marginalized or deemed 'unauthentic' (Gibbings, 2005). Such a discourse prioritizes women's gender interests over other interests constructed around class, religion, ethnicity or political/ideological orientation, thereby often creating new structures of inequality.

Nevertheless, whilst such a discourse is essentializing of women's experiences and potentially exclusionary, there are some Iraqi women activists who have benefited in order to obtain access to international funding for the purpose of establishing NGOs and, in some cases, to obtain access to international forums, such as the UN, to promote the case for supporting Iraqi women. In the words of two Iraqi women activists addressing the UN Security Council meeting on the fifth anniversary of UNSCR 1325: 'Resolution 1325 has been instrumental in giving women a voice in the process [of establishing peace and justice in Iraq] and we thank you and hope we can count on your continued support' (Edwar and Fakri, 2005). Such access to international/transnational forums has become progressively more important as women become increasingly marginalized within Iraqi political life under US occupation, as we discuss later.

Diaspora women and the 'new Iraq'

Anyone who spent time with diaspora Iraqis in the first couple of years after the invasion would have been struck by the amount of travel and flurry of activities. Many women we talked to in late 2003 and throughout 2004 were seriously considering returning to Iraq permanently. The energy, enthusiasm and hopefulness even reached some of those women who had fervently opposed the invasion. They also wanted to be part of the 'new Iraq'. Sanaa M. told Nadje during a cultural event in London in the fall of 2003:

> You know I was against this war. But now that Saddam is gone, I hope to be able to return and help my country. We have been waiting for this moment. I would like to set up a small project to help orphans in Baghdad. There are so many of them after all these wars. Throughout the sanctions period I used to send money and medicines to my relatives in Iraq. I want to continue my work but now I can actually spend time within the country. Maybe I will even return for good? I never felt at home in London and I miss Iraq all the time.

Many women, similar to Sanaa, visited Iraq with the wish to help rebuild the country and improve living conditions for ordinary Iraqis. While some only went for short visits, others had more long-term plans. However, it was mainly the pro-invasion women who initially got involved in political processes and projects linked to reconstruction. On both sides of the Atlantic, those women who had advocated a military invasion to topple the regime of Saddam Hussein were sought after by government officials and institutions eager to show their commitment to 'women's liberation'. Iraqi diaspora activists were perceived to be the legitimate mediators and bridges to reach a wider population within Iraq.

As mentioned earlier, many pro-war Iraqi women activists in the USA received high-profile support and media attention in the run up to the war and in the immediate aftermath. Sumaya R., who was involved with the Women's Alliance for a Democratic Iraq (WAFDI), in April of 2005 described with enthusiasm and hope the close cooperation with US government bodies and non-governmental organizations:

> Our group is part of a network that was established in 2002. My husband was very active and involved in this. It is a network of Iraqi-American organizations, now consisting of about 17 or 18 organizations, including Kurdish and Islamist organizations. The first time we had a conference was in June 2002. Kanan Makiya[3] was involved, and people from the State Department. After the conference the State Department established a working group on Iraq. Then Iraq was liberated. In September 2003, we organized another conference and [head of al-Dawa party, Ibrahim] Al-Jafa'ri came. There were many senators and again people from the State Department. ... For the first time now, women are able to spread their wings. They are forming groups, they are speaking their minds. They are expressing themselves. We are organizing together with the Higher Council of Women inside Iraq. You can't imagine how our women are excited about these events. A lot of them are going outside the country for training. Now they have their freedom! (Al-Ali and Pratt, 2009: 150)

A flurry of meetings, workshops and conferences bringing together diaspora women and women from the inside marked the early phase of post-Saddam Hussein Iraq. Diaspora women became involved in charity organizations, humanitarian assistance, training programmes, advocacy around women's issues, democracy and human rights and wider political issues both inside Iraq and in their countries of residence. Several Iraqi diaspora organizations and individual activists based in the USA and the UK were instrumental in facilitating and encouraging Iraqi women's political mobilization inside Iraq in the early period.

In London, numerous meetings, workshops and seminars brought together Iraqi women of different political, ethnic and religious backgrounds. These meetings were often facilitated, if not initiated, by UK government bodies, such as the Department for International Development (DFID), or by the former UK Secretary of State for Trade and Industry and Minister for Women's Affairs Patricia Hewitt. In the beginning of July 2003, nearly one hundred women participated in a conference entitled 'the Voices of Iraqi Women', which was sponsored and supported by Patricia Hewitt as well as the US Undersecretary of State for Global Affairs Paula Dobriansky. Although uninvited, Nadje and other members of Act Together: Women's Action for Iraq attended one of the preparatory meetings in London, during which most of the women expressed their gratitude to the British government for 'liberating Iraq'. Those few women activists, like members of Act Together, who expressed more critical views and questioned the idea that diaspora women could either represent or liberate Iraqi women, were clearly sidelined (Al-Ali and Pratt, 2009: 149).

Funding for 'women's empowerment'

When Nicola visited Washington DC in March–April 2005, a number of people were keen to stress the US administration's commitment to support women's 'empowerment' in Iraq and to see them play a role in the country's future. As one former member of the Coalition Provisional Authority (CPA) in Baghdad, Janet W., said, 'From the time that I arrived at the CPA, [Paul L.] Bremer always talked about including women. He met with lots of women.' Indeed, the CPA included an Office for Women's Affairs. Similarly, Leslie F., a senior State Department official, stated: 'We are committed to women in Iraq and we've put our money where our mouth is' (Al-Ali and Pratt, 2009: 57).

It is difficult to find exact figures that would identify the amount of money allocated to supporting Iraqi women. This is partly because funds are channelled through different government institutions (SIGIR, 2007: Appendix G). Also the vast majority of funding is gender-neutral – that is, it is expected that funding for the re-habilitation of infrastructure (water, electricity, oil industry, transport and communications) and security and law enforcement should benefit all Iraqis, regardless of gender. The USA has spent money on the education sector ($1.15 billion) and the health sector ($530 million) in programmes that mention women and girls specifically as beneficiaries, such as accelerated learning for children out of school (USAID, n.d.) and the rehabilitation of a maternity hospital in Baghdad (SIGIR, 2007: 96). However, one of the major problems in the post-invasion period has been the lack of actual improvement and reconstruction of severely debilitated basic services and infrastructure (Al-Ali and Pratt, 2009: 58).

Despite the absence of disaggregated data with regard to the number of Iraqi women benefiting from US reconstruction funds, we found plenty of evidence of Iraqi women being targeted through programmes and projects in Iraq. The United States Institute for Peace (USIP) is a US-based NGO that initially received $10 million directly from Congress, in October 2003, to participate in rebuilding Iraq. Congress did not specify that any of the $10 million should be directed for the support of women. Nevertheless, Peter K. at USIP, echoing some of the assumptions of UNSCR 1325, told Nicola: 'We see women's inclusion as important ... women are 60 per cent of the population. They have a moderating impact on politics.' Meanwhile, Sara J. at USIP told Nicola that a focus of their small grants scheme is to promote women's empowerment and USIP had allocated six grants (out of a total of thirty-four), worth between $5,000 and $20,000, to women's organizations (Al-Ali and Pratt, 2009: 58–9).

Another way in which women have been beneficiaries of US funding is through efforts by US agencies and NGOs to bring women together in conferences and workshops. In the first year following the fall of the Ba'th regime, Janet W., in the Women's Affairs Office of the CPA, helped to organize several conferences in different parts of Iraq which were funded by the USA:

We assisted a group of women in organizing a small conference in Baghdad in July 2003 [Voices of the Women of Iraq]. The women selected their own steering committee. The conference discussed all sorts of issues, such as constitutional reform, social welfare, education, the economy, etc. They presented these recommendations to the [Iraqi] Governing Council. Following this Baghdad meeting, regional meetings were held in the south, south-central, the north, etc. We provided the support that they requested. They had a lot of ideas about what they wanted. (Al-Ali and Pratt, 2009: 59)

Women Waging Peace and the Woodrow Wilson School brought Iraqi women together in several workshops in the USA and in Beirut to discuss how to involve women in post-conflict reconstruction and how to guarantee women's rights in the constitution. Hind S., working on the Middle East programme at Woodrow Wilson, told Nicola:

> Our role was to facilitate discussion and reach out to these women. The women were from different religious and ethnic backgrounds. Some were active at the grassroots level. They were well-received by the US administration – Bush, Wolfowitz and others – they were very receptive to meeting the women. And money has been allocated for programs targeting women. (Al-Ali and Pratt, 2009: 60)

The vast majority of funding in support of women appears to have been directed for the 'training' of women as participants in political, civil and economic processes. This approach to women's empowerment is based on the assumption that Iraqi women need training to bring them into the public sphere: '[Iraqi] Women are capable and they need knowledge and skills', as Lesley at the State Department told Nicola (Al-Ali and Pratt, 2009: 60). Such an approach fails to recognize that Iraqi women participated in the public sphere before 2003 and that the socio-economic and political context – particularly war and occupation – undoubtedly impacts upon women's opportunities for public involvement. A key example of such an approach is the twenty women's centres that the CPA and USAID funded throughout Iraq. The first of the nine Baghdad centres, supported by a grant of $1.4 million, was opened on 8 March 2004 (International Women's Day) by CPA head L. Paul Bremer. The centres were meant to offer women training in vocational and business skills, computers and the English language, as well as providing legal advice. However, we both encountered criticisms about their sustainability. For example, Ziba H., seconded to Iraq by the UK government between September 2003 and April 2004, told Nicola:

> There was no ownership over these centres in the local communities. They would be suspicious of the centres – what are they for?

What are our women doing there? There was a flawed consultation
process. (Al-Ali and Pratt, 2009: 61)

The concept behind the women's centres reflected not only particular assumptions about Iraqi women's needs but also the US
administration's desire to support Iraq's transition to a market-based
economy. The USA has endeavoured to train and support Iraqi
women as 'entrepreneurs'. For example, the Center for International
Private Enterprise (CIPE), a US-based NGO that receives funds from
the National Endowment for Democracy, worked throughout 2005
with two women's organizations: the Iraqi Business Women's Association (IBWA), established in 2004, and the Iraqi Professional
Women's Association (IPWA), established at the beginning of 2005.
According to Fares J. of CIPE, who spoke to Nicola in Washington:

> We are doing training and capacity building, raising awareness
> about economic reform. … We have provided start up costs for
> furniture, etc. … We bring them to Amman for training in corpo-
> rate governance.[4] (Al-Ali and Pratt, 2009: 61)

Similarly, the US government also established the US-Iraqi Businesswomen's Partnership, bringing 'American women entrepreneurs
together with Iraqi counterparts in a virtual mentoring program'
(US Department of State, 2007).

Iraqi women have also been 'trained' to take part in the political
process as candidates, voters and advocates of women's rights. On
8 March 2004, then Secretary of State Colin Powell announced an
allocation of $10 million for the 'Iraqi Women's Democracy Initia-
tive'. According to Undersecretary of State for Global Affairs Paula
Dobriansky, the initiative aimed 'to help women become full and
vibrant partners in Iraq's developing democracy' (USINFO, 2004).
Implicitly revealing US concerns that regime change in Baghdad
was not resulting in women's 'liberation', Richard T. at the US State
Department, who was charged with the process of managing the
allocation of grants, said: 'We were under pressure for immediate
results. Deputy Secretary of State Armitage said, "No dilly-dallying.

We need results." There was a need to bring women into the political process immediately' (Al-Ali and Pratt, 2009: 63). The grants were given to NGOs to carry out democracy education, leadership training, political training, NGO coalition-building, organizational management, media training and 'teaching entrepreneurship' (Office of the Senior Coordinator for International Women's Issues, 2004). Since then, the Women's Democracy Initiative has been extended to $24.5 million, with a new focus on the elimination of violence against women, 'economic capacity building' for widows and women and peace-building (US Department of State, n.d.).

Transnational women's rights activism

Women's organizations and initiatives started to mushroom all over Iraq in the aftermath of the invasion. Many of these organizations, like the National Council of Women (NWC), the Iraqi Women's Higher Council (IWHC), the Iraqi Independent Women's Group or the Society for Iraqi Women for the Future, for example, have been founded by members of the major political parties or prominent professional women with close ties to political parties. Many organizations, such as the Organization for Women's Freedom in Iraq, were initiated by returnees – that is, Iraqi women activists who had been part of the diaspora before 2003. While mainly founded and represented by elite women, some of the organizations have a broad membership and have branches throughout the country. The Iraqi Women's Network ('Al-Shabaka'), for example, consists of thirty-seven women's grassroots organizations spread throughout Iraq. Their activities revolve around humanitarian and practical projects, such as income generation, legal advice, free healthcare and counselling, as well as women's rights advocacy and lobbying. Many of the initiatives fill the gap in state provision of welfare and health services and are often related to religiously motivated organizations and groups.

The main issues that have publicly mobilized women of mainly educated middle-class background throughout Iraq are: (1) the attempt to replace the relatively progressive personal status law governing marriage, divorce, child custody and inheritance with a more conservative law (Article 137 in 2003, and Article 41 of the 2005 constitution); (2) the issue of a women's quota for political representation – women's demands were for a 40 per cent quota in the Transitional Administrative Law (TAL), but they managed to achieve a 25 per cent quota; (3) the struggle against sectarianism and for national unity; (4) the struggle against Islamist encroachment by political parties, militias and terrorist organizations; (5) the debate about the Iraqi constitution, mainly with respect to the role of Islam, the personal status laws and the demand to include an article recognizing international human rights conventions, including CEDAW;[5] and (6) the targeted assassinations of professional women and women's rights activists.

One of the first issues was the campaign around the women's quota. The Bush administration refused to support quotas for women – despite establishing de facto quotas for different communal groups on the Iraqi Governing Council (IGC), a consultative body of limited authority created in July 2003. Indeed, Bremer appointed only three women to the IGC – a move regarded by many as tokenistic. Despite Bremer's opposition, Iraqi women activists achieved the compromise of a 25 per cent target for women's participation in elected assemblies in the Transitional Administrative Law and the permanent constitution. The women's quota in parliament was put into practice by obliging every third candidate in party lists to be a woman. As a result, following the January 2005 elections, the 25 per cent quota was exceeded and the newly elected assembly was more than 30 per cent women. However, in the December 2005 elections, the percentage of women elected was reduced to 19 per cent, due to changes in which Iraq as a single constituency was replaced by the drawing-up of multiple constituencies. In order to meet the 25 per cent target, women's presence in parliament was augmented by the allocation of compensatory seats. However, as we discuss later, the organization of the quota has not necessarily guaranteed the protection of women's rights.

Iraqi women's perseverance was also crucial in helping to stop the passage of Decree 137 in early 2004. The proposed decree, suggested in December 2003 by members of the IGC under the rotating chairmanship of 'Abd al-'Aziz al-Hakim, leader of the Supreme Council for the Islamic Revolution in Iraq (SCIRI), could have replaced Iraq's unified personal status code with more conservative interpretations of Sharia (Islamic jurisprudence) with regard to matters of marriage, divorce, child custody and inheritance.[6] The passing of the decree was shrouded in some mystery and was not leaked to the press until 13 January 2004 (Various, 2004). It quickly resulted in the mobilization of women – not only inside Iraq but also transnationally – in order to oppose it. Many Iraqi women activists (though by no means all) vehemently opposed Decree 137 as a retrograde step for women's position in Iraq (see Agency staff, 2004a; Various, 2004). Lina P., an Iraqi woman living in the USA for over thirty years, was working temporarily for the Iraqi Reconstruction and Development Council when Decree 137 was issued. She told Nicola:

> I was sitting in my office when my colleague came to me and said, here, read this. I couldn't believe my eyes. I called Judge Hakki[7] and we spoke to the media. We went to speak to Bremer to ask him not to ratify it. Over the following forty-eight hours, we contacted a lot of groups and we spoke to the BBC. The next day, we saw [Minister] Nesrine Berwari.[8] The following week, a protest was organized.

Women activists inside and outside Iraq issued press releases outlining the implications of the decree, which was distributed widely by email. They lobbied the IGC, the CPA and international bodies to prevent the proposal from passing into law. Forty-four US lawmakers, from both parties, wrote a letter to George Bush urging the administration 'to take steps now to protect the rights of Iraqi women' (Lobe, 2004). In Baghdad and the Kurdish region, thousands of women protested, calling for the decree to be repealed (Al-Jazeera and agencies, 2004). Following several weeks of protests, Bremer did not ratify the resolution, thereby preventing it from becoming law.

Many supporters of women's rights criticized Bremer for taking so long to cancel the proposal. Yet they also recognized that Decree 137 was significant in forming new transnational networks of solidarity for women's rights in Iraq.

This moment of upsurge in women's activism has been identified as an important turning point for the Iraqi women's movement. Women's protests contributed to overturning Decree 137; to ensuring the inclusion of a 25 per cent quota (a compromise figure) in the Transitional Administrative Law, signed in March 2004 (and later the permanent constitution); and to the appointment of six women cabinet ministers and seven deputy ministers within the transitional government of Iyad Allawi (June 2004–April 2005). As a result, there was a feeling for a while among certain people that women were making gains in post-invasion Iraq and that their public presence would help to guarantee their rights.

For the US and UK governments, the political gains made by Iraqi women are seen as a vindication of their policies. As they see it, Iraqi women have benefited from US, UK and other international efforts to support civil society through grants to organizations, including women's organizations and human rights organizations. The rights to association and expression that appeared in the initial period after the fall of the Ba'th dictatorship provided many women with the opportunities to mobilize publicly. Some Iraqi women have celebrated these achievements as a testimony of their determination to be part of post-invasion politics and reconstruction, despite the fact that US support has been ambiguous in their eyes.

However, as time has passed, more and more women activists with whom we spoke were increasingly less celebratory. Leila H., a women's rights activist still living inside Iraq, told Nadje while visiting Amman for a short respite during the hot summer months of 2005:

> Initially many of us were very hopeful. We did not like foreign soldiers on our streets, but we were happy Saddam was gone. Once the general chaos and the looting settled down a bit, women were the first ones to get organized. Women doctors and lawyers started

to offer free services to women. We started to discuss political issues and tried to lobby the American and British forces. But especially the Americans sent people to Iraq whose attitude was: 'We don't do women'. Bremer was one of them. Iraqi women managed to get a woman's quota despite the Americans who opposed it. Their interpretation of women's issues was to organize big meetings and conferences and to build modern women's centres. Do you think anyone went to visit these centres? What we need are more women in all aspects of governance. But the problem is that some of the women that are appointed are actually very conservative and are against women's rights. (Al-Ali, 2007b: 256)

Leila, like many others, increasingly expressed her disillusionment with a political process that has become characterized by sectarian politics, growing conservatism and increasing violence – to the detriment of women's participation and women's rights.

Communal politics versus women's 'empowerment' under occupation

The rise in sectarian/communal politics has operated to erode women's rights since the fall of Saddam Hussein. Sectarianism is not inherent to Iraqi society but is the result of specific historical processes. Whilst sectarian prejudices certainly existed under the Ba'th and official measures were pursued to prioritize the Sunni Arab character of Iraq at the expense of the Shi'a and Kurds, all opponents of the regime, regardless of religious or ethnic background, suffered persecution. Indeed, it is the destruction of an Iraqi (national) civil society through persistent persecution of activists of all ideological stripes that ended the processes of national integration that had begun with the formation of the Iraqi state at the beginning of the twentieth century (Sluglett and Farouk-Sluglett, 1993: 90). The regime's brutal repression led to feelings of alienation from the state and increased identification with non-state entities – such as ethnic and religious communities and tribes. These non-state entities represented a source of protection from the state. These trends grew under sanctions, from

1991 onwards – partly because Saddam Hussein actively encouraged the growth of religion and tribes in public life and also because individuals came to rely on communal/familial/tribal networks for economic survival. Meanwhile, state institutions disintegrated from lack of funds, and their withdrawal from people's lives enabled non-state actors, largely rooted in particularistic identities of religion, ethnicity and tribe, to fill the vacuum.

Whilst the former regime, especially under sanctions, provided the environment for the growth of sectarian sentiments and informal networks, the US-led occupation has institutionalized sectarian and ethnic politics. This is a result of the further undermining of national state institutions together with the creation of new political arrangements that have enabled the emergence of a de facto confessional system. State institutions have been undermined by the CPA de-Ba'thification order, which removed not only top Ba'th officials but also a whole section of experienced and qualified members of Iraq's state institutions; the CPA disbanding of the national army and the slow progress in training a new one; the failure of reconstruction and rehabilitation of basic services and infrastructure; insufficient oversight to stop corruption; and the introduction of market reforms and attempts to dismantle the dominant state role in production and distribution (for further details, see Al-Ali and Pratt, 2009; Herring and Rangwala, 2006). Together, these measures have rendered state institutions less capable and less relevant in the lives of Iraqi citizens. In a survey of a sample of Iraqi women, 12.7 per cent said that religious institutions had 'done something in the past year to improve their lives', compared to only 5.5 per cent of women who thought that the government had done so. Indeed, 16 per cent of women said that 'the government has done something to make their lives much worse over the past year', whilst only 8.4 per cent of women 'blamed worsened conditions on religious institutions' (Women for Women International, 2005: 18).

Sectarian and ethnic-based politics became significant in post-Ba'th governing arrangements with the introduction by L. Paul Bremer of sectarian and ethnic quotas to the Iraqi Governing Council in July 2003. Subsequently, competition for political power along ethnic and religious lines has largely determined political behaviour in Iraq. Political party lists formed in preparation for the January and December 2005 elections vied for power not on the basis of ideological distinctions but on the basis of communal affiliations. Indeed, those groups that won no or very few seats were those that shunned sectarian politics, such as Adnan Pachachi's newly formed Independent Iraqi Democrats.

The introduction of a proportional representation electoral system has meant that no one group can dominate the political scene – a fear of the CPA (Herring and Rangwala, 2006: 13–19). However, the division of power among groups competing along communal lines has created a de facto confessional system. Cabinet posts and the major positions of president, vice presidents, prime minister and deputy prime ministers have been allocated to enable a sectarian and ethnic balancing act. Indeed, following the elections of December 2005, in which Sunni parties reversed their previous decision to boycott elections, increased Sunni representation in parliament led to an increase in the number of cabinet posts in order that all parties could be accommodated in the government.

The USA assumed that the accommodation of political forces on the basis of ethnic and sectarian identifications would keep these forces within the formal political system (rather than opposing it from outside). However, de facto ethnic and sectarian quotas work against women's participation – even where, as in Iraq, there is a 25 per cent quota for women's representation in parliament. The sharing out of top political posts to enable sectarian and ethnic balancing is enabled through back-room negotiations between the most powerful politicians in each grouping, at the expense of those who are less powerful – who are, generally, women politicians. Indeed, the number of female members of Iraq's cabinets since 2004 has decreased as sectarian and ethnic politics has become more en-trenched. The interim cabinet of Iyad Allawi (June 2004–April 2005) contained five women ministers and six women deputy ministers out of total of thirty-one posts. The cabinet formed in April, following the January 2005 elections, contained six women out of thirty-six posts. The cabinet formed in May 2006, following the December 2005 elections, contained only four women out of forty-two posts. Irrespective of the democratic veneer of competitive elections, as lauded by the USA and its allies, political decision-making is subject to trading of competing communally based interests rather than the result of parliamentary deliberations. Members of parliament are instructed which way to vote by their political leaders. Women MPs, who are elected through a party list system, are beholden to male politicians for their positions. This means that the 25 per cent quota reinforces rather than challenges competition along sectarian and ethnic lines. This is particularly problematic when it comes to the issue of protecting and promoting women's rights. The majority of women MPs were elected on the Shi'i Islamist list, the United Iraqi Alliance. They have supported measures that Suzan R., elected to the Baghdad parliament on the Kurdistan Alliance list, considers as 'against their interests' as women (Al-Ali and Pratt, 2008: 79).

However, it is inaccurate to represent the majority of women MPs as dupes of sectarian political leaders. Rather, they do not see themselves or their interests as autonomous from the communally based parties that promote political interests based on sectarian identity. For women within the Shi'i parties, the promotion and affirmation of a Shi'i religious identity is intrinsically linked to the ability of their 'community' to promote the interests of the Shi'i majority and prevent a repetition of the brutal repression that many Shi'i suffered under Saddam Hussein. Within this context, the concept of gender equality promoted by secular-oriented women activists contradicts their Shi'i identity and, therefore, is perceived as counter to their interests.

Similarly, women MPs elected on the Kurdistan Alliance list also see their interests in line with those of male political leaders – that is, autonomy for Kurdistan through a federal political system and the inclusion of Kirkuk within the Kurdistan region. However, Kurdish identity is not based primarily on religious affiliation and beliefs but rather on ethnicity. Kurdish nationalism is more secular- rather than religious-oriented. One of the ways in which Kurdish political leaders have historically differentiated Kurds from Arabs is on the basis that Kurdish women are accorded more freedom in Kurdish society (Mojab, 2004: 115). Therefore, not only are Kurdish national politics able to accommodate women's demands for greater rights but Kurdish politicians consider support for women's rights within Iraq as a means of differentiating themselves from competing political forces within Iraq. Yet the instrumentalization of women's rights within the Kurdish national agenda means that they are easily sacrificed for the greater political goals of federalism and Kirkuk. This political trading was particularly notable during the process of drafting the constitution over the summer of 2005. The USA supported the political objectives of Shi'i Islamist and Kurdish nationalist parties, since these coincided with US aims to prevent supporters of the ex-Ba'th party from regaining political power.

Political bargaining, women's rights and the constitution

The negotiations between the sectarian and ethnic-based political groupings over the permanent Iraqi constitution in 2005 demonstrate how women's rights have become compromised. The constitution ratified in October 2005 predominantly reflected the objectives of the Shi'i Islamist and the Kurdish nationalist parties, which dominated the drafting committee and were largely supported by the USA. The Shi'i Islamist parties wanted to guarantee that the numerical dominance of the Shi'i would translate into future political dominance – thereby reversing their historical marginalization within Iraqi nation-state building processes. This meant writing a constitution that would give the national legislature (where Shi'i Islamist parties would probably be in the majority) significant leeway to shape the future of the political system. Connected to this, the Shi'i Islamist parties sought to reshape the identity of the new Iraq to reflect their majority status – that is, by promoting their Islamist ideology through the law-making process. The Kurdish political leaders wanted to guarantee the continuation of their de facto political control of Iraqi

Kurdistan through the establishment of a federal political system. Linked to this, they sought to fix the borders of the Kurdistan region and to decide the status of the oil-rich province of Kirkuk – which they claimed as part of the Kurdish region. Linked to the consolidation of an autonomous Kurdistan, they wished to ensure a claim to oil revenues.

Whilst not the source of legislation (which was opposed by secular-oriented members of the drafting committee), Islam was defined in the constitution as the official religion and a basic source of legislation. Moreover, no law can be passed that contradicts the 'undisputed rules' of Islam.[9] The body charged with overseeing the constitutionality of federal laws is the Supreme Federal Court. This is to be made up of 'a number of judges and experts in Sharia and secular law, whose number and manner of selection will be defined by a law that should be passed by two-thirds of the parliament members'. In other words, the interpretation of the rules of Islam depends upon the nature of parliament – the majority of whose members are part of the Shi'i Islamist bloc. Whilst Islam does not necessarily stand in contradiction to women's rights, in other Muslim countries, certain interpretations of Islam have been used, variously, to justify domestic violence, to prevent women travelling without a male guardian and to stop women becoming judges, and so on.[10]

The other constitutional article of particular concern to secular women activists is the organization of family law, Article 41, which states that 'Iraqis are free in their adherence to their personal status according to their own religion, sect, belief and choice, and that will be organized by law.' This realizes the worst fears of many women's rights activists in that it opens the way for a Lebanese-type system, in which family law is governed according to respective membership of a religious sect. This gives powers to religious leaders to interpret family law, significantly reduces protection for women's rights in family matters, and codifies sectarianism within the legal system. However, the increased role for religious leaders in interpreting family law is in line with Shi'i parties' objectives to increase the public role of Islam in the new Iraq.

Since family law is not the preserve of central government and the wording of the constitution is substantially loose, this devolves authority to the regions to specify family law.[11] Kurdish political leaders are generally perceived to be more secular in orientation, and the Kurdish parliament rejected Decree 137 when it was proposed by the IGC at the end of 2003 (Agency staff, 2004b). In other words, the current constitution enables a system in which women are not necessarily divided by sect but that allows different regions of Iraq to implement different family laws. The outcome could be a more secular-oriented family code in Kurdistan and a religiously inspired conservative family code in the Shi'i south. Such an outcome would violate universal citizenship rights for women. Unsurprisingly, many women activists are lobbying hard to repeal this article of the constitution to allow the continuation of the unified family code that has been in place, with some amendments, since 1959. However, the potential for regional differences has also led women activists in the Kurdish region to focus more on achieving federalism than on overturning an article that could violate women's rights. Indeed, certain secular-oriented women activists in northern Iraq backed the constitution in the national referendum because of its guarantees for federalism, which, they believe, will ensure that women's rights are respected in the Kurdistan region.

US pressure on the parties to complete and ratify the constitution by the deadlines previously proposed in the TAL meant that there was almost no time to accommodate the demands of Sunni parties, which came late to the drafting process. The Sunni politicians, representing Islamist and secular parties, sought to protect the Arab character and integral nature of the state and, therefore, were hostile to federalism and the majoritarian power of the Shi'i parties. They also sought to prevent further de-Ba'thification (which they considered to be a cover for the exclusion of Sunnis from government), and to ensure that oil revenues would be centrally distributed (thereby guaranteeing oil revenues for the Sunni-majority areas with no oil reserves). In a last-minute effort to win support for the constitution in Sunni majority areas, the drafters inserted a clause to establish a Constitutional Review Committee (CRC) to examine the disputed issues of de-Ba'thification, federalism, the distribution of oil revenues, the status of Kirkuk and the nature of personal status laws.

At the time of writing, the CRC continues its deliberations. Women activists feel that they will not succeed in amending Article 41 because of trading over other issues deemed more politically important by the leaders of the different political groupings – in particular, the likelihood that the Kurdish politicians, who, in principle, are amenable to supporting demands to retain the unified personal status code, will trade Article 41 for their political ambitions with regard to Kirkuk. Rawan H., a deputy minister and part of the list headed by Iyad Allawi, as well as a women's rights activist, was very pessimistic when she spoke to Nadje in August 2007:

> There was a huge pressure by women activists to abolish Article 41, but we feel that we have reached an impasse. ... There is not enough support from the UN, international NGOs and the media. ... We have managed to change the position of some political parties, including Fadila. We are working on the Sadrists. The most hardcore are SCIRI and Da'wa. ... Abbas al-Bayati [of the UIA] has said that he would rather abolish the whole constitution than Article 41. ... He and others argue that Article 41 is about personal freedom and that it is the most democratic article in the constitution. Most of the Islamist Shi'i women are for the article and against the unified personal status code. (Al-Ali and Pratt, 2009: 118)

It is significant that family law has become an important arena of contestation. Ba'thist measures sought to dismantle the authority of the male heads of family, clan and tribe over women and to replace it with the authority of the state (Joseph, 1991: 176–200). The new constitution replaces state authority over women with the authority of communal leaders of the different regions of Iraq – whether Shi'i, Sunni or Kurd (Al-Ali and Pratt, 2006). Family law is one of the mechanisms for consolidating a post-Ba'th state on the basis of regulating religious-ethnic difference within the private sphere. By devolving family law to the regions, the state encourages the loyalty of communal leaders to the state, despite fragmenting authority and weakened national institutions. Family law becomes part of a 'social contract', trading communal autonomy for women's rights.[12]

Women's activism and shifting gender identities in Iraq

Not unsurprisingly, and largely due to the deteriorating security situation, women's activism in Iraq has been seriously impeded. As middle-class professionals and foreign passport-holders have been key targets of frequent kidnappings for ransom as well as targeted assassinations by militias seeking to impose 'traditional' gender roles or by insurgents punishing those with any connections to the USA and its allies, Iraqi women returnees have been particularly vulnerable. Moreover, the lack of credibility of the large number of former exiles now holding key political positions, and who have been disproportionately represented in the various governments, has also contributed to a growing resentment towards women returnees who have been involved in women's organizations and political processes and reconstruction in general.

Najwa R., a middle-aged professional woman who had been living in exile for over thirty years, first in London and then Amman in order to be closer to Baghdad, her home town, told Nadje:

> Many Iraqis who lived outside wanted to come inside to help rebuild the country, but we faced this hatred, this anger: 'You did not see it! You did not live it! Why should you come now?' They are very bitter about it. I even felt it with my own family. There is bitterness towards those of us who did not live through the misery. (Al-Ali, 2007a: 144)

Others were much less understanding in their assessment and account of their experience inside Iraq. Widad M., a doctor and activist in her fifties who lived in London for twenty-five years and who worked for the Coalition Provisional Authority in 2003 and 2004, said:

> It was very shocking, even my family had problems accepting me as I am. The characters changed, they seem to have closed up. At

one time, I organized a meeting between students and the Ministry of Education. They wanted to discuss things. The first thing they wanted to discuss was young girls turning up at the university with short sleeves or short skirts or dresses. The mentality went so wrong. Why is this so important to them? (Al-Ali, 2007b: 255)

Like many other women to whom we spoke, Widad feels very disillusioned. She was not the only one to tell us that she was giving up because her efforts were not appreciated by people inside Iraq, and also because things had just gone from bad to worse. Leila A., a researcher in her mid-forties, who used to be very active in promoting health issues among the Iraqi refugee population in London and was one of the most outspoken diaspora women trying to influence UK policies on Iraq in 2003, told Nadje:

I am totally fed up. Why am I giving up, because I am boiling with anger. There is so much corruption, so much undermining of local initiatives. International NGOs are trying to project themselves instead of trying to support local initiatives. DFID[13] is spending lots of money on useless things. I put my life at risk, every time I go, and all I see are things getting worse, and I get criticism on top of it.

On the other hand, several women who never left Iraq complained about 'all these women who lived outside for forty years and now want to tell us what we should do'. Many, although one has to stress not all, diaspora women are perceived to be patronizing and detached from realities on the ground. Amal R., a pharmacist who did not leave Iraq and who was one of the co-founders of the Knowledge for Iraqi Women Society, a women's organization based in Baghdad that is providing classes in literacy, English, computers and Koranic recitation, mainly to widows and young women, complained:

I participated in a workshop on the constitution. They asked us to come to Amman. There was a big problem: most of the women who participated are women who have lived outside for 40 years. ... I was surprised to hear what they were saying. They said women had no rights before. They have not been to school, not to university. I asked them whether they lived in Iraq. Most had just returned after 40 years. I told them: 'Look, all the women here are over 35 years old. We all have college degrees, our education was free. I was in the college of pharmacy. In that college, women were in the majority.' They were saying all the bad things about Saddam. I said: 'We have to tell the truth. Not everything was bad.' (Al-Ali, 2007b: 247)

Some pro-war diaspora women have been involved in a widely publicized campaign supported by the US government stressing the previous regime's poor record on women's rights. Without wanting to play down the atrocities of Saddam Hussein and his regime, some of the alleged claims contradict the accounts of the majority of women we interviewed. One especially absurd example is the assertion of some pro-war activists that women were not allowed to enter university under Saddam.

However, in the context of the specific debate about the Iraqi constitution, it became obvious that some of the discrepancies between diaspora women's attitudes and women 'from the inside' had more to do with lack of actual information about the content of the constitution and its implications rather than deeply entrenched political or 'cultural' differences. On several occasions women from inside Iraq told us that they were happy with the call for the implementation of Sharia. Azza A., for example, told Nadje, 'We are Muslims. Of course we want Islamic law' (Al-Ali and Pratt, 2006). However, when Nadje began to discuss the possible implications of this, such as the man's right to unilateral divorce, restrictions on freedom of movement, increased polygamy and changes in existing child custody laws, most women expressed shock and acknowledged that they had been unaware of these implications. As many people involved in non-governmental organizations and women's groups commented to us, the short timeline for drafting the constitution did not allow any public discussion of women's rights protection and the role of Islam.

It is unfortunate that, except for a relatively small number of activists inside Iraq, many Iraqi women construct their differences with the predominantly secular diaspora activists as a contestation between an 'authentic' Iraqi/Muslim culture and values, on the one side, and the imposition of foreign values and political agendas, on the other. The trend to associate feminism and women's rights with Western agendas is, of course, not unique to the Iraqi context, but has been a continuous challenge and difficulty for feminists in the region since the emergence of women's movements at the turn of the twentieth century. Yet, such construction of difference is amplified in a context of foreign occupation and a political system where political interests are defined and resources accrued on the basis of ethnic and sectarian identities.

Conclusion

The invasion and occupation of Iraq have created new transnational networks with various implications for women activists and gender relations in Iraq. For its part, the previous US administration forged links with Iraqi diaspora women as a means of implicitly justifying its invasion and occupation of Iraq. It provided funding and technical support for projects and programmes, implemented through various NGOs, aimed at supporting the participation of women in the 'new Iraq' as symbolic of its efforts to 'liberate' Iraqi women from the regime of Saddam Hussein. Their ability to point to women's participation, through the presence of women in civil society and political institutions, was held up by US officials as an indicator of the success of deposing Saddam Hussein, as well as enabling the USA to display its 'civilizing' credentials in a context where the international community increasingly promotes the importance of women's involvement in peace building. However, the objective of the Bush administration was not to reform gender relations in Iraq but 'to construct a war story that ... has thus camouflaged the realities of war for women [in Iraq]' (Hunt, 2007: 66). The US administration sought to control Iraq's political development for the purpose of US national security. In pursuing its strategic interests, it accommodated and augmented the power of Iraqi political actors who seek to restructure gender relations in order to buttress their authority within the new Iraq, with negative consequences for women's rights and participation.

There is evidence to suggest that the promotion of women's rights and participation by the US administration and the Iraqi diaspora have contributed to constructing new notions of cultural and national differences among some Iraqi actors – both men and women. The transnational is not viewed as a cosmopolitan space in which actors of different nationalities operate on an equal footing, but rather as a means for Western governments and non-governmental actors to impose 'their' ideas about gender relations onto Iraq through the vehicle of local women's rights activists. In the context of foreign occupation, the rejection of women's rights by a range of Iraqi actors represents an attempt to assert national sovereignty in a context of occupation through evoking notions of national/religious difference.

As various and more powerful actors have appropriated women's bodies as symbolic capital in the reconstruction of Iraq, women activists have attempted to carve out their own agency. Some have allied themselves with the US mission in Iraq, whilst others have benefited from the interest of international NGOs and other agencies to establish themselves in Iraqi political life. Simultaneously, other women activists have allied themselves with certain communal leaders as a means of securing their interests. This includes militia leaders, conservative Islamist leaders and armed groups resisting the occupation. In all cases, although women's agency continues to exist, its ability to transform gender relations in ways that guarantee women's long-term participation and rights is currently severely undermined.

Notes

1. According to the Foundation for the Defense of Democracies (FDD), the neoconservative institute that provided funding for the group, 'The campaign's media placements are estimated to have reached over 50 million Americans'. www.defenddemocracy.org/programs/programs_show. htm?doc_id=192125&attrib_id=10014; accessed 21 March 2006. The FDD

defines itself as a non-partisan institute. However, its founding members include Steve Forbes and James Woolsey, two of the signatories of the Project for a New American Century; Jack Kemp, founder of the neoliberal advocacy group, 'Empower America'; Jeanne Kirkpatrick and Newt Gingrich. For a discussion of FDD and their links with WFFI, see Zangana, 2006.

2. That is not to say that women enjoyed equality or that social conservatism did not exist in Iraq. For a detailed study, see Al-Ali, 2007b.

3. Author of *Republic of Fear* and *Cruelty and Silence*, books documenting the brutality of the Saddam Hussein regime. The former was originally published under the pseudonym of Samir al-Khalil.

4. IBWA has a website at: www.ibwa-iraq.org/index.html.

5. The Convention on the Elimination of All Forms of Discrimination against Women (CEDAW); see, for example, www.un.org/womenwatch/daw/cedaw/.

6. For more details, see Efrati 2005.

7. Judge Zakia Hakki was the first female judge appointed in Iraq in 1959 and was also a member of Women for a Free Iraq.

8. Nesrine Berwari was the minister for municipalities and public works in the first interim cabinet and the only woman minister in that cabinet. In June 2004, she was reappointed minister in the cabinet of the Iraqi Transitional Government.

9. Of course, it is not clear what the undisputed rules of Islam are.

10. This differs between Muslim countries. For details of legislation affecting women in Middle Eastern countries, see Nazir, 2005.

11. We thank Nathan Brown for pointing out that personal status laws are not designated by the constitution as among the areas to be defined by the central government. Pers. comm. September 2005.

12. Lisa Hajjar makes a similar argument with regard to Israel and India in Hajjar, 2004. See also Martina Kamp in this volume.

13. (UK) Department for International Development.

References

Agency staff (2004a) 'Iraqi Women Protest Proposed Changes to Family Law', Agence France Presse, 13 January.

Agency staff (2004b) 'Kurdish Parliament Defies Baghdad', Associated Press, 6 February.

Al-Ali, N. (2007a) 'Iraqi Women in Diasporic Spaces, Political Mobilisation, Gender and Citizenship', *Revue des Mondes Musulmans et de la Méditerranée* 117/118: 137–56.

Al-Ali, N. (2007b) *Iraqi Women: Untold Stories from 1948 to the Present*. London: Zed Books.

Al-Ali, N., and N. Pratt (2006) 'Women in Iraq: Beyond the Rhetoric', *Middle East Report* 36: 18–23.

Al-Ali, N., and N. Pratt (2008) 'Women's Organizing and the Conflict in Iraq since 2003', *Feminist Review* 88: 74–85.

Al-Ali, N., and N. Pratt (2009) *What Kind of Liberation? Women and the Occupation of Iraq.* Berkeley: University of California Press.

Al-Jazeera and agencies (2004) 'Iraqi Women Divided Over Family Law', 21 January. www.occupationwatch.org/print_article.phpandid=2686; accessed 19 October 2004.

Bush, G. (2005) 'State of the Union address'. www.whitehouse.gov/news/releases/2005/02/print/20050202–11.html; accessed 31 March 2006.

Cloud, D.L. (2004) '"To veil the threat of terror": Afghan Women and the "Clash of Civilisations", in the Imagery of the U.S. War on Terrorism', *Quarterly Journal of Speech* 90(3): 285–306.

Cockburn, C. (2007) *From Where We Stand: War, Women's Activism and Feminist Analysis.* London: Zed Books.

Cockburn, P. (2002a) 'Iraqi Opposition Gathers to Plot Saddam's Fall', *Independent*, 16 December: 9.

Cockburn, P. (2002b) 'Opposition Summit Papers Over Rivalries', *Independent*, 18 December: 11.

Edwar, H., and B. Fakri (2005) United Nations Security Council 'Arria Formula' Meeting: 5th Anniversary of Security Council Resolution 1325 on Women, Peace and Security, New York, 25 October. http://www.peacewomen.org/un/5thAnniversary/Arria%20Statements/HanaaEdwar.pdf.

Efrati, N. (2005) 'Negotiating Rights in Iraq: Women and the Personal Status Law', *Middle East Journal* 59(4): 577–95.

Gibbings, S. (2005) 'Governing Peace, Governing Women: A Study of the Women, Peace and Security Agenda at the United Nations', International Studies Association annual meeting, Honolulu.

Gordan, E. (2005) 'Our Friend in the Gallery: Safia al-Suhail and the New Iraq', *National Review Online*, 4 February.

Hajjar, L. (2004) 'Religion, State Power and Domestic Violence in Muslim Societies: A Framework for Comparative Analysis', *Law and Social Inquiry* 29(1): 1–38.

Herring, E., and G. Rangwala (2006) *Iraq in Fragments: The Occupation and Its Legacy.* London: Hurst.

Hunt, K. (2007). '"Embedded Feminism" and the War on Terror', in K. Hunt and K. Rygiel, eds, *(En)gendering the War on Terror*, pp. 51–72. Aldershot: Ashgate.

Joseph, S. (1991) 'Elite Strategies for State Building: Women, Family, Religion and the State in Iraq and Lebanon', in D. Kandiyoti, ed., *Women, Islam and the State*, pp. 176–200. Philadelphia: Temple University Press.

Keck, M., and K. Sikkink (1998) *Activists beyond Borders: Advocacy Networks in International Politics.* Ithaca: Cornell University Press.

Lobe, J. (2004) 'Iraq: U.S. Lawmakers Say Council's Plan Curbs Women's Rights', 23 February. www.peacewomen.org/news/Iraq/Feb04/right.html; accessed 23 February 2006.

Makiya, K. (1993) *Cruelty and Silence: War, Tyranny, Uprising, and the Arab World*. London: Jonathan Cape.

Mojab, S. (2004) 'Women in Iraqi Kurdistan', in W. Giles and J. Hyndman, *Sites of Violence: Gender and Conflict Zones*, pp. 108–33. Berkeley: University of California Press.

Nazir, S., ed. (2005) *Women's Rights in the Middle East and North Africa: Citizenship and Justice*. New York, Freedom House.

Office of the Senior Coordinator for International Women's Issues (2004) 'US Commitment to Women in Iraq', 23 September. www.state.gov/g/wi/rls/36751. htm; accessed 15 March 2005.

Shepherd, L. (2006) 'Veiled References', *International Feminist Journal of Politics* 8(1): 1–23.

Shepherd, L.J. (2008) *Gender, Violence and Security*. London: Zed Books.

SIGIR (Special Inspector General for Iraq Reconstruction) (2007) *Quarterly and Semiannual Report to Congress*. Washington DC, 30 January.

Sluglett, P., and M. Farouk-Sluglett (1993) *Iraq since 1958*. London: I.B. Tauris.

Spivak, G. (1988) 'Can the Subaltern Speak?', in C. Nelson and L. Grossberg, eds, *Marxism and the Interpretation of Culture*, pp. 271–313. London: Macmillan.

USAID (United States Agency for International Development) (n.d.) 'Assistance for Iraq: Support to Iraqi Women'. www.usaid.gov/iraq/accomplishments/women.html; accessed 20 June 2007.

US Department of State (2003) 'Human Rights and Women in Iraq: Voices of Iraqi Women', 6 March. www.state.gov/g/rls/rm/2003/18477.htm; accessed 12 June 2007.

US Department of State (2007) 'US–Iraqi Businesswomen's Partnership Launched', 28 June. www.state.gov/r/pa/prs/ps/2007/jun/87521.htm; accessed 25 August 2008.

US Department of State (n.d.) 'Iraqi Women's Democracy Initiative'. www.state. gov/g/wi/iraq/index.htm; accessed 25 August 2008.

USINFO (2004) 'Iraqi Women Receiving Democracy Training Ahead of Elections', 27 September. www.state.gov/mena/Archive/2004/September/27–387029. html; accessed 15 March 2005.

Various (2004) 'Iraqi Women Reject Decision no. 137 Passed by the Iraqi Governing Council on 29/12/2003', 20 January. www.occupationwatch. org/print_article.phpandid=2651; accessed 19 October 2004.

Wadley, J.D. (2006) 'Reclaiming Masculinity: The Connection Between State-Level Emasculation and Foreign Policy', Annual Meeting of the International Studies Association, San Diego, 22–25 March.

Wolfowitz, P. (2004) 'Women in the New Iraq', *Washington Post*, 1 February.

Women for Women International (2005) *Windows of Opportunity: The Pursuit of Gender Equality in Post-War Iraq*. Washington DC.

Zangana, H. (2006) 'Colonial Feminists from Washington to Baghdad: "Women for a Free Iraq" as a Case Study', in J. Ismael and W. Haddad, eds, *Barriers to Reconciliation: Case Studies on Iraq and the Palestine–Israel Conflict*, pp. 63–84. Lanham MD: University Press of America.

THREE

'Post-war Reconstruction', Imperialism and Kurdish Women's NGOs

Shahrzad Mojab

Destruction and reconstruction are integral components of life in the Middle East. While destruction is by no means a uniquely Middle Eastern phenomenon, it has been, for quite a long time, the rule rather than the exception in the region. What distinguishes the region is a rather unique relationship between reconstruction and destruction. Here, (re)construction lags behind destruction, and seriously constrains the enormous resources available for renewal and survival. This situation, I will argue, reproduces the conditions of destruction.

A host of factors are at work in the contemporary dynamics of destruction and reconstruction in the Middle East. The state, including Western powers and their inter-state organ, the United Nations, as well as non-state actors such as oppositional political groups and non-governmental organizations (NGOs), are all involved in the process of destruction in complex ways that are not difficult to comprehend. This chapter looks critically at the reconstruction projects in Iraqi Kurdistan. The evidence for this study is based on my three decades of close involvement with Kurdish women in the region as well as diaspora and, in part, on field research in Iraqi Kurdistan in 2000 and 2005. I will use the evidence to reflect on both the theory and the practice of 'post-war' reconstruction, and offer ideas that are relevant for the renewal of progressive, feminist and anti-imperialist nation-state building in the Middle East.

I will argue that 'post-war' reconstruction projects reproduce, and even embody, conditions of violence against the majority of the populations. Democratic and effective state structures have not been allowed to emerge in most of the Middle East, in particular in Iraqi Kurdistan. When NGOs are encouraged, as in the case of northern Iraq, to play a significant role in reconstruction, they fail to act effectively. In the case of the Kurdish region, the NGOs are, in fact, promoted to constrain the evolving of an effective, sovereign, Kurdish state. In Iraqi Kurdistan, some NGO and even UN-based agency operations have created conditions of dependence, and even destruction of the indigenous agriculture and local orders of production and consumption. More significantly, in Iraq today a regime of fragmented religious-feudal rule subverts serious efforts at constructing democratic state power and civil society.

Destruction/reconstruction occurs in the context of changing international relations, aspects of which are conceptualized as 'transnationalism', 'postcolonialism', 'post-nationalism' and 'globalization'. While the literature on the nature of this changing world is diverse, it highlights a set of widely shared claims about the institution of the state. One claim is the withering away of the state, which is weakened by emerging sub-national and supra-national entities. A related claim is the retrogressive nature of the state and the progressive nature of private property, free enterprise and free markets. These theories often treat the market as the source of life – that is, democracy, freedom, transnational cooperation, prosperity and peace. However, the evidence from the Middle East casts serious doubt about the validity of these claims.

Drawing on a critical transnational feminist analytic, this chapter opens up new ways of thinking about nationalism, citizenship, homeland and the conception of gender as the layered subject in the nation-building project. It brings into focus contemporary conjunctures and disjunctures in the materialization and historicization of women's lived experiences of militarism, colonialism and imperialism. Through this analytic, I will attempt to interrogate forms of colonial/imperial feminism with goals to 'liberate' and promote 'democracy' through women's NGOs and argue that this feminized 'rescue' mission has re-orientalized Kurdish women and has failed to challenge structural-patriarchal violence and the ways in which war, occupation and imperialism have impoverished them. The main argument is that destruction is a trend in the changing international order based on the supremacy of capital and 'free' markets. Far from withering away, the institution of the state, both in the West and in the Middle East, leads, plans and thrives on expanding markets. I will argue that violence is embedded in, rather than alien to, the rule of 'free' markets. A transnational 'free' market regime thrives on stability, which is difficult to achieve under conditions of widespread poverty. Disparities, famine, poverty, despotism, corruption and injustice generate conflict. The management of international and regional conflicts in the Middle East is increasingly conducted by the United States, which uses military intervention frequently in order to move towards that desired political stability. Very simply, but not simplistically, the maintenance of the 'world order' demands violence, and thrives on it. Harvey aptly conceptualizes this process as a contradictory feature of neoliberalism by naming it 'creative destruction' and 'accumulation by dispossession' (Harvey 2003, 2006). Quite often reconstruction or development projects involve violence – political, social, psychological and economic – in so far as they maintain a political order which has produced destruction.

In Iraqi Kurdistan, people cherish the fall of Saddam Hussein. However, Ba'th power has been replaced by a regime of political, economic, psychological and physical violence in which the two Kurdish political parties, the UN, the NGOs, the Turkish army, the US-led occupying forces, as well as Iranian, Syrian and Turkish state power, play diverse roles. Under these conditions, the political structural order that produced destruction and violence in the past has been replicated in more complex ways in Iraqi Kurdistan.

Iraq: a state born in war

The Iraqi state is a product of World War I and colonial rivalry. Before the war ended in 1918, the territories that now constitute Iraq were provinces of the Ottoman Empire. Britain and France, the two powers that led the dismantling of the Ottoman Empire, decided to create a Kurdish state. Provisions for this state-building project were inscribed in the Treaty of Sèvres, which was signed by the defeated Ottoman government in 1920. Western plans changed, however, largely due to the revival of the Turkish army under the leadership of Mustafa Kemal (Ataturk) and the establishment of Soviet power in the Caucasian region by 1921. The Kurds of Iraq resisted integration into the Iraqi state, but Kurdish rebellions were put down by the British–Iraqi army.

The Kurds revolted in 1961, and conducted an armed struggle for autonomy, which continued until the Gulf War of 1991. Western powers, Israel and Iran, among others, supported or opposed it during its long history. In 1970, the Kurds reached a settlement with Iraq, which, if implemented, would have created an autonomous Kurdish region by 1974. However, the United States, Israel and Iran encouraged the Kurdish leadership to reject the settlement. The USA was concerned about Baghdad's close relations with the Soviet Union, and its border disputes with Iran. Baghdad declared war on the Kurds by the end of the four-year truce. The USA, Israel and Iran provided the Kurds with arms and logistics. However, they abandoned the Kurds after a year of destructive war when Iran and Iraq resolved their differences. The Kurdish side was defeated. This war inflicted extensive damage on life and property. It created waves of refugees, estimated at more than 100,000, who fled to Iran, Turkey and Western countries.

After the defeat of the Kurds, the Iraqi government created a buffer zone on its borders with Iran. This was done through the destruction of mountain villages along the border. All village buildings and springs of water, which were the lifeblood of the community, were destroyed; millions of landmines were planted in the villages and their farms so that no one, peasants or guerrillas, could resettle there.

The Kurdish armed resistance resumed, however. The government pursued a policy of revenge rather than amnesty and reconstruction. State violence led to armed revolt, and to more violence and destruction. In the aftermath of the 1979 Iranian Revolution, Iraq attacked the Islamic state, and unleashed the longest war of the region, which led to enormous destruction in the two countries. The United States intervened by helping Iraq.

The two major Kurdish political parties leading the armed struggle continued their war against Baghdad, although one of them, the Patriotic Union of Kurdistan (PUK), tried in vain to negotiate a deal. During the last phases of its destructive war with Iran, Iraq conducted a genocidal campaign against the Kurds in 1988. The genocide, known as 'Anfal', eliminated an estimated 180,000 people and resulted in the destruction of about 4,000 villages in Kurdistan. Iraq also used chemical bombs against the Iranian army and its own citizens in the Kurdish town of Halabja, which led to the killing of about 5,000 (for a comprehensive history of modern Kurdistan, see Bird, 2004; Hiltermann, 2007; McDowell, 2000).

The Gulf War of 1991 was a war of the colonial type to the extent that the major Western power, the United States, led its European allies and some of the states in the region in punishing a disobedient state. The fact that it was conducted under the banner of the United Nations cannot disguise its (neo)colonial mission. The war did not end when the two sides declared its ending. Saddam's army violently attacked the Kurds and the Shi'a, and almost the entire Kurdish population fled to the mountains in the cold days of April, trying to escape into Turkey and Iran. Although Washington initially ignored the conflict, it soon intervened, and declared a major part of the Kurdish region a 'no-fly zone', banning the deployment of the Iraqi army and its air force (Schorr, 1991). The result was the creation of a 'Safe Haven', to which the refugees returned. The creation of the 'safe haven', protected by the US and its European allies, was for Kurdish nationalists like the realization of the dream for autonomous or independent status. Within a year, there were elections for a provincial Kurdish parliament, and a government was established.

Since the second US war on Iraq, in 2003, the USA has failed to install a stable government in Baghdad, leading to speculation about the parcelling of Iraq into three mini-states – one of which would be Kurdish. However, Western powers and the UN recognize the sovereignty of the Iraqi state, and are officially committed to protect its 'territorial integrity'. Therefore the Kurdish state, as a sovereign entity, may not emerge under the current circumstances. The present regime established in the northern parts of the Kurdish territory has been called a 'de facto UN state', 'de facto autonomous state', or 'Regional Authority' (Ahmed and Gunter, 2003, 2007; Natali, 2005; Stansfield, 2003; van Bruinessen, 2005).

The (re)production of destruction: the case of the 1991 war

In telling the story of my visit to Iraqi Kurdistan in 2000, I have often said that all sides – including Iraq, Turkey, Iran, the USA, Kurdish political parties in power, the NGOs – are in one way or another involved in the destruction of the social web of life in this region. This was my impression based on intensive observation and detailed discussions with people from all walks of life (Mojab, 2001). In 2000, the majority of the Kurdish population expressed deep concern with UN agencies. The problems identified were poverty, huge bureaucracy, corruption and lack of accountability. There was a lack of coordination among UN agencies, a lack of sufficient authority and technical capacity among the UN staff, and intimidation of the UN staff by the Iraqi government in particular, if they seemed to be friendly with Kurds.

In order to illustrate the seriousness of these problems, I quote from a report by Alastair Kirk and Gary Sawdon entitled *The Household Economy: Understanding the Situation of Kurdish Livelihoods*:

More households are extremely vulnerable to external shocks, including unplanned changes in the sanctions system…. Many poor people are reliant on the economic activity of the richest groups, and are vulnerable to changes in their income….

The sanctions and ration regime created by the UN Security Council has undermined and distorted markets and livelihoods and destroyed normal economic life for the vast majority…. The rations system instituted by UN Security Council Resolution 986 has created unprecedented levels of dependency. Sanctions have undoubtedly impoverished the Iraqi population: the SCR986 Programme, however, has not overcome that impoverishment, but rather has raised dependency to internationally unprecedented levels. In the many near-destitute households, up to 90% of food comes from the SCR986 ration…. Poor people could not afford to feed themselves if the SCR986 ration was suddenly removed….

SCR986 rations have destroyed the livelihoods of most people, and diminished their capability to develop new livelihoods….

The SCR986 ration system has facilitated state domination of food supply … SCR986 relief rations have allowed the Government of Iraq to reassert its dominance over food systems, and seriously undermined the development of sustainable agriculture in Northern Iraq. Although rations in Kurdistan are distributed by the UN's World Food Programme (WFP), the Government of Iraq (GOI) is responsible for importing most staples and milling flour. That means the GOI is able to control the content of the ration; carbohydrate staples and tea and sugar instead of protein – both in Northern Iraq as well as in the South. (Kirk and Sawdon, 2002: 43–5)

Kirk and Sawdon's research supports my observations of the structural constraints on reconstruction in Iraqi Kurdistan. In 2000 there was at least a consensus that something was seriously wrong with international humanitarian assistance. One must admit, however, that in spite of the enormity of problems facing both the Kurdish political parties and individuals, there was considerable effort to rebuild the destroyed Kurdish region. And some of this rebuilding was the work of devoted individuals, in particular women. A prominent case is the protest of women against the civil war of 1994 between the two rival parties sharing government, the Kurdistan Democratic Party (KDP) and the Patriotic Union of Kurdistan. A group of women marched from Sulaimaniya to Irbil in protest against what they called a fratricidal war (birakuji). Another grassroots initiative was women's protests against the violence that was unleashed against them in the aftermath of the war. There was an unprecedented rise in killing women for reasons of 'honour' (for a detailed account of these cases, see Mojab, 2002). The Kurdish government refused to criminalize these atrocities and arrest or punish the murderers. Government authorities justified their policy by arguing that they had to abide by the personal status laws of the Ba'thist regime in Baghdad. Women demanded a repeal of these laws, but the parliament, dominated by males and especially the conservative KDP, refused to initiate new legislation. While killing continued, women expanded their struggle against this violence. They established shelters and exposed the gender politics of the two ruling parties. In 2000 the PUK was forced, by the rising oppositional voices of women in the diaspora and the pressure of women in the homeland, into issuing two resolutions that treated 'honour killing' as a punishable crime. The PUK government was not, however, in a position to implement the resolutions, especially in villages where tribal and kin organizing is strong and where the PUK relies on the loyalty of tribes and feudal lords.

While poverty and violence against women were serious problems, the transfer of power from the Ba'th to the Kurdish political parties led to other changes. For example, mass media proliferated in the Kurdish region. Intellectuals have for a long time struggled for communication rights such as the right to publish and the right to read. Under Saddam's rule, all media, including the press, were state-owned. By contrast, in the 'Safe Haven,' political organizations were allowed to launch their own broadcasting; there was an unprecedented growth of print media. The situation had the semblance of a public sphere, although the two parties dominated the media and other public outlets.

To the extent that there was a civil society in the Kurdish region, it was largely the achievement of social movements. The two ruling Kurdish political parties have strong statist tendencies. Moreover, the UN and even the NGOs do not rely on or even recognize the social movements. Much could be achieved in reconstruction efforts if people were allowed to participate in changing the conditions under which they suffered. For instance, in the case of the clearing of landmines, if the people who were potential victims of the landmines were allowed to participate in the de-mining effort, much progress could be made within a few years. This observation was, in fact, made in a project proposal that I received in 2000 from an organization called Hoshiar. The draft proposal stated that

> Currently there are de-mining activities in Kurdistan but they are not properly organized. Each organization's priorities is set according to their understanding. Sometimes a specific minefield is cleared by one of them, then after a while another organization will start working in the same minefield. So to avoid these problems it is necessary to have a network in Kurdistan. The network will establish priorities for the minefields depending on previous data, which has been collected by survey teams and the government plan for the Reconstruction and Rehabilitation of Kurdistan.

Ala Noori Talebani, who was advocating this plan, told me in an interview:

> I am planning to involve women in this project. Women are the victims of landmines, whilst the burden of care-giving to disabled family members as a result of landmines is on their shoulders. Therefore, if they learn about how to avoid landmines and learn how to visually identify them it would be great for the community. But the response of NGOs and the government to my proposal of engaging women and mobilizing the community in de-mining activities has been disappointing. They argue that the information on landmines, their pattern of distribution, and their types constitute military information which cannot be made available to civilians. This response is heartbreaking for me! (October 2000, Sulaimaniya)

The picture offered here is obviously a disturbing one. The Iraqi state under Ba'thist rule committed genocide against its people, destroyed thousands of villages, and used chemical weapons. It also destroyed

the marshlands of southern Iraq in an attempt to control the population. This level of destruction would not have been possible without
the use of new technologies of destruction provided by Western
powers. Until the Gulf War of 1991, the authorities committed
genocide and ecocide with impunity. As Leo Kuper argues, 'the
sovereign territorial state claims, as an integral part of its sovereignty,
the right to commit genocide ... and ... the United Nations, for all
practical purposes, defends this right' (1981: 161).

The formation of the 'Safe Haven' has been treated by many
observers as a radical breach of the principle of state sovereignty
which is to be protected by the United Nations. In other words, the
UN itself violated its foundational principle by allowing the United
States to create such a state within the state. The UN also sanctioned
the destructive war waged by the coalition forces in 1991. However,
rather than indicating that the UN is prepared to override sovereignty
in the name of protecting human rights, these developments point
towards the formation of an interstate order controlled by one power
– the United States.

Iraq, like much of the Middle East, has enormous resources,
human and natural, to build a viable democratic society that can
readily solve the problems of poverty, illiteracy and disease. Indeed,
Iraq under the Ba'th regime was, alongside Turkey, the most secular
nation in the Middle East and its treatment of the Kurds was, overall,
better than their treatment by Turkey (for a useful discussion of this
issue, see the documentary by McKiernan, 2000). Similarly, by most
measurement indices, Iraq was a leader in the Middle East in terms
of healthcare and education, especially for women (Al-Ali, 2007;
Zangana, 2007). No doubt a host of factors prevented the realization
of this potential in the aftermath of the 1991 war in the Kurdish
region. It is important, however, to emphasize that destruction,
much like war, is a source of capital renewal – that is, profit-making
– in part through the creation of investment opportunities. It is also
important to note that the market, much like the state, thrives on
both war and destruction and, therefore, at its core is the logic of
the 'Shock Doctrine' (Klein, 2007).

Disentangling contradictions in women's NGOs:
the context of the 2003 war and occupation

So far, I have attempted to establish the links between construction, deconstruction and reconstruction in the context of the 1991 war in the Kurdish region of Iraq. In 2003 the United States launched a war of 'regime change' in order to install in Baghdad a regime of its own. The Kurdish leadership played an active role in this project, which led to the fall of the Ba'thist regime and further consolidation of the status of the Regional Government of Kurdistan. The USA devoted greater resources, economic, military and diplomatic, to its second war. The process itself and its outcomes were destruction on a much larger scale.

My focus in this section will be on Kurdish women's NGOs, which are thriving following the 2003 occupation of Iraq. The detailed analysis of the role of women's NGOs in the 'post-war' reconstruction will assist us in explicating the interconnectedness of an imperialist gender project, one which is constructed on notions such as 'democracy', 'freedom', and 'civil society', and its link to the larger imperialist agenda of regional and global domination. I invite readers to rethink and reconsider the contexts in which notions such as 'civil society', 'NGOs', 'freedom' and 'democracy' are used uncritically. Under the condition of war, occupation and imperialism, we need to develop a more sophisticated theoretical understanding of social relations, local and global institutional structures and powers, divisions of labour and habits of life. I intend to open spaces for a more critical engagement with the role of women's NGOs in war zones and their participation in what I prefer to call *assembling spoils of war*, rather than the euphemism of 'post-war reconstruction'.

As a result of my fieldwork in war zones and in diaspora communities and women's NGO in contexts such as Palestine, Turkey, Iran, Iraq and Egypt, I deeply appreciate the resiliency of women, their sacrifice and their absolute devotion to their just cause. This acknowledgement, however, has never prevented me from critical engagement with women organized in NGOs. Inspired by Cynthia Enloe's (2004) idea of 'being curious by our lack of feminist curiosity', I have been curious about women and therefore have been able to see patriarchy in collusion with capitalism, militarism, racism, colonialism and imperialism. This means that my critical transnational feminist framework aims at rupturing the normalcy in neoliberal notions of the 'inevitability' of capitalism and imperialism, in civilizational privileging of the West over the East, and in the 'naturalization' of the separation of political rights – that is, democracy and freedom – from economic rights (for further articulation of this point, see Meiksins Wood, 2006).

My main focus in this section will be on unravelling the ideo-logical underpinning of the project of imperialist powers in the 'post-war reconstruction' of Iraq through drawing on the results of my fieldwork among women's NGOs in the Kurdish region in 2005. My aim is not one of evaluation or assessment of the NGOs operating in the region; I will, rather, attempt to track the US 'reconstruction' policy and the role that NGOs, knowingly or unknowingly, play within this project. I believe that it is critical for the left, anti-war, anti-globalization activists to understand the intricacies of the specific project of reconstruction in Iraq, and how it fits into a larger neo-liberal agenda that is transnational in scope. A perfect summary of this policy can be found in the description of the US Department of State's 'Middle East Partnership Initiative' (MEPI). MEPI operates in a 'four pillar structure': '(1) political governance and participation (2) economic liberalization and opportunity (3) educational quality and access (4) the empowerment of women.' Under the 'women' pillar, four initiatives are listed: 'Fostering Empowerment', 'Women's Survey', 'Women and the Law', and 'Women Business Summit' (see MEPI, 2008).

It is also important to keep in mind that I differentiate between women's NGOs and the women's movements in the region. The women's movements, as opposed to NGOs, encompass a diversity of positions and relationships to the state, are often more politically oriented, and allow for a more critical assessment of external involvement in the region. In some cases, women's NGOs are mobilized by the state and external actors to weaken, depoliticize, or even crush the women's movements (for a similar argument in the context of the USA and Palestine, see Smith, 2007b).

It is difficult to make sense of NGOs if we do not look at the historical context of the idea and practice of NGOs. By historical context, I mean raising questions such as: When and why did the phenomenon of NGOs emerge? Where do NGOs stand in the structure of power relations, locally, nationally, internationally and transnationally? Whose particular interests do NGOs serve or address? Why is there so much academic and political interest in this set-up? My argument is that if we do not pursue these questions, we are more likely to miss the social, political, historical and economic ties that bind colonialism and imperialism to the rise of nationalisms, fundamentalisms and racism.

While non-governmental organizations have existed since the beginning of the formation of modern nation-states, in the current political environment they are a rather new phenomenon. They can be traced to the late 1980s and early 1990s, and the aftermath of the fall of the Soviet bloc. Western governments and many liberal and conservative intellectuals hoped that West European or American style democracy would reign in Eastern Europe and the former Soviet Union. Thus 'civil society', 'the public sphere' and 'NGOs' were promoted as venues for establishing capitalist democracy, in which the absolute rule of the state would be replaced by the absolute rule of the market. In much of this discourse, whether one calls it neoconservative or neoliberal, 'market' and 'democracy' are used as synonyms (for a critical survey of these concepts, see Meiksins Wood, 1990; and Elyachar, 2005, for an extensive analysis in the context of Cairo, 2005).

Meiksins Wood, in 'Democracy as Ideology of Empire', raises a pertinent question: 'How is it that freedom, equality, and universal human dignity can seem a convincing justification for imperialism and war?' (Meiksins Wood, 2006: 11). Her response is in what she calls the coexistence of economic and non-economic powers:

Both capital and labour can have democratic rights in the political sphere without completely transforming the relation between them in a separate economic sphere; and much of human life is determined in the economic sphere, outside the reach of democratic accountability. Capitalism can, therefore, coexist with the ideology of freedom and equality in a way that no other system of domination can. (Meiksins Wood, 2006: 11)

Now, let me apply these ideas and concepts in the context of the Middle East, where colonialism followed by pro-American dictatorships has devastated the lives of citizens for decades. The violence of these dictatorships led to resistance by many, especially women, workers, peasants, indigenous peoples, students, religious leaders, intellectuals, human rights groups and journalists. However, the USA and Western powers treated these resistances as communist and 'terrorist' and therefore went as far as engaging in military or paramilitary interventions to eliminate them. Focusing on the history of the Middle East in the twentieth century, we see the peoples of the region engaged in extensive and relentless struggle to change the difficult conditions of their lives. They had many successes, but in every step towards independence and economic development, they were suppressed through the intervention of Western powers that allied with local feudal, tribal and religious leaders, and the emerging capitalist class. This history is a history of unceasing struggle, success and defeat. Today, the people of the Middle East are subjected to more violence and more poverty. There are more theocratic states, more imperialist wars and greater violence against women. Not surprisingly, US wars have helped the re-traditionalization and re-tribalization of society, terms that are appearing in Amnesty International (2005) and Human Rights Watch reports (2003).

Under the rubrics of 'reconstruction' and building 'civil society', the USA has opened up a new front in its expansionist desire in the region. Elite, educated, skilled and activist women are absorbed into numerous and often well-financed NGOs. Haifa Zangana, an Iraqi woman novelist, activist and writer, sees in today's Iraq diverse colonial sources; they include 'NGOs, missionaries, and women's organizations. Unlike military invasion and violence, the work of these organizations is directed at the very fabric of society and has received much less publicity' (Zangana, 2006a; see also 2006b).

Women NGOs that I have studied in the Kurdish region of Iraq manifest the same symptoms as other NGOs studied in Latin America, Palestine and Europe (e.g. Alvarez, 1999, 2000; Hammami, 2000; Jad, 2004; Lang, 2000; Mendoza, 2002; Roy, 2000). They have a short-term agenda and their contribution is often piecemeal, curative, limited and dependent on the agenda of donors. By contrast, women's movements pursue long-term goals such as reform or radical change of patriarchal relations in both civil society and the state. While the two should not be seen as mutually exclusive, states in the Middle East as well as the USA and other Western powers are more tolerant of women's NGOs than women's movements. It is not surprising, therefore, that the United States takes the promotion of NGOs as a pillar of its foreign policy. According to Barry Lowenkron, the US Assistant Secretary for Democracy, Human Rights, and Labor (Lowenkron, 2006):

> When NGOs are under siege, freedom and democracy are under-mined. How then can we best support and defend the work of NGOs in countries across the globe? The United States must con-tinue to stand up for what President Bush calls 'the non-negotiable demands of human dignity' and that includes the exercise by individuals of their rights to freedom of expression, association and assembly through their membership in NGOs.... Second, we need to ensure that NGO protection is an integral part of our diplomacy. We must highlight the protection of NGOs as a legitimate issue on our government-to-government agenda.... The Secretary raises our concerns in her bilateral meetings as do I and many of my colleagues at the State Department. When I travel, I insist on seeing NGO representatives, as does the Secretary.

It is interesting to contrast the statement above with the results of the United Nations Development Fund for Women (UNIFEM) 2005 report entitled 10 Years After Beijing: The Role and Contribution of the Arab NGOs, which states that

the number of NGOs working in the field of development in the
Arab World has increased from 175,000 in 1995 to 225,000 in
2003.... While considering the diverse political climate in the
region, Arab NGOs can rarely be regarded as powerful players
capable of influencing the development and future of their societies. (UNIFEM, 2005: 8, 10)

Even if the NGOs are not yet 'powerful players', they are increasingly becoming venues for the implementation of the foreign
policy of the USA (and other Western states), ostensibly at 'arm's
length'. As we will see, this occurs through funding arrangements
and through the co-option of progressive and/or elite women into
NGOs. The cultural ideology of neoliberalism is promoted through
this hegemonic process that equates the notion of democracy in civil
society and the market, a locus not hospitable to political rights and
social justice. NGOs, while in appearance autonomous from the state,
end up acting as its appendage. Let us closely consider the case of
women's NGOs in Iraqi Kurdistan.

Kurdish women's NGOs under US occupation

Following the creation of the 'Safe Haven', as detailed above, Iraqi
Kurdistan was soon flooded by NGOs of all kinds. UN agencies, the
European Union and NGOs based in European countries provided
funding. My data indicate a limited involvement of the USA in
funding NGOs in the period 1991–2003, a fact to note when we
discuss the relationship between the US 'democracy' plan for Iraq
and the role of Kurdish women's NGOs in this project.

I visited Iraqi Kurdistan for the second time in 2005. I began my
research by visiting women's NGOs in the Sulaimaniya region, with
theobjective of understanding the inner dynamics of women's NGOs at
three interrelated levels: organizational structure; the social and political location of women leaders of NGOs; and the transnational sphere
of relations and connections, in particular the link with diaporic
Kurdish women's activism. I slightly changed my research plan, as
early into the fieldwork I was able to map out a pattern indicating

the history, actors, connections, sphere of influences, funding and the inner dynamics of the NGOs, especially the class locations and political affinity of women leaders. Therefore, instead, I decided to engage with NGO workers and activists at the level of analysis: to interrogate deeply what is going on; to turn the moment into a feminist transnational praxis where the production of knowledge become relational and feminist desire for change the interlocutor of the conversation. So, I mapped out my analysis and pointed to how, where and what I saw as challenges and problems. We engaged in some deep and often difficult conversations, and amazing contradictions became apparent. I engaged in this frank discussion with women involved with the following NGOs: Aram Shelter; Asuda (Organization for Combating Violence Against Women); The Cultural and Social Centre of Khanzad; Women's Information and Culture Centre; Civilization Development Organization (CDO); and Rasan, which publishes a Kurdish women's newspaper under the same name.

In discussing the role, function, structure and status of women's NGOs with those intimately involved with them, we agreed on the following points. First, there is a lack of feminist consciousness, by which I specifically mean the absence of the notion of patriarchy as a system entangled with other imposing forces such as militarism, capitalism, fundamentalism and nationalism. Therefore, after more than a decade of hard work on women's issues, patriarchy, in its harsher form of religious–feudal nationalism, has remained intact, and indeed has taken a new, harsher form in response to external forces of militarism and occupation. In a comprehensive report released in 2007, the Kurdish Human Rights Project (KHRP) concludes that

> [A]lthough some positive changes may have occurred for the better in the lives amongst a select group of elite women, usually with strong tribal and political ties, the majority of the population has seen a regression in terms of freedom of movement, right to life and the ability to live free from violence. (KHRP, 2007: 49)

The report documents the rise of violence against women in the form of suicide, 'honour killing' and self-immolation in the Kurdish regions of Turkey and Iraq. The report concludes: '[I]t became clear during the course of the mission that discussion of women's rights has been limited almost exclusively to that of stopping violence, but not about women's rights in their entirety' (KHRP, 2007: 75).

In my discussion with these women, I asked them about an extensive survey conducted by the Rural Rehabilitation and Community Development Program of the Norwegian People's Aid (NPA) in 2002 in the Kurdish region. To my astonishment, they either were not aware of the existence of this massive survey or did not bother to learn from it. This survey, to my knowledge, is one of the most comprehensive studies on the social, economic and political situation of women in northern Iraq. To collect the data, twenty-three organizations and five ministries were involved; 20,134 women of 15 years and above were interviewed; and the result is a two-volume report of 1,546 pages of data and analysis. The study covered eleven areas of education and learning; culture; health; psychology; women's status in the family; human rights and legal awareness; marriage; political participation; violence; economic independence; and widows. The research undertaken and the data collected for this expansive survey and the lack of awareness of its results all show that most women's organizations and NGOs in Kurdistan have little or no informed awareness of the situation of Kurdish women. They do not have much contact with people at the grassroots level; nor do they rely on concrete evidence about women. The elites, or 'pioneers' as they are called in the report, rely on information generated by mainstream intellectuals, other elites or the political parties with which they are often associated. These two streams of the women's movement, the grassroots and the elite, are completely disconnected. According to this report, women are the 'great losers' of the last decades in Iraq. Despite the claims of the elite women's organizations that they have addressed the concerns of Kurdish women, the patriarchy prevailing in Kurdish society has not been addressed. This is evident in the statistics presented in the report: 37 per cent of women in Kurdistan are illiterate; most women marry under the age of 19 because women over 23 are considered past their prime for marriage, and consequently few women move on to higher education; the few women who manage to gain higher education, participate in politics or have a job that does not revolve around the family are no longer respected in their communities; 50 per cent of women do not possess adequate knowledge about women's health – there is no health education in school or at home, and there is no structural or systemic means of obtaining information; 14 per cent of women face violence on a daily basis; and 7 per cent of women have been threatened with 'honour' killing, the majority of which threats (64 per cent) come from family members. In all aspects of women's lives, it is evident from the data presented in this report that Kurdish women are far below the average when it comes to the quality of life and provision of basic needs and services for women. Most distressingly, there has been no successful intervention by NGOs on behalf of the 'Anfal widows', the widows of victims of the Ba'thist genocide. After a decade, these women still have no inheritance, property or custody rights, let alone the right to remarry. Borzou Daragahi, in a report in the *Los Angeles Times* (9 September 2007) under the title 'Kurdish Widows' Lives Frozen in Time', captures their despair:

> Patience, the mothers begged their children. Saddam Hussein will fall. Liberty will come. Your father will return. Years went by. The regime fell. Prison doors were opened. Mass graves were unearthed. Still, the women wait.

Furthermore, there has been little change in terms of the representation of gender relations in textbooks or in media portrayal of women.

The results of the NPA study reflect the conclusion of a survey published by the Brussells Tribunal in 2007 that states (Al-Azzawi, 2007: 27):

> The major conclusion is that the USA occupation of Iraq has intentionally created a catastrophic collapse in the social inter-related structure, infrastructure services, education and healthcare system, and security. All of which have a direct detrimental impact on women's living conditions and women's rights in Iraq. The

occupation of Iraq has taken women back to the dark ages. By ending the occupation, Iraqi women have a better chance to earn back what they previously accomplished.

In August 2005, at the time of my visit, almost all women's NGOs were preoccupied with discussing the draft of the Iraqi constitution. They complained about 'being workshopped out' of the constitution. This constitutional rousing was a response to the US administration plan to legitimize its own rule in Iraq. The then Secretary of State Colin Powell, in announcing the recipients of grants for reconstruction of Iraq, said that each of the grantees 'will work with Iraq partners on the ground to prepare women to compete in Iraq's January 2005 elections, encourage women to vote, train women in media and business skills, and establish resource centres for networking and counselling'. Kurdish women were seriously concerned about the 'religious nature' of the constitution. Despite their efforts in lobbying the Kurdish Regional Government to write to the drafting committee, and discussing the constitution in the Kurdish media and women's press, the current constitution of Iraq is based on Sharia, confirming the creation of a theocratic state in Iraq. The Kurdish leadership even made concessions on the issue of women's rights versus federalism. Isobel Coleman writes,

> As the arguments dragged on, US Ambassador Zalmay Khalilzad finally intervened to avoid a stalemate. To gain concessions in other areas, he supported provisions that strengthened Islam's influence. Ultimately, the Kurds acquiesced too, both because they had other priorities to defend and because they recognized that conservative Shiites were not going to capitulate. (Coleman, 2006)

Article 2 of the constitution makes Islam the official religion of the state and the basic source of legislation. What became apparent was that the presence of women in the public sphere, such as NGOs, does not necessarily guarantee a progressive change in gender relations; there is a need for feminist consciousness, a women's movement and a collective struggle. For Kurdish and Arab women of Iraq undoubtedly this will be a long and arduous struggle. Noga Efrati, tracing women's participation in changing the Personal Status Law, depicts a bleak future when she writes:

> Women's rights activists have been forced to channel energies under chaotic war-time conditions into preserving a law which ignored many of their long-sought demands: outlawing polygamy, equal rights in divorce and inheritance, and further extending maternal child custody. Thus preoccupied, feminists were hindered from advancing personal status issues as they had in the past when regimes perceived as favorable had assumed power. A valuable opportunity was lost. In the 'new Iraq' women have found themselves running just to stay in place. (Efrati, 2005: 594–5)

Second, in discussing my observation with Kurdish women's rights activists, we engaged in a heated debate on the notion of NGO 'autonomy'. Their definition of 'autonomy' was limited to independence from political parties or the state. The Kurdish women activists consider themselves part of the growing civil society in Kurdistan. They refused to see the ties between the civil society sector and the larger political, military and economic projects of capitalism, imperialism and globalization. These women acknowledged, but wilfully ignored, the connection between their personal privileged location and the sources of power in social and political structures of Kurdish society. The Kurdish political parties may have an arms-length relationship with these NGOs, but there are many ties that bind them to forces in the state, the market and the transnational imperialist gender politics. These include funding sources, the political composition of their board of directors, and their connection to the international donor and women's communities. A case in point is Asuda (Organization for Combating Violence Against Women), whose coordinator is among a handful of Kurdish women from Iraq dominating the international scene of conferences, workshops and training provided by the World Bank, UNIFEM, Women for Women International, Independent Iraqi Women and Independent Women's Forum, among many others. The Asuda board of directors includes politically and socially well-connected women, among them Narmin Othman, former minister of education in the PUK administration and currently Iraqi minister of environment; Roonak Rauf, mother of Dr Barham Salih, prime minister of the Kurdish Regional Government (under the Patriotic Union of Kurdistan), deputy prime minister of the Iraqi Interim Government, the minister for planning and co-ordination in the Iraqi Transitional Government, and deputy prime minister in the government of Nouri al-Maliki (Roonak Rauf is also the president of the Women's Information Center); and Shirin Amadi, secretary general of the Kurdish Women's Union and the highest ranking politician in the Kurdish Democratic Party. The argument here does not concern the merit of these women. Quite the contrary; these are women who have earned their status as 'leaders' in their own right, mainly through long-standing involvement in supporting and providing services to women and waging a difficult fight for women's rights in Kurdistan. They have shown extraordinary courage and their gains have been significant and symbolically important ones. The point that I am trying to make is, rather, related to the very nature of NGOs. James Petras's articulation of the structure of NGOs as 'internally elitist, externally servile' is relevant here. He argues that NGOs are hierarchical, non-democratic, with a 'self-appointed elite' of directors whose role is to 'supervise and ensure conformity with the goals, values and ideology of the donors as well as the proper use of funds' (Petras, 1999: 433–4).

As an example of positive action, one might mention Asuda, which has produced an impressive array of educational materials and has been ingenious in producing anti-violence materials. A matchbox-sized card with the full contact information and street address of Asuda was distributed among the taxi drivers in the city of Sulaimaniya to direct women passengers in distress to the organization. The act of distributing the cards was used as a method to raise awareness on violence against women. My point, however, is that these remain isolated initiatives which fail to reverse the rise of patriarchal violence against women. These acts, in other words, are not being turned into a tool for mobilizing women and men, activists and politicians, to change the structural conditions conducive to the (re)production of violence.

Asuda has been one of the regular receivers of funds from the National Endowment for Democracy, the International Republican Institute and USAID, all funded by the USA. Most of the Kurdish women in the leadership of NGOs have taken part in conferences, meetings or workshops organized by the Independent Women's Forum, also funded by the USA, in Iraqi Kurdistan or Amman, Jordan. The Independent Women's Forum (IWF) was the recipient of a portion of the $10 million grant from the US State Department in 2004 to implement the 'Iraqi Women's Democracy Initiative', aimed at providing leadership training, democracy education and coalition-building assistance to Iraqi women. Strong opposition was expressed to this deal by US feminist groups such as the National Organization for Women (NOW) and the Feminist Majority Foundation. NOW, the largest American women's organization, in their 15 October 2004 communication, called the IWF 'Halliburton in a Skirt', and Kim Gandy, the NOW president, stated 'If the United States really wants to educate Iraqi women about issues as important as democracy and civil rights, the IWF is an embarrassing place to start.' The mission statement of the IWF reads: 'IWF builds support for a greater respect for limited government, equality under the law, property rights, free markets, strong families, and a powerful and effective national defence and foreign policy' (IWF, 2008). The IWF has strongly opposed the US affirmative action and Violence Against Women Act, and the UN Convention for the Elimination of All Forms of Discrimination Against Women (CEDAW), on the grounds that they mandate governments to enforce laws guaranteeing equal pay for equal work, maternity leave with pay, and childcare facilities.

The question we need to ask is, what are the 'democracy' lessons that Kurdish women have to learn from an anti-feminist organization? Why are Kurdish women's national and feminist aspirations being harnessed by a colonial, racist and anti-feminist agenda? As long as Kurdish women remain devoted to the cause of the nation/nationalism and its dream of building a masculine, patriarchal and bourgeois modern state, they will inevitably compromise the cause of women's emancipation. Women in leadership positions in NGOs are not leaders of a women's movement; they, rather, constitute a new transnational technocratic elite class with the power to create the best local conditions for transnational capitalist reconstruction projects (Robinson, 1996: 372).

Third, the point over which we were able to reach the most consensus was on the future of NGOs and long-term gender projects in Kurdistan. Women activists collectively expressed a sense of social fatigue, fragmentation, chaos, competition and corruption in the process of 'NGOization' of women's movements and the gender justice agenda in the region. They were quite conscious of the fact that they have become the femocrats of the reconstruction industry, though were not willing to accept it as such and did not see any other alternatives. Each organization is fighting for a piece of the reconstruction dollar pie, and is thus surviving on short-term, piecemeal, project-by-project plans. Critical feminists reviewing the experience of women's movements globally since the rise of neoliberalism in the early 1980s have conclusively argued that the outcomes of the NGOization of the women's movement were bureaucratization, professionalization, institutionalization and depoliticization of the movement. In the absence of strong state-based public policies and social cohesion, NGOs, in particular women's NGOs, provide social services which also function as a mechanism of control of social dissent. In the context of Palestine, Khalili Nakhleh argues that development and reconstruction through NGOization is a form of 'coercion and persuasion', which takes economic, military, political and cultural forms (Nakhleh, 2004: 7). Thus, no wonder that the younger generation of Kurdish women was complaining about being excluded from the activities of NGOs or any opportunities for being trained as the next cadres of the women's movement.

My study concurs with Sarah Roy's observation (2000: 30) that NGOs are a response to 'burning issues' and they act as a 'fire-extinguisher' of burning social problems. Kurdish women's NGOs have produced numerous reports and volumes on the issues of 'honour killing', female genital mutilation (Rahimi, 2004) and 'suicide' as forms of crimes against women, all of which certainly require immediate action. Asuda has produced powerful posters and flyers for raising public awareness on the issue of male violence. Women's groups have initiated the setting up of several life-size statues of women in major squares in the city of Sulaimaniya depicting images of women breaking their chains of oppression. Despite these limited actions and public pedagogical instances, these forms of violence against women have been on the rise since the 1991 war and are regularly being reported in the Kurdish press.

Concluding remarks: women's NGOs, anti-feminism and colonial feminism

The Kurds of Iraq have lived since 1961 in one of the most enduring war zones of our time. Here, war constructs colonies, nations and states through enormous acts of destruction, massacres, genocide and ecocide. However, the particularity of the Kurdish case reveals, rather than conceals, universal trends in the theory and practice of women's NGOs. In spite of the diverse contexts of Latin America, Asia, Africa, it is difficult to find visible variance in the goal and outcomes of NGOization.

NGOization, in the Kurdish case, is a direct outcome of the US-led war of 1991. In Iraq, under the Ba'th Party, where the state was the ultimate power, there was no room for non-government initiatives beyond the confines of the home or a small private enterprise. Once the Ba'th regime was driven out of the no-fly zone of Kurdistan in April 1991, the Kurdistan Regional Government took over the administrative structure that was left vacant.

Relieved from the patriarchal gender politics of the Ba'th regime, Kurdish women were now in conflict with the traditional patriarchy of Kurdish society and the new government. Decades of war, and especially the Anfal genocide of 1988, destroyed the very fabric of Kurdish society and unleashed patriarchal violence everywhere. However, Kurdish nationalism, calling for the unity of the nation regardless of gender and class differences, acted as a political and ideological obstacle to conscious feminist intervention. Nationalism was in conflict with feminist consciousness. The Kurdish government, which claimed to be a negation of Ba'thist political power, continued to uphold Saddam's personal status law, which sanctioned 'honour killing'. The women's NGOs, which emerged in the wake of the Ba'th Party's departure, were now in the shadow of the emerging Kurdish government. If ideologically women's NGOs were more nationalist than feminist, they were logistically rather insignificant in the prevailing no-war-no-peace environment.

The Bush Jr administration conferred on women's NGOs an active role in promoting US foreign policy objectives. Equally significant was the gender politics of this administration. In gender relations, anti-feminism was the rule. Through funding an anti-feminist group such as the Independent Women's Forum, Washington provided training for Iraqi women and made other interventions in Iraq's gender politics on the basis of one of the most conservative anti-feminist agendas in the United States. The project was to train Iraqi women leaders as anti-feminist neoconservatives capable of shaping gender policy in the country.

This study, much like previous critical literature, has demonstrated the limitations of NGOization: their short-term, piecemeal agenda; their failure to engage in long-term planning; their elite and non-grassroots leadership; their role as alternatives to women's movements and as agents of depoliticization and control. While one may add to this list, the main limitation is the politics that guides their agenda – they do not turn their political and intellectual energy vigorously against patriarchy as a system. They deal with the products of patriarchy, with its effects and its consequences, only. Even when they address violence against women, they do not see it as the product of a regime of gender relations, as a system that is social, economic, political, cultural, religious and ideological; and as a system that not only produces male domination but is able to reproduce itself.

Women's NGOs are not the only loci of reformist or reductive gender politics. Some women's movements, also, may not pursue radical encounters with patriarchy. More than two centuries of feminist and women's struggles in the West have visibly democratized gender relations. However, patriarchy still rules. Critical transnational feminist analyses argue that the co-optation of women's NGOs into the state gender agenda has depoliticized the women's movement worldwide. Penny Johnson and Eileen Kuttab show that in the post-Oslo era in Palestine international donors shifted resources away from the highly political women's movement towards absorbing women leaders into ministries and channelling funds away from women's organizations whose goals were political transformation and the national liberation struggle (Johnson and Kuttab, 2001). Darwiche shows how this process of depoliticization is not limited to Palestine but stretches across the entire Middle East (Darwiche, 2001). Indeed, we can argue that since the release of the Beijing Platform in 1995, women's movements that were associated with national liberation and anti-colonial struggles shifted their activities towards gender training and advocacy based on this platform. In reviewing the 1995 Beijing conference, Spivak terms it a 'global theater' and 'repressive ideological apparatus' (Spivak, 1996). She notes how the framework of such conferences does not deal with the internal divisions within nations and the power differences between North and South. It is this power divide that urges some feminist scholars to caution us about the unproblematic use of the term 'transnational' in feminist scholarship. Delia Aguilar asserts that using the word 'transnational' when referring to feminism has a 'falsely leveling effect' between imperialist and non-imperialist countries and between women of different class backgrounds. Aguilar is critical of transnational feminist analysis that culturalizes ruling relations of capitalism, colonialism and imperialism and reduces resistance against them to 'everyday spontaneous individual acts with not much political deliberation' (Aguilar, 2006).

The 2003 war brought market-centred anti-feminist politics to Kurdish women active in the NGOs and government. The introduction of this brand of colonialist feminism into Kurdistan, where feminist theoretical inquiry is of recent origin, calls on feminists and women activists to engage in struggle over the interplays of patriarchy, imperialism, capitalism, religion and nationalism. Kurdish women in Iraqi Kurdistan have already experienced living under the rule of 'their own' nation and are being exposed to colonial feminism. One can only predict that many Kurdish feminists will rise up against both national and colonial patriarchies.

Note

This chapter is part of a larger study funded by the Social Sciences and Humanities Research Council (SSHRC) of Canada. **The author is responsible for the contents of this study.**

References

Aguilar, Delia (2006) 'Current Challenges to Feminism: Theory and Practice'. http://mrzine.monthlyreview.org/aguilar181006P.html.

Ahmed, M.A., and M. Gunter, eds (2003) *The Kurdish Question and the 2003 Iraqi War*, Costa Mesa CA: Mazda, Kurdish Studies Series.

Ahmed, M.A., and M. Gunter, eds (2007) *The Evolution of Kurdish Nationalism*. Costa Mesa CA: Mazda, Kurdish Studies Series.

Al-Ali, Nadje Sadig (2007) *Iraqi Women: Untold Stories from 1948 to the Present*. London: Zed Books.

Al-Azzawi, Souad (2007) *Deterioration of Iraqi Women's Rights and Living Conditions under Occupation*. Survey published by the Brussells Tribunal, Baghdad.

Alvarez, Sonia (1999) 'Advocation Feminism: The Latin American Feminist NGO "Boom"', *International Feminist Journal of Politics* 1(2): 181–209.

Alvarez, Sonia (2000) 'Translating the Global: Effects of Transnational Organizing on Local Feminist Discourses and Practices in Latin America', *Meridians: Feminism, Race, Transnationalism* 1(1): 29–67.

Amnesty International (2005) *Iraq: Decades of Suffering, Now Women Deserve Better.* London.

Bird, Christiane (2004) *A Thousand Sighs, A Thousand Revolts*. New York: Ballantine.

Cohen, Robin (1997) *Global Diaspora: An Introduction*. London: UCL Press.

Coleman, Isobel (2006) 'Women, Islam, and the New Iraq', *Foreign Affairs* 1(85), January/February: 24–38.

Darwiche, N. (2001) 'Women in Arab NGOs', *Feminist Review* 69, Winter: 15–20.

Efrati, Noga (2005) 'Negotiating Rights in Iraq: Women and the Personal Status Law', *Middle East Journal* 59(4), Autumn: 577–95.

Elyachar, Julia (2005) *Markets of Dispossession: NGOs, Economic Development, and the State in Cairo*. Durham NC: Duke University Press.

Enloe, Cynthia (2004) *The Curious Feminist: Searching for Women in a New Age of Empire*. Berkeley: University of California Press.

IWF (2008) www.iwf.org/about/; accessed February 2008.

Hammami, Rema (2000) 'NGOs: The Professionalisation of Politics', *Race and Class* 37(2): 51–63.

Harvey, David (2003) The New Imperialism. Oxford: Oxford University Press.

Harvey, David (2006) 'Neo-liberalism as Creative Destruction', Swedish Society for Anthropology and Geography 88B(2): 145–58.

Hiltermann, Joost R. (2007) A Poisonous Affair: America, Iraq, and the Gassing of Halabja. Cambridge: Cambridge University Press.

Human Rights Watch (2003) 'Climate of Fear: Sexual Violence and Abduction of Women and Girls in Baghdad', Human Rights Watch 15(7), July.

Jad, Islah (2004) 'The NGOization of the Arab Women's Movements', Review of Women's Studies, vol. 2, Institute of Women's Studies, Birzeit University.

Johnson, Penny, and Eileen Kutlab (2001) 'Where Have All the Women (and Men) Gone? Reflections on Gender and the Second Palestinian Intifada', Feminist Review 69, Winter: 21–43.

KHRP (Kurdish Human Rights Project) (2007) The Increase in Kurdish Women Committing Suicide. London: European Parliament's Committee on Women's Rights and Gender Equality.

Kirk, Alastair, and Gary Sawdon (2002) The Household Economy: Understanding the Situation of Kurdish Livelihoods. London: Northern Iraq Country Programme and the Food Security and Livelihoods Unit, and Save the Children UK.

Klein, Naomi (2007) The Shock Doctrine: The Rise of Disaster Capitalism, New York: Knopf.

Kuper, Leo (1981) Genocide: Its Practical Use in the Twentieth Century. New Haven CT: Yale University Press.

Lang, Sabine (2000) 'The NGO-ization of Feminism: Institutionalization and Institution Building within the German Women's Movements', in Bonnie G. Smith, ed., Global Feminisms since 1945. London and New York: Routledge.

Lowenkron, Barry (2006) 'The Role of NGOs in the Development of Democracy', Remarks to the Senate Foreign Relations Committee, Washington DC, June 8. www.scoop.co.nz/stories/WO0606/S00277.htm.

McDowell, David (2000) A Modern History of the Kurds. London: I.B. Tauris.

McKiernan, Kevin, dir. (2000) Good Kurds, Bad Kurds: No Friends but the Mountains. Film.

Meiksins Wood, Ellen (1990) 'The Uses and Abuses of "Civil Society"', Socialist Register 1990, pp. 60–84. London: Merlin.

Meiksins Wood, Ellen (2006) 'Democracy as Ideology of Empire', in Colin Moers, ed., The New Imperialists: Ideologies of Empire, pp. 9–23. Oxford: One World.

Mendoza, Breny (2002) 'Transnational Feminisms in Question', Feminist Theory 3(3): 295–314.

MEPU (2008) http://mepi.state.gov/outreach/index.htm; accessed January 2008

Mojab, Shahrzad (2001) 'Kurdish Women in the Zone of Genocide and Gendercide', Al-Raida Magazine 21(103): 20–25. Institute for Women's Studies in the Arab World, Lebanese American University.

Mojab, Shahrzad (2002) 'No "Safe Haven" for Women: Violence against Women in Iraqi Kurdistan', in W. Giles and J. Hyndman, eds, Sites of Violence: Gender and Identity in Conflict Zones, pp. 108–33. Berkeley: University of California Press.

Nakhleh, Khalili (2004) *The Myth of Palestinian Development: Political Aid and Sustainable Deceit*. Jerusalem: Palestinian Academic Society for the Study of International Affairs.

Natali, Denise (2005) *The Kurds and the State: Evolving National Identity in Iraq, Turkey, and Iran*. Syracuse: Syracuse University Press.

Petras, James (1999) 'NGOs: In the Service of Imperialism', *Journal of Contemporary Asia* 29(4): 429–40.

Rahimi, Runak F. (2004) *Kurdish Community and Female Genital Mutilation: A Social Field and Theory Research in Southern Part of Kurdistan*, trans. Nasreen I. Rahim. Sulaimaniya: Women's Information Center.

Robinson, Williams (1996) *Promoting Polyarchy: Globalization, US Intervention, and Hegemony*. Cambridge: Cambridge University Press.

Roy, Sarah (2000) 'The Transformation of Islamic NGOs in Palestine', *Middle East Report* 214: 24–32.

Schorr, Daniel (1991), 'Ten Days that Shook the White House', *Columbia Journalism Review*, July–August: 21–3.

Smith, Andrea (2007a) 'Introduction: The Revolution Will Not Be Funded', in INCITE! Women of Color Against Violence, eds, *The Revolution Will Not Be Funded: Beyond the Non-Profit Industrial Complex*, pp. 1–18. Cambridge MA: South End Press.

Smith, Andrea (2007b) 'The NGOization of the Palestine Liberation Movement: Interviews with Hatem Bazian, Noura Erekat, Atef Said, and Zeina Zaatari', in INCITE!, eds, *The Revolution Will Not Be Funded: Beyond the Non-Profit Industrial Complex*, pp. 165–82. Cambridge MA: South End Press.

Spivak, Gayatri Chakravorty (1996) '"Woman" as Theatre', *Radical Philosophy* 75, January/February.

Stansfield, C. (2003) *Iraqi Kurdistan: Political Development and Emergency Democracy*. London: Routledge.

Sussman, Gerald (2006) 'The Myths of "Democracy Assistance": US Political Intervention in post-Soviet Eastern Europe', *Monthly Review* 58(7): 15–29.

UNIFEM (United Nations Development Fund For Women) (2005) *10 Years After Beijing: The Role and Contribution of the Arab NGOs*. Amman: Arab State Regional Office.

Van Bruinessen, Martin (2005) 'Kurdish Challenges', in Walter Posch, ed., *Looking into Iraq*, Chaillot paper 79, pp. 45–72. Paris: Institute for Security Studies, European Union.

Zangana, Haifa (2006a) 'The Unfinished Struggle: Priorities of Iraq Women under Occupation', paper presented at the international conference on Women, War and Learning, University of Toronto.

Zangana, Haifa (2006b) 'Colonial Feminists from Washington to Baghdad: Women For a Free Iraq as a Case Study', in Jacqueline Ismael and William Haddad, eds, *Barriers to Reconciliations*. Washington DC: University Press of America.

Zangana, Haifa (2007) *City of Widows: An Iraqi Women's Account of War and Resistance*. New York: Seven Stories Press.

PART II

Revisiting Transnational Women's Activism
in the Context of Conflict, Post-conflict
Reconstruction and Peace-building

FOUR

Gender Mainstreaming and Feminist Organizing in the Middle East and North Africa

Isis Nusair

In this chapter I examine the ways in which gender mainstreaming has been implemented in the Middle East and North Africa (MENA) by European Union and United Nations bodies. In addition, I examine the strategies used and the challenges faced by various feminist and women's groups and illustrate how gender mainstreaming is most effective when it involves, mobilizes and establishes solidarity networks with other local, regional and transnational groups. I argue that the local remains the main site for action for women's and feminist groups as a result of structural conditions and limitations imposed on their work by state and non-state actors. I analyse the intersection between local, regional and transnational economic and political power structures that fuel and benefit from the promotion of masculinized and militarized discourses of domination while keeping gender orders intact. The aim is to develop effective networking and gender mainstreaming processes that question these gender orders and support feminist and alternative solutions and transformations.

Gender mainstreaming

Gender mainstreaming originated in development policies in the 1970s and was adopted by the United Nations (UN) Platform for Action created in the Fourth World Conference on Women in Beijing in 1995 and taken up by the European Union (EU) and its member states. The concept of gender mainstreaming was first developed by feminists working in the European Commission in their efforts to promote gender equality policies among member states (Hawkesworth, 2006). The fundamental premiss of gender mainstreaming is that gender perspectives are essential to all programmes and issues. As a social change strategy, then, gender mainstreaming requires that all 'decision-making processes take gender into account, exploring the implications of proposed policies for men and women, and investigating differential gender impacts and disparate gender outcomes of existing and proposed programs' (96). In the language developed by the United Nations Economic and Social Council, gender mainstreaming is a 'strategy for making women's as well as men's concerns and experiences an integral part of the design, implementation, monitoring, and evaluation of policies and programs so that women and men can benefit equally and inequality is not perpetuated' (96–7). This definition emphasizes the need for the integration of women's concerns on all levels of policy and programmes, and the creation of equal conditions for realizing their full rights. Within this context, gender mainstreaming has involved 'new forms of political practice and alliances' (Walby, 2005: 467). It involves 'elected women in parliament, the development of specialized gender machinery in government, as well as gender expertise in civil society from universities to grassroots organizations' (467).

Gender mainstreaming has been transnational from the start, and dependent on gender relations and the national political context (Eveline and Bacchi, 2005). It goes beyond comparing the 'disadvantaged position of women with the privileged position of men', and aims to 'subject and broaden all policy areas to gender equality practices' (Walby, 2005: 456). It is an example of a policy development that is 'not a simple process of diffusion from core countries to the periphery but rather one in which there is a complex hybridization and development in form in different locations' (458). Gender mainstreaming in the MENA region has involved initiatives by governments, EU and UN bodies, as well as women's and feminist groups and organizations. I assess these initiatives while paying particular attention to the Palestinian case.

EU and UN gender mainstreaming initiatives

In November 1995, the European Union and twelve Mediterranean partner countries adopted the Barcelona Declaration, thereby agreeing to establish the Euro-Mediterranean Partnership (EMP). In the Barcelona Declaration, the parties undertook to act in accordance with the United Nations Charter and the Universal Declaration of Human Rights, as well as other obligations under international law (Naciri and Nusair, 2003). They furthermore committed themselves to respect human rights and fundamental freedoms and to guarantee these freedoms without discrimination on grounds of race, nationality, language, religion or sex.

It was agreed that gender mainstreaming should be incorporated into all three baskets of the EMP – that is, political and security cooperation, economic as well as cultural and human exchange. In addition, gender analysis should guide all development activities, programmes and projects at all stages. A follow-up mechanism should be established to assess the implementation of gender-sensitive policies within the EMP, and gender mainstreaming and affirmative action should be used as complementary strategies to ensure that women and men achieve their full potential, using gender disparities as a main indicator of policy performance in the region (Naciri and Nusair, 2003: 10).

However, despite the EMP's commitment to human rights, women's rights issues have initially received little attention in the EMP.[1] Neither the Barcelona Declaration nor the Association Agreements which govern the EMP explicitly recognize the indivisibility of women's rights, human rights and democracy. Although all parties to the EMP have positive obligations to implement gender mainstreaming into all aspects of the EMP, women's rights have been confined to the social and economic spheres (Naciri and Nusair, 2003: 8). As a result, women's rights projects have not been well funded through the MEDA programmes.[2] Given the many constraints against them, women's rights organizations – particularly South-based ones – often lack information on EU procedures and structures, making any EU funding difficult to access (9).

The partners at the Euro-Mediterranean Ministerial Conference on 'Strengthening the Role of Women in Society', which was held on 14-15 November 2006 in Istanbul and based on shared international, regional and national commitments, agreed to work to strengthen women's role in political, civil, social, economic and cultural spheres, as well as to fight against discrimination.[3] The conference adopted a Five Year Plan of Action to lead the Euro-Mediterranean Partnership work on the promotion and protection of women's rights. It was then stated that partners would adopt 'measures to achieve gender equality, preventing all forms of discrimination and ensuring the protection of the rights of women', while taking stock of the Rabat Preparatory Conference that was held on 14–16 June 2006 (Ministerial Conclusion). It was agreed that the Euro-Mediterranean partners need to include women's political, civil, social, economic and cultural rights in their dialogues, including in the framework of the Association Agreements, in the European Neighbourhood Policy action plans, and in the EU programmes and projects (Naciri and Nusair, 2003: 2).

In order to achieve gender mainstreaming, Euro-Mediterranean partners should move beyond minimum standards to full integration and equality in application of programmes and allocation of funds. To do so, they have to question cultural conceptions of women's rights and transform them into a well-defined and integrated gender mainstreaming approach. The 'promotion of gender equality and human rights, democracy and development are indivisible', and gender mainstreaming should involve a 'dual approach of systematic integration of gender issues in all policies and at all levels and stages promoting male–female equality – as well as affirmative action for women to ensure that they have the same access as men' (Abu Habib, 2006: 7). The initiative should also 'stress the importance of regular and systematic dialogue' with civil society and especially women's rights non-governmental organizations (NGOs) on issues relating to gender equality (7). The aim is to promote gender equity via a mainstreaming process that is both 'technical, involving tools and procedures that can be carried out by policy makers, and political in that it includes women's participation in defining what gender equality means in different political arenas and contexts' (Grosser and Moon, 2005: 533). Equal access and participation by all parties are essential for the development and success of this process.

In addition to EU policies and programs for gender mainstreaming in MENA, the United Nations Development Fund for Women (UNIFEM) has been involved with national committees in the region in preparing national strategies and gender mainstreaming in programmes and national budgets. UNIFEM was also involved in 'preparing a system for the evaluation and follow-up of national strategies, and in the evaluation of achievements and obstacles' (ESCWA, 2003: 6). These involved the preparation of national reports and training materials and guides, and particular attention was given to the feminization of poverty as a major challenge. This required an updating of economic policies in order to have a positive impact on the employment of women in the official and non-official sectors. It also included the 'establishment of social security systems, the strengthening of capacities for analysis that focused on gender issues, and the mobilization of all parties involved in the development process' (6). In addition, laws governing the political rights of women needed to be amended and updated to include either a quota system or a system based on the granting of opportunity, in order to increase the representation of women (3). This includes the creation of democratic institutions and practices in MENA countries that could make a genuine attempt at gender mainstreaming, and the strengthening of women's movements and civil society organizations.

To achieve this, funds need to be allocated for gender mainstreaming at both government and non-governmental levels (5).

Gender mainstreaming and women's and feminist organizing

Feminists in different parts of the world, including the MENA region, have made effective use of the merging institutions of global governance, utilizing UN processes and expanding the discourse of human rights (Walby, 2005: 459). This approach 'contrasts with the development of gender mainstreaming in employment and related economic domains, which, in European countries at least, have been far more dependent upon developments within the EU than at the global level' (459).[4] Therefore, gender mainstreaming is a 'leading-edge example of the potential implications of globalization for gender politics', and is a practice that is at least well developed (if not better) in the global South than in the North (464). Often, and as is the case in the MENA region, activists face opposition by their governments to gender mainstreaming and they have to deal with biases against them in the global North. There is a tendency by governments in the global North, as well as within the EU to regard women's rights in MENA in general as a domestic issue and not the concern of the international community or regional bodies. Furthermore, women from MENA countries, and especially Muslim women, are often stereotyped in the global North as being passive and without agency (Russo, 2006; Abu-Habib, 2006; Naciri and Nusair, 2003; Abu-Lughod, 2002).

The women's movement in MENA has benefited from the practical knowledge and experiences that the various women's groups acquired in the national liberation movements, in political groups and trade unions, and in participating in the UN international conferences on women's rights.[5] Such conferences highlighted the concerns of women's rights activists and organizations and facilitated local, regional and transnational advocacy on women's rights. They also encouraged mobilization on initiatives such as raising the minimum age for marriage, combating violence against women, and lifting reservations to CEDAW. NGOs promoting women's rights in MENA have also gained from establishing and joining regional coalitions and networks in the Maghreb, Mashreq and Mediterranean countries as well as transnationally (Naciri and Nusair, 2003). Since the beginning of the 1990s, aiming to improve the effectiveness of their work, women's rights groups and organizations have started to look beyond their national frontiers to develop regional and trans- national solidarities, and to use United Nations legal instruments to disseminate information about discrimination and violence against women (Basu, 1995).

As a social movement, women's activism in MENA includes strate- gies in the public sphere that do not 'reproduce Western frameworks' but employ 'cultural worldviews to feed into a global synergy' (Moghadam and Sadiqi, 2006: 2). It is only through 'understandings of intercultural worldviews and various meanings of "pragmatism" that MENA women's rights tactics can be appreciated globally' (2). Yet, in most MENA countries, access to the public sphere does not necessarily translate into gender equality or women's achieve- ment of their political, economic and legal rights (Skalli, 2006: 39). Despite the increasing number of women in schools, private and public sectors of activities, political structures, and decision-making positions, 'the significance of these numbers is threatened by the vigilant eye of the political regime and Islamist groups and often negated by conservative family laws institutionalizing discrimination' (39). Thus, while the sources of resistance to gender mainstreaming remain numerous, 'women are forced to be more strategic in their interventions and creative in their actions and alliances if they want to transform their realities in a meaningful way' (39).

There has been an increase in the number of NGOs in MENA during the 1990s due to national and international economic and political developments and policies (Carapico, 2000). The increase in women's organizations is due in particular to cuts in state pro- grammes, urbanization, and an increase in women's education and international aid (Kandil, 2002). Yet El-Gawhary (2000) raises questions about the capability of NGOs in Egypt, for example, to produce significant political and social transformations. The question remains as to whether NGOs are able to constitute continuous and sustained social movements as a result of the 'fragmentation of the issues that they deal with, the temporality of these issues and resources, and their weak networks' (Jad, 2003: 38). In spite of this, Carapico (2000:15) contends that NGOs have helped call attention to important issues such as human rights abuses, family violence, environmental degradation, and the deterioration of public works and welfare mechanisms.

The strategies of feminist and women's groups in MENA during the past two decades have become more diverse and dynamic. Activists in the region work on many fronts. They 'raise consciousness, engage in grassroots mobilization, conduct research, and collect and publish data that serves as a basis for advocacy work' (Skalli, 2006: 39). These efforts are increasingly expressed on the pages of newspapers, magazines and periodicals, on television and radio programmes, in documentaries and feature films, and on the Internet. In this way, 'women use different mediums to articulate their needs and multiply the opportunities of creating alternative discourses on womanhood and citizenship' (39).

The impact of women's interventions and initiatives is often more 'subtle and symbolic than openly radical or revolutionary – this is precisely how women activists bargain with structures of patriarchy in the MENA region' (Skalli (2006: 53).[6] Skalli adds that attempts to measure women's interventions by standards of achievement in regions with different politico-economic and socio-cultural realities are simply counterproductive. Taken together, these efforts and initiatives have managed to start the process of 'mainstreaming gender issues, raising awareness about women's complex realities, and interrogating the silence around family laws and other forms of institutionalized physical, mental and psychological violence' (54).

One of the main challenges to gender mainstreaming in the MENA region relates to the reform of family laws. Personal status codes and other issues related to women's roles in society have been publicly debated in Arab countries since the nineteenth century. These debates 'changed the terms of participation and made women and gender issues a matter of national dialogue and contention' (Sadiqi and Ennaji, 2006: 86). Sadiqi and Ennaji focus in particular on the case of Morocco and the mobilization during the 1990s by women's rights activists to change personal status laws. Although Moroccan women's rights activists have succeeded in accessing the Moroccan public sphere by politicizing women's issues, the 'litmus test' for Moroccan women's activists relates to the extent to which the reformed Personal Status Code will be 'implemented and enforced unequivocally' (Abu Habib, 2006: 8). This will require putting in place measures and mechanisms that will ensure that the new code is adequately interpreted and that the implementation mechanisms ensure women's full access to justice 'including equal rights to inheritance' (8).

Across the MENA region, women and civil society organizations have organized campaigns demanding reforms in such critical areas as violence against women, early marriage, reform of nationality laws, lifting the reservations on CEDAW, and ratifying the United Nations Optional Protocol. I will describe and assess below recent initiatives promoted by women's rights activists in the region.[7]

The coalition '20 Years Barakat', which contributed very significantly to putting reform of the Algerian Family Code on the agenda, was achieved through a media and consciousness-raising campaign. The Coalition consisted of several Algerian women's rights organizations supported by women's organizations in Morocco and Europe (8). Consequently, the Algerian parliament introduced in March 2005 a number of changes and reforms to the Family Code.[8] In Syria, significant change in the Personal Status Code allowed divorced mothers four additional custody years for their children, so that children remain in the custody of their mothers until the age of 15 years for girls and 13 years for boys. In Jordan, the personal status code was amended in 2001 with improvement for women in relation to alimony and further restrictions on polygyny (9). Recently, there was a campaign against early marriage that included workshops, discussions with religious men, and theatre performances at schools and summer camps. In Lebanon, there was a campaign to raise the age for mothers to retain custody of their children to 13 for males and 15 for females. Finally in Tunisia, there was a campaign to change inheritance laws.

In addition, NGOs have operated women's assistance centres in Morocco, Jordan and Tunisia. In Morocco, the Anaruz Network, a network of forty associations and centres, aims at raising awareness of the concept of gender-based violence. It also aims at 'fighting its cultural and social impunity as well as lobbying for legislative reforms and improving women's access to justice' (15). Activists have organized symbolic courts and radio campaigns on violence against women. Jordanian NGOs, including the National Commission for Human Rights, launched the campaign '16 Days of Activism against Gender Violence' in November 2005. The V-Day Karama Programme was established in 2006 in order to examine the impact of violence against women in nine Arab countries in all aspects of life including economics, politics and the judicial system.[9] Finally, the Salma Network, established as a follow-up to the Salma Project of 2003–05, aims to continue the national and regional campaigns on violence against women and create a sustainable network of Arab Women's NGOs active on the subject. The Network aims to facilitate communication, foster coordination, and exchange expertise on the local and regional levels.[10]

Women's rights activists have been promoting a regional campaign to lift reservations to CEDAW and to ratify the Optional Protocol. Under the slogan 'Equality without Reservation', representatives of NGOs from the Euro-Mediterranean gathered at a conference in Rabat in June 2006 to launch a regional campaign in all Arab countries to achieve gender equality. The objective of the campaign is to make states lift all reservations to CEDAW and sign up to the Optional Protocol. According to Abu Habib, despite encouraging development, MENA countries still 'lag behind other regions in the area of women's public and political participation and representation' (Abu Habib, 2006: 19). In some places, previous positive steps have even been reversed. She argues that the progress of political representation will be slow if not accompanied by gender mainstreaming and specific gender equity measures such as the adoption of quota systems. 'Where these and other affirmative actions have been taken', as is the case in Jordan, 'there has been a positive development toward more involvement of women in political decision-making' (19).

Attempts at establishing local and regional networks and coalition-building in MENA have been increasing in the last two decades. The Maghreb Equality 95 Collective (Le Collectif 95 Maghreb Egalité), set up in 1991/92 and still in existence today, was the first network of independent women's rights associations in the region.[11] Despite the difficulties associated with the political situation in Algeria and Tunisia, the Collective has been able to continue to grow, in part because of its 'flexible organizational structure and its decision-making procedures built on consensus' (Naciri and Nusair, 2003: 39). The Collective's plan of action for 2001–06 included writing parallel reports to the CEDAW Committee on Algeria and Tunisia's compliance with the CEDAW Convention, as well as a comprehensive study on Maghreb societies' acceptance of values of equality.

Aisha is another network established in 1993, composed of independent women's organizations from Algeria, Egypt, Jordan, Lebanon, Morocco, Palestine, Sudan and Tunisia. It aims to develop a regional feminist agenda that challenges discriminatory laws and practices.[12] Aisha's work has been paralysed recently as a result of lack of funding and coordination between its members. The Court of Arab Women is another initiative that addresses discrimination and violence against women. The Court was established in 1996 in Lebanon by NGOs from several Arab countries. It works to combat violence against women both in legislation and in practice, and has pressured governments in the region to take measures to protect and support women survivors of violence. In 1999, the Court launched a campaign calling for gender equality, especially in regard to women's access to divorce.

Finally, the first Sisterhood is Global Institute was established in Jordan in 1998. The institute is the first technology and communications-training centre in the region, providing courses on the use of computers and the Internet for research and advocacy on women's human rights, as well as training in basic interactive teaching and learning skills. The institute launched a website, and established a resource centre on violence against women.[13] In addition, the Maghreb/Mashreq Network for Information and Training on Gender unites Egypt, Lebanon, Morocco, Syria, Tunisia, Yemen and, very recently, Algeria. Established in 2000, this network provides a forum for debate, learning and exchange of information on women, gender and development. In March 2002, the Network launched a regional campaign on nationality laws and the right of women who are married to foreigners to transfer their nationality to their children.[14]

Other networks function unofficially in the region, such as the centres for legal aid and counselling for survivors of violence. Activists who run these centres in Algeria, Morocco and Tunisia meet regularly to exchange ideas and consolidate their experiences. Electronic networks have also sprung up over recent years, and have been developed more in the Mashreq than in the Maghreb, which lacks appropriate technological infrastructure, especially in Algeria, and is subject to stricter state censorship, as is the case in Tunisia. Although women's and feminist activism in MENA has been growing in the last few decades, it still faces major challenges. One of the main challenges relates to making gender mainstreaming a transformative project that addresses gender relations and power structures in both conflict and non-conflict situations.

Gender mainstreaming in conflict situations

I analyse in this section the prospects and challenges of gender mainstreaming in conflict situations in the MENA region with a particular focus on the Palestinian case. There has been an increased acknowledgement in recent years of the impact of conflict on women and of women on conflict (Zuckerman and Greenberg, 2005: 70). As emphasized in the Women and Armed Conflict section in the Beijing Platform for Action, government commitments in the Beijing

+5 review, and Security Council Resolutions 1325 and 1820, there is a need to examine the gendered impacts of war and women's contributions to conflict resolution and sustainable peace. As gender discrimination in conflict situations continues 'through political exclusion, economic marginalization and sexual violence, achieving sustainable peace requires a more permanent transformation of social norms relating to violence, gender and power' (79). The drafting of new constitutions and the 'transformation of legal systems at the conclusion of a peace agreement provides opportunities for mainstreaming gender into all state institutions, including the executive, legislative, judiciary, security service and education system' (Etchart and Baksh, 2005: 32).

The participation of more women directly or indirectly in a peace process, however, 'does not in and of itself ensure the inclusion of women's concerns in the substance of any agreement reached' (Onubogu and Etchart, 2005: 36). Therefore 'gender balance in participation must be accompanied by gender mainstreaming' (36). Onubogu and Etchart argue that what is relevant to a gendered analysis of the conflict is the social, economic and political position of women before and during the conflict, and the transition to post-conflict (36). Analysing the continuum of violence in the private and public sphere and in conflict and non-conflict situations allows for an understanding of the processes entailed in the gendering of hierarchical and exclusionary systems of power, and the re-examination of terms like 'post-conflict' and 'reconstruction' (Cockburn, 2007, 2004; Kelly, 2000). Without addressing the different forms of violence that permeate women's lives in so-called peace times, it is hard to achieve transformative relations for achieving gender equality.

In order to achieve gender equality, 'institutions must be transformed and energy and resources must be given to the implementation and institutionalization of policies' (Stiehm, 2001: 44). As the 'women and security' regime has established clear norms in terms of principles and a few implementation imperatives (Carey, 2001: 63), the challenge remains on how to 'increase focus, strengthen the rule of law institutions, and improve respect for human rights in post conflict environments' (Skjelsbaek, 2001: 81). Therefore 'gender mainstreaming should move beyond being an instrument for improving operations' (Whitworth, 2004).

Most of the formal recognition of women's vulnerabilities in conflict situations focuses on women as victims of sexual violence and not as agents in their own right. Far less common in the UN accounts is any acknowledgement of the 'relationship between insecurity and economic liberalization, or the ways in which the international division of labour is itself a violent process' (133). Peterson (2003) and Enloe (2000) analyse how the war economy has affected patterns of gender inequality and contributed to gender-based violence. 'The dynamics of gendered disadvantage, the erosion of local livelihoods, the criminalization of the economy and insecurity at the hands of armed groups and factions combine seamlessly to produce extreme forms of female vulnerability' (Kandiyoti, 2007a: 511). Therefore, attempts at addressing issues of gender justice through institutional and legal reforms need to acknowledge these interactions and their long-term effects (511).

Critical questions, not bureaucratic ones, should inform feminist work on gender mainstreaming. A larger and more focused effort must be made to 'challenge the role and limitations of the UN in framing contemporary debates on gender and security' (Whitworth, 2004: 121). 'Women's rights and the gender "mainstreaming" agenda that informs donor-assisted post-conflict reconstruction packages usually adopts a technocratic approach to address what are fundamentally political problems' (Kandiyoti, 2007a: 514). Within this context, 'pleas for the inclusion of women in peace building as a means of enhancing security is reminiscent of a type of instrumentalism evident in earlier arguments about promoting gender equity to better achieve economic growth and environmental sustainability' (514). Gender mainstreaming should not by any means contribute to militarism. Whitworth (2004) points to the potential radical strategy of gender mainstreaming rather than its simple liberal policies.

The invocation of women's rights for political purposes in the context of the 'war on terror', as was the case in Afghanistan and

Iraq (Abu-Lughod, 2002; Russo, 2006; Hatem, 2003), tended to breed scepticism in the MENA region about the Bush regime's commitment to women's rights. Using democracy and human rights to justify the 2003 invasion of Iraq caused mistrust in the human rights regime viewed by many in MENA as a new form of colonialism and imperialism. This in addition to the crackdown, in the aftermath of the 11 September 2001 attacks, by states in the region like Egypt and Tunisia on human rights activists in the name of protecting national security. This complicates and has serious negative implications on coalition-building and solidarity work among local women's and feminist groups and transnational networks in the region.

The Palestinian case

The Palestinian case raises serious questions about the possibility and success of gender mainstreaming in conflict situations. Within this context, and as was the case in Afghanistan and Iraq, 'the legal and technical solutions offered by gender mainstreaming may be at odds with the "real politics" of highly volatile and insecure environments' (Kandiyoti, 2007a: 514). The cases of Afghanistan and Iraq illustrate how a rights-based agenda could be 'compromised by the nature of the interventions that purport to uphold them and by the corrosive, long-term effects of prolonged conflict and endemic insecurity' (504). In the next section I briefly describe the history of the Palestinian women's movement, its achievements and the challenges it currently faces. In addition, I analyse the strategies used for gender mainstreaming since the Palestinian Authority came to power in parts of the West Bank and Gaza in 1994.

The First Intifada

The first Palestinian Intifada (uprising) in 1987 created new organizations that mobilized Palestinian youth, workers, women and students. It also included the creation of various specialized committees like the voluntary work committee, agricultural committees and health committees. These structures, according to Kuttab (1993: 73), became an 'organic part of the Palestine national movement and opened a new horizon for national awakening and identity consciousness. Because these forces were inspired by democratic principles, they provided a new ideological platform for gender and class issues.' Kuttab adds that this 'new' movement, which was mainly 'initiated by a group of progressive women of different political ideologies and of petit bourgeois origin, established new mass-based associations capable of organizing and mobilizing women in villages and refugee camps' (73). They generated literacy and consciousness-raising campaigns and were instrumental in strategizing national boycotts of Israeli products. During the Intifada, they were behind the emergence of household-based and small-scale economic cooperatives run by women. Furthermore, the Intifada witnessed the establishment of independent feminist centres (Abdo, 1999).

The second stage of the Intifada showed a 'relative decline and retreat in the intensity of the struggle that automatically generated negative repercussions for women's political participation' (Kuttab, 1993: 82). Instead of 'accumulating their experience in order to develop a qualitative change, new social and economic conditions emerged which neutralized women's activism and alienated them from their own achievements'. The 1988 Declaration of Independence in one way or another suggested that 'liberation was close by and that what was required was more emphasis and concentration on the building of the Palestinian state' (82). In 1991, the Palestinian women's movement raised publicly the concern that political fundamentalism sanctioned by conservative nationalist forces was imposing new repressive conditions on women (Giacaman et al., 2006). As a result, the achievements of women in general and the women's movement in particular 'failed to contribute to a real drastic and qualitative change in the status of women within Palestinian society' (Kuttab, 1993: 81). The Intifada left women's groups with a 'legacy of heightened consciousness and failed initiatives exemplified by the closure of many of the small-scale women's production projects' (Giacaman et al., 2006: 96).

The Palestinian National Authority and the Second Intifada

Despite the decline of and limitations on women's activism during the second part of the First Intifada, they still expected more participation in the decision-making bodies of the new political structures of the Palestinian National Authority (PNA) (Abdo, 1999). Between 1987 and the signing of the Oslo Accords in 1993, there was a reliance on NGOs to provide services, and they in turn became stronger actors than their parent political parties (Jad, 2007a). With the regression in the role of political parties, women's groups started looking for funding, and as a result technocratic institutions emptied the women's institutions from its cadres, which had an impact on the capacities and strategies used by women's and feminist organizations.[15]

While the PNA has developed as a governing body resembling the formal bureaucracy of a nation-state, in fact it remains politically, economically and geographically dependent on Israel (Abdo, 1999). This absence of sovereignty and geographical cohesion results in the absence of an independent and functioning civil society.[16] Despite this, the women's movement began to focus on legal issues as the prospects of a state and a national legal system became more realistic.[17] In 1995, the Women's Centre for Legal Aid and Counselling (WCLAC) launched a national and regional campaign of legal literacy to discuss women's status and the need to change existing laws. This was one of many programmes culminating in 1998 in the Model Parliament.

The PNA's lack of commitment to gender issues and its fragility both internally vis-à-vis civil society and externally towards Israel led many NGOs to shift their work from the national to the local and from the general to the individual (Jad, 2007a). In their urgent search for a viable strategy for the new era, Palestinian women activists seized, perhaps too quickly, on concepts developed elsewhere such as the need for 'gender training' (Giacaman et al., 2006). This clearly appealed for two reasons, as cadre women were eager to advance their own abilities to understand and deal with gender issues, and they hoped to influence their male colleagues (Giacaman et al., 2006). 'Despite political polarization, the Palestinian women's movement, with other social and political groups, actively negotiated rights with the PNA' (94).

The mixed experience of the women's committees and the women's movement during the First Intifada were the backdrop for examining the strategies proposed by women's activists in the early period following the coming of the PNA to power. The Women's Technical Committee, headed by Zahira Kamal, was among the first quasi-governmental bodies to be established. The Committee formed subcommittees to examine issues such as legislation, education and employment, with the aim of making policy recommendations. The gender mainstreaming experience of the Women Unit in the Ministry of Planning and International Cooperation has adopted 'participation, empowerment and cooperation as procedures to govern the relationship between management and voluntary and Government women's institutions'. The Unit saw its role as 'providing the impetus for gender mainstreaming in legislation, policies, plans and programmes' (ESCWA, 2003: 7). The development of the Ministry of Women's Affairs' mandate and its experience in gender mainstreaming was illustrated in three stages. The first focused on building the capacities and institutions of management. The second related to the practical application of gender mainstreaming in policies and plans of three ministries, namely the Ministry of Local Government Affairs, the Ministry of Labour and the Ministry of Agriculture. The third stage focused on the empowerment of women. Yet, there were limitations on the ability of the ministry to influence political decisions as it 'emphasized the exercise of influence rather than a more public contest for equality' (Giacaman et al., 2006: 97).

As the PNA focused primarily on policing functions, leaving the development of social policies and services to international aid and non-governmental organizations, there was a need to 'emphasize and realize the significance of NGOs in developing innovative and effective programmes for service provision, and in promoting democratization and community action essential for the growth of civil society' (Giacaman et al., 2006: 104). In particular, the women's movement was 'a leading force in widening and redefining social, rather than private, issues and needs'. Yet, 'the objective constraints of the transitional stage, the inexperience of the PNA, and the limitations on national resources were constraining factors' (104). This combined with the exacerbating conditions on the ground as illustrated by Israel's continued occupation policies even in areas within the jurisdiction of the PNA.

Women's advancement and effective gender mainstreaming were impeded by entrenched patriarchal structures, the militarization of the Second Intifada that started in 2000, and the prioritization of national security discourse. The question remains how to achieve gender equality and sustainable networking under conditions of extreme instability and insecurity and with diminishing prospects of finding a peaceful and just resolution to the Israeli–Palestinian conflict. A case in point is the paralysis in the work of the Palestinian Legislative Council since 2006. With many council members imprisoned by the Israeli authorities and many others not allowed to cross from Gaza to Ramallah, it has been quite impossible to make progress on reforming the penal and personal status codes. The main challenge for gender mainstreaming has to do with the limited space for action for women's rights organizations, and the need to recognize and address the demands of the different Palestinian constituencies. There remains a tension in the work of NGOs on how best to meet the demands of the national and the feminist, and how to balance community struggle with the provision of services.[18] The struggle for power between Hamas and Fatah factions have a negative effect on the morale of Palestinian society and its vision for an independent state, not to mention Israel's building of the separation wall, and its continued policies of occupation and cantonization of Palestinian areas, resulting in economic strangulation and de facto discontiguity on the ground.

Although Palestinian women's groups and NGOs have been able despite these conditions to network and lead pioneering programmes on the local and regional levels, networking on the transnational level remains limited. This was illustrated in the establishment of recent local and regional coalitions to reform personal status laws and introduce new family protection laws. In addition, local communication and civil associations' forums were established to support women's issues, and to prevent and eliminate violence against women.[19] Mais Warad said in response to my question about the persistent activism of women's rights groups in the West Bank that when dealing with women's issues in court, it matters more who the judge is rather than whether Hamas or Fatah are able to reconcile their differences.[20] She argues that work on law reform should continue despite economic, social and political limitations.

The challenge on the local level remains how to involve rural, refugee and poor women not as beneficiaries but as active participants in decision-making processes. It is not enough to rely on NGOs to provide services as they are not always able to address social and economic inequalities, especially within short-term projects dependent on foreign funding. Jad warns against the bureaucratization of relations between NGOs and local constituencies, and argues that the 'potential for NGOs to foster participatory developments beyond the grassroots level is fairly small, given the transitory nature of projects' (2007b: 187). She concludes that individual and universal women's rights approaches, including gender mainstreaming, need not ignore home-grown locally developed feminisms, and the historical realities of different layers of colonialism and occupation. There is still a need for a different form of organization with a different locally grounded vision and more sustainable power base for social change (Jad, 2007b). Yet, the establishment of national gender machinery and women's rights organizations that could produce critical thinking and change on the ground remains in question in the absence of an independent Palestinian state.

Challenges for gender mainstreaming and feminist organizing in MENA

As discussed earlier, one of the main challenges for gender mainstreaming is to turn it into a transformative project of gender order and relations of power and not descend into technocratic language and processes (Kelly, 2005: 473). In addition, there is a need to make international law 'permeate down into the realm of everyday life' without loosening the 'foundation of feminist analysis and under- standings' (489). The main critique against gender mainstreaming is that it could foster adaptation and change without transformation, especially in conflict situations, as is currently the case in Iraq and the Palestinian Occupied Territories. Working within or parallel to state institutions should be accompanied by alternative visions and strategies in order to confront the prevailing political culture and create more democratic structures and ways of doing politics (Al-Ali, 2003). In addition, gender mainstreaming and gender sensitivity should avoid becoming 'mechanistic quick fixes, which assume that problems of gender inequality can be addressed by redirecting some resources toward women's and girl's education, skills development, access to health services, or improvement of communication between men and women' (Hawkesworth, 2006: 100).

With their civic commitment, activists promoting the human rights of women in MENA are involved in an ongoing struggle for the democratization of their respective societies, which in turn could strengthen gender mainstreaming. In addition to the difficulties of maintaining human and material support for their projects, gaining and preserving independence in their work remains a daily struggle. The challenge goes beyond reforming laws that discriminate against women to ensuring their implementation as well. There is an urgent need to change the poor representation of women in elected bodies in MENA that contributes to their exclusion from decision-making positions. The aim is not to add women and stir but to integrate gender conceptually and in practice on both state and non-state levels. Or, as put by Eveline and Bacchi (2005), it is important to focus on the process of gendering where gender-awareness mainstreaming may well create more than a vision.

In conclusion, the agendas of local, regional and transnational feminist groups need to establish a plan for periodic and systematic evaluation of gender mainstreaming. They also need to examine their mobilization strategies and dependence on outside sources for

funding. They need to remain connected to grassroots efforts even while negotiating with official state bodies. Elitism is a recipe for alienation, and local and regional networks and collectives in MENA have proved most effective when coordinating their activities and advocacy strategies. Cooperation with transnational groups has also proved effective in creating alliances, as was the case when French, Italian and Spanish feminist and women's groups stood in solidarity with women during the civil strife in Algeria in the 1990s.

Finally, it is important to address structural hierarchies and power relations or the pyramid of marginalization when creating informational and solidarity networks.[21] The focus should be on networking, making the discourse practical, and linking theory with practice. As the local remains the site for action more than the regional and the transnational, the challenge for feminist and women's rights activists remains how to build effective networking under these conditions. Although feminist and women's groups in MENA have been quick to condemn the 2003 US-led invasion and occupation of Iraq and the continued Israeli occupation of the Palestinian Territories, they have been slow in forming regional and transnational solidarity networks to analyse the budgetary and the gendered socio-political implications of the security discourse, and war-waging and masculinized militarization processes in the region.

Notes

1. Specific reference to women's rights is only made in the economic and financial chapter of the Barcelona Declaration stating the need for overall improvement in the living and working conditions of the populations in the Euro-Mediterranean region. It was not until November 2001 that gender issues were mentioned in the final conclusions of the Euro-Mediterranean Partnership Summit. Furthermore, the Partnership's work programme has only marginally acknowledged the importance of women's rights, and these rights were inconsistently addressed in the Euro-Mediterranean National Strategy paper and the National Indicative Programmes (Naciri and Nusair, 2003).

2. The MEDA programme is the principal financial instrument of the European Union for the implementation of the Euro-Mediterranean Partnership. For further elaboration on the Euro-Mediterranean initiatives on women, see

http://ec.europa.eu/comm/external_relations/euromed/women/index.htm; accessed 15 January 2007.

3. See for further reference: http://ec.europa.eu/comm/external_relations/ euromed/women/docs/conclusions_1106.pdf; accessed 15 January 2007.

4. According to Walby (2005), the EU has become a transnational actor that is very important for the contemporary development of gender mainstreaming, with strengths in promoting the policy in abstract, but with weaknesses in implementation. The USA, on the other hand, is noteworthy for the absence of gender mainstreaming among its gender equality policies, and the transfer of the policy is thus not simply from the most powerful countries to weaker ones, but takes a more horizontal form that hybridizes according to local conditions.

5. See for further elaboration: Al-Ali, 2000; Chatty and Rabo, 1997; Lazreg, 1994.

6. See, for further elaboration, Hatem, 2005; Joseph, 2000; Kandiyoti, 1997, 1991.

7. This section is based on Abu Habib 2006.

8. Key changes included the introduction of the same legal age for marriage for both men and women, and of a legal requirement for a divorced man to provide housing for his former wife if she has custody of the couple's underage children. Homelessness among divorced women and their children has been recognized as a growing problem. The new law also rescinded the legal duty of a wife to obey her husband and introduced equal rights and duties for men and women during marriage. However, numerous provisions which discriminate against women were maintained, including restrictions on female guardianship, polygyny, the husband's unilateral right to divorce his wife, as well as the discriminatory provisions governing inheritance rights (Abu Habib, 2006).

9. See, for further reference, www.vday.org/contents/vday/vcampaigns/ amea/karama.

10. Interview with Hiba Al-Taibi, project coordinator, Heinrich Böll Foundation, Ramallah, 14 August 2008.

11. The section describing regional organizations in MENA is based on Naciri and Nusair 2003: 39–40.

12. The network has worked on monitoring Arab countries' compliance with their international obligations; documenting abuses against women; support-ing the independence of women's rights organizations from governmental and political parties; mobilizing for women's rights campaigns; supporting the establishment of women in decision-making positions; and examining the representation of women and girls in textbooks and in the media.

13. The Institute's website is: www.amanjordan.org.

14. See for further reference, Moghadam, 2005: ch. 6.

15. Zahira Kamal, Sharek Center, Ramallah, 14 August 2008.

16. Interview with Dr Nahla Abdo, Ramallah, 13 August 2008.

17. Ibid.
18. Ibid.
19. See, for further reference, www.wclac.org/about/partners.php.
20. Interview with Mais Warad, lawyer, Center for Legal Aid and Counselling, Ramallah, 16 August 2008.
21. Interview with Nabila Espanioly, director of Al-Tufula Center, Nazareth, 8 August 2008.

References

Abdo, Nahla (1999) 'Gender and Politics under the Palestinian Authority', *Journal of Palestine Studies* 28(2): 38–51.

Abu Habib, Lina (2006) *Achieving Gender Equality in the Euro-Mediterranean Region: Change is Possible and Necessary*. Denmark: Euro-Mediterranean Human Rights Network.

Abu-Lughod, Lila (2002) 'Do Muslim Women Really Need Saving? Anthropological Reflections on Cultural Relativism and Its Others', *American Anthropologist* 104(3): 783–90.

Ahmed, Leila (1992) *Women and Gender in Islam*. New Haven: Yale University Press.

Al-Ali, Nadje (2000) *Secularism, Gender and the State in the Middle East: The Egyptian Women's Movement*. Cambridge: Cambridge University Press.

Al-Ali, Nadje (2003) 'Gender and Civil Society in the Middle East', *International Feminist Journal of Politics* 5(2): 216–32.

Al-Ali, Nadje (2007) *Iraqi Women: Untold Stories from 1948 to the Present*. London: Zed Books.

Basu, Amrita, ed. (1995) 'Introduction', *The Challenge of Local Feminisms: Women's Movements in Global Perspective*, pp. 1–21. Boulder CO: Westview Press.

Carapico, Sheila (2000) 'NGOs, INGOs, GO-NGOs: Making Sense of Non-governmental Organizations', *Middle East Report* 214: 12–15.

Carey, Henry (2001) 'Women and Peace and Security: The Politics of Implementing Gender Sensitivity Norms in Peacekeeping', in Louise Olsson and Torunn Tryggestad, eds, *Women and International Peacekeeping*, pp. 49–67. London: Frank Cass.

Chatty, Dawn, and Annika Rabo, eds (1997) *Organizing Women: Formal and Informal Women's Groups in the Middle East*. Oxford: Berg.

Cockburn, Cynthia (2004) 'The Continuum of Violence: A Gender Perspective on War and Peace', in Wenona Giles and Jennifer Hyndman, eds, *Sites of Violence: Gender and Conflict Zones*, pp. 24–44. Berkeley: University of California Press.

Cockburn, Cynthia (2007) *From Where We Stand: War, Women's Activism and Feminist Analysis*. London: Zed Books.

El-Gawhary, Krista Masonis (2000) 'Egyptian Advocacy NGOs: Catalysts for Social and Political Change?', *Middle East Report* 214: 38–41.

Enloe, Cynthia (2000) *Maneuvers: The International Politics of Militarizing Women's Lives*. Berkeley: University of California Press.

ESCWA (Economic and Social Commission for Western Asia) (2003) 'Workshop on Gender Mainstreaming in the ESCWA Region', Beirut, 23 December. www.escwa.un.org/divisions/ecw_editor/Download.asp?table_name=other%20andfield_name=id%20andFileID=%2084; accessed 14 July 2008.

Etchart, Linda, and Rawwida Baksh (2005) 'Applying a Gender Lens to Armed Conflict, Violence and Conflict Transformation', in Rawwida Baksh et al., eds, *Gender Mainstreaming in Conflict Transformation: Building Sustainable Peace*, pp. 14–33. London: Commonwealth Secretariat.

Eveline, Joan, and Carol Bacchi (2005) 'What Are We Mainstreaming When We Mainstream Gender?', *International Feminist Journal of Politics* 7(4): 496–512.

Giacaman, Rita, et al. (2006) 'Gender, Citizenship, and the Women's Movement in Palestine', in Joel Beinin and Rebecca Stein, eds, *The Struggle for Sovereignty: Palestine and Israel 1993–2005*, pp. 94–104. Stanford: Stanford University Press.

Grosser, Kate, and Jeremy Moon (2005) 'The Role of Corporate Social Responsibility in Gender Mainstreaming', *International Feminist Journal of Politics* 7(4): 532–54.

Hatem, Mervat (2003) 'Discourses on the "War on Terrorism", in the US and its Views of the Arab, Muslim, and Gendered "Other"', *Arab Studies Journal* 6(2)/7(1), Fall/Spring: 77–97.

Hatem, Mervat (2005) 'In the Shadow of the State: Changing Definitions of Arab Women's "Developmental" Citizenship Rights', *Journal of Middle East Women's Studies* 1(3): 20–45.

Hawkesworth, Mary (2006) *Globalization and Feminist Activism*. New York: Rowman & Littlefield.

Jad, Islah (2003) 'The 'NGOization' of the Arab Women's Movements', *Al-Raida* 20(100): 38–47.

Jad, Islah (2007a) 'NGOs between Buzzwords and Social Movements', *Development in Practice* 17(4–5): 622–9.

Jad, Islah (2007b) 'The NGO-isation of Arab Women's Movements', in Andrea Cornwall et al., eds, *Feminisms in Development: Contradictions, Contestations and Challenges*, pp. 177–90. London: Zed Books.

Joseph, Suad, ed. (2000) *Gender and Citizenship in the Middle East*. New York: Syracuse University Press.

Kandil, Amani (2002) 'Women in Egyptian Civil Society: A Critical Review', *Al-Raida* 19(97–98): 30–37.

Kandiyoti, Deniz (1997) 'Beyond Beijing: Obstacles and Prospects for the Middle East', in Mahnaz Afkhami and Erika Friedl, eds, *Muslim Women and the Politics of Participation: Implementing the Beijing Platform*, pp. 3–10. Syracuse: Syracuse University Press.

Kandiyoti, Deniz (2007a) 'Between the Hammer and the Anvil: Post-Conflict Reconstruction, Islam and Women's Rights', *Third World Quarterly* 28(3): 503–17.

Kandiyoti, Deniz (2007b) 'Old Dilemmas or New Challenges? The Politics of Gender and Reconstruction in Afghanistan', *Development & Change* 38(2): 169–99.

Kandiyoti, Deniz, ed. (1991) *Women, Islam and the State*. Philadelphia: Temple University Press.

Kelly, Liz (2000) 'Wars against Women: Sexual Violence, Sexual Politics and the Militarized States', in Susie Jacobs et al., eds, *States of Conflict: Gender, Violence and Resistance*, pp. 45–65. London: Zed Books.

Kelly, Liz (2005) 'Insiders Outsiders: Mainstreaming Violence against Women into Human Rights Discourse and Practice', *International Feminist Journal of Politics* 7(4): 471–95.

Kuttab, Eileen (1993) 'Palestinian Women in the Intifada: Fighting on Two Fronts', *Arab Studies Quarterly* 15(2): 69–86.

Lazreg, Marnia (1994) *The Eloquence of Silence: Algerian Women in Question*. London: Routledge.

Moghadam, Valentine (2005) *Globalizing Women: Transnational Feminist Networks*. Baltimore: Johns Hopkins University Press.

Moghadam, Valentine, and Fatima Sadiqi (2006) 'Women's Activism and the Public Sphere: Introduction and Overview', *JMEWS* 2(2): 1–7.

Naciri, Rabéa, and Isis Nusair (2003) *The Integration of Women's Rights from the Middle East and North Africa into the Euro-Mediterranean Partnership*. Denmark: Euro-Mediterranean Human Rights Network.

Onubogu, Elsie, and Linda Etchart (2005) 'Achieving Gender Equality and Equity in Peace Processes', in Rawwida Baksh et al., eds, *Gender Mainstreaming in Conflict Transformation: Building Sustainable Peace*, pp. 34–55. London: Commonwealth Secretariat.

Peterson, V. Spike (2003) *A Critical Rewriting of Global Political Economy: Integrating Reproductive, Productive and Virtual Economies*. London: Routledge.

Russo, Ann (2006) 'The Feminist Majority Foundation's Campaign to Stop Gender Apartheid – The Intersection of Feminism and Imperialism in the United States', *International Feminist Journal of Politics* 8(4): 557–80.

Sadiqi, Fatima, and Moha Ennaji (2006) 'The Feminization of Public Space: Women's Activism, the Family Law, and Social Change in Morocco', *JMEWS* 2(2): 86–114.

Skalli, Loubna (2006) 'Communicating Gender in the Public Sphere: Women and Information Technologies in the MENA Region', *JMEWS* 2(2): 35–59.

Skjelsbaek, Inger (2001) 'Sexual Violence in Times of War: A New Challenge for Peace Operations', in Louise Olsson and Torunn Tryggestad, eds, *Women and International Peacekeeping*, pp. 69–84. London: Frank Cass.

Stiehm, Judith Hicks (2001) 'Women, Peacekeeping and Peacemaking: Gender Balance and Mainstreaming', in Louise Olsson and Torunn Tryggestad, eds, *Women and International Peacekeeping*, pp. 39–48. London: Frank Cass.

Walby, Sylvia (2005) 'Introduction: Comparative Gender Mainstreaming in a Global Era', *International Feminist Journal of Politics* 7(4): 453–70.

Whitworth, Sandra (2004) *Men, Militarism, and UN Peacekeeping: A Gendered Analysis*. Boulder CO: Lynne Rienner.

Zuckerman, Elaine, and Marcia Greenberg (2005) 'The Gender Dimensions of Post-Conflict Reconstruction: An Analytical Framework for Policymakers', in Caroline Sweetman, ed., *Gender, Peacebuilding and Reconstruction*, pp. 70–82. London: Oxfam.

FIVE

'Here, it's not about conflict resolution –
we can only resist': Palestinian Women's Activism
in Conflict Resolution and Non-violent Resistance

Sophie Richter-Devroe

Since the passing of UN Security Council Resolution 1325 in 2000, which calls upon member states to mainstream gender in all aspects of conflict prevention, management and resolution, there has been a strong focus on the contribution that women could potentially make to positive conflict transformation. While the UN heralds the Resolution as a landmark document that promises to protect women's rights and guarantee their equal participation in peace processes (UN, 2004), others criticize it for promoting essentialist binaries between women/peacemaker/victim and men/warrior/protector (Väyrynen, 2004) and for merely adding women to existing gender-discriminate frameworks without challenging the war system from a feminist, gender or human rights perspective (Cohn et al., 2004; see Cockburn, 2007: 147–55).

Besides such theoretical criticism, the Resolution faces challenges in implementation. While practitioners call for the enactment of monitoring, accountability and enforcement mechanisms 'to give "teeth" to the Resolution 1325' (D. Steinberg, 2008), those women on the ground whose peace-building work the Resolution is supposed to strengthen often prefer not to be associated with what either they themselves or their societies at large perceive 'to be part of a Western plot to destroy [their] society's traditional culture and values' (Al-Ali, 2005: 743). Since women are often reified as bearers of cultural authenticity (Yuval-Davis and Anthias, 1989), an intervention by international actors that presses links between women's issues and conflict resolution is viewed sceptically, particularly by societies whose conflict history was or still is dominated by foreign occupation. The difficulty of implementing 1325 and reconciling it with local women's peace and conflict-resolution agendas raises several questions. What impact do international gender and conflict interventions, transnational feminism and women's solidarity initiatives have on local women's movements in situations of conflict and foreign occupation? Do they advance or hinder processes of women's empowerment and conflict resolution? More particularly, when and why do local women perceive international interventions such as UNSCR 1325 to be part of rather than a solution to the conflict? Given these controversies, what should be the basis of women's transnational solidarity movements striving for political and social change: a shared gender, feminist or political agenda?

Palestinian women's peace-building activism provides a rich case study for addressing these questions. Studying the impact that international agendas have in this local setting reveals the power structures that exist not only *between* but also *within* the different international and local feminist agendas and women's strategies. On the one hand, international donors and some local NGOs support women's participation in joint Palestinian–Israeli peace projects, often advancing a women's rights agenda and aiming for reconciliation between the two sides. On the other hand, the majority of Palestinians reject such dialogical conflict-resolution initiatives, considering them foreign-imposed and elitist policies that, at best, affect cosmetic personal changes only, while leaving the political root causes of the conflict and people's everyday needs unaddressed. Instead they support and participate in various forms of non-violent resistance, finding that such action-oriented political activism has more potential to bring about and sustain social and political change.

The first part of this chapter consists of an overview of the historical development of the different types of Palestinian women's political activism. In the second, third and fourth parts I compare the different organizational forms, the aims and the strategies chosen, in, respectively, joint Palestinian–Israeli conflict-resolution initiatives (mainly foreign-funded), and non-violent resistance activities (mainly Palestinian-initiated), inquiring into their respective transformative potential. While most international, Israeli and also a few Palestinian organizations claim that joint conflict resolution is most empowering for women, I argue that in the Palestinian case women's participation in resistance activism is more broadly mobilizing and empowering. As a non-violent, gender-friendly, widely supported and inclusive form of political activism, it offers a promising but much neglected bargaining strategy for female political agency and, as such, might prove more conducive than joint conflict resolution to gender and peace development.[1]

Historical overview of Palestinian women's peace activism

Women's public activism in Palestine dates back to the early twentieth century. While early organizations were restricted to charitable work and joined only by a minority of middle- and upper-class women from the cities (Jad, 1990), the establishment of the Israeli state in 1948 and the subsequent wholesale destruction of Palestinian social, political and economic structures necessitated women's increased public presence. In 1967 the Israeli occupation led to the politicization of the entire Palestinian society. The Union of Palestinian Women's Working Committees was founded in 1978,[2] enjoyed extensive grassroots support[3] and, in addition to its charitable and political motivations, started gradually to address gender issues as well (Kamal, 1998). Women's activism, however, remained mainly within Palestinian society. The very few tentative contacts with Israeli activists which were made through the first (mainly communist) joint Palestinian–Israeli underground political parties (Ashrawi, 1995: 32, 51; Nasser-Najjab, 2004) were based on a joint political, not gender, agenda.

The First Intifada, 1987–93

Women participated strongly in non-violent resistance activism during the First Intifada. They organized demonstrations, provided relief work, took over jobs left vacant by detained men and formed women's co-operatives to support the production process (Abdo, 1994). With their resistance activities women not only confronted the occupation, but also challenged societal norms and patriarchal practices which hinder their more personal liberation as women. Palestinian women's political and social struggles are thus interlinked, with the former having had an exceptional and, at least in parts, positive impact on the latter.[4]

The Intifada also encouraged joint peace activities between Israeli and Palestinian women in, for example, dialogue groups, local and international conferences and joint solidarity protests (Sharoni, 1995: 134–5). The first contacts were mainly solidarity-based demonstrations or street actions. With their shared goal of ending the occupation they were successful in achieving some bonding across the Israeli–Palestinian divide, but remained unofficial and without much publicity. The first official public encounter took place in a television debate in 1988. Hanan Ashrawi participated in the Palestinian debating team. Her hesitation and discussions with leaders of the Palestinian political factions before the televized debate point to one of the major difficulties of joint encounters, which up until today remains 'to persuade the various factions that such an event could be carried out without conceding the "normalization" of relations between occupier and occupied' (Ashrawi, 1995: 48). The Popular Front for the Liberation of Palestine (PFLP) refused to participate or lend official support to public Palestinian–Israel dialogue, while the Communist Party was its strongest supporter. Fatah and the Popular

Democratic Front for the Liberation of Palestine (PDFLP)[5] remained ambiguous in their stance towards dialogue with the Israeli side (Ashrawi, 1995: 48). The Women's Committees reflected the position taken by their political parties.

The Intifada had attracted increased attention from international women's groups and activists to the plight and activism of Palestinian women. Prominent female leaders, such as Simone Süsskind from Belgium and Luisa Morgantini from Italy, began officially supporting joint Palestinian–Israeli women's conflict-resolution initiatives. In 1989 Süsskind organized an international women's peace conference in Brussels entitled 'Give Peace a Chance: Women Speak Out' (Sharoni, 1995: 143–4; Jad, 2004: 193) which was attended by over 150 women from around the Mediterranean. Palestinian women participated as Committee representatives or as independent experts. The PFLP-affiliated Union of Palestinian Women's Committees (UPWC) boycotted the conference (Ashrawi, 1995: 60–61). In an interview in 1991 Maha Nassar, the Union's director, expressed her scepticism toward joint women's dialogue groups asking: 'what kind of bridges [do] you want to build, between whom and leading to what?' (Nassar quoted in Sharoni, 1995: 142). This crucial question was to dominate joint encounters, particularly so after the Oslo Accords when internal divisions as well as external pressure mounted and joint peace initiatives took on new forms and content.

The Oslo Peace Process, 1993–2000

After the signing of the 1993 Oslo Accords joint Palestinian–Israeli civil society peace projects received increased financial support from international donors. Joint projects thus multiplied, and – more importantly – became institutionalized in the 1995 Israeli–Palestinian Interim Agreement on the West Bank and Gaza Strip. In its Annex VI the Agreement stipulates the Israeli–Palestinian Cooperation Program including a specific People-to-People Program in Article VIII which calls upon the two sides to 'cooperate in enhancing dialogue and relations between their peoples' (Oslo II, 1995).

The fact that the Cooperation Programme is added almost as an afterthought to the Agreement in the Annex reveals the two theoretical traditions embedded in the Accords: a top-down approach of peacemaking as manifest in the official peace process at high political level, and a bottom-up approach of peace-building which was introduced to mainstream conflict resolution by Boutros-Ghali's Agenda for Peace in 1992 and found expression in the Israeli–Palestinian People-to-People Program. By bringing together constituencies from both sides of the conflict and allowing them to present their different perspectives on the conflict, the latter hoped to enhance mutual relations and build stability, trust and cooperation between the two sides. It aimed at affecting attitudinal and relational change, while structural change was supposed to be implemented from above.

Norway and its Institute for Applied Social Science, Fafo, were the official administrators of the People-to-People Program, but other local, bi- and multilateral organizations such as USAID, CIDA, EU, SIDA and Belgium Aid quickly joined the post-Oslo peace market. It is estimated that between September 1993 and September 2000 alone in the region of $20–$25 million was allocated to civil society organizations for joint Palestinian–Israeli peace-building (IPCRI, 2002: 2). These projects could take the form of one-time single events or long-term, continuous series of meetings. Often groups were assembled according to shared identities other than national, such as age, profession or gender. A special focus was put on marginalized groups; women thus became a specific target group for joint encounters (Nasser-Najjab, 2004). The Jerusalem Link, an alliance between the (Palestinian) Jerusalem Centre for Women (JCW) in East Jerusalem and the (Israeli) Bat Shalom in West Jerusalem is one such cooperative peace-building project that emerged under the institutional support of the Oslo peace process. Already under discussion in the 1989 Brussels meeting, the Link was established in 1994. It has since received broad media and academia attention (e.g. Cockburn, 2007; Farhat-Naser, 2005; Wrege, 2008) and has often been showcased as a model for women's peace and feminist activism (e.g. Powers, 2007).

On the Palestinian side, however, women's joint peace-building was perceived more critically. The PFLP, the Islamic Resistance Movement and Hawatmeh's faction of the Democratic Front for the Liberation of Palestine (DFLP) (and their affiliated women's committees) openly opposed the peace process and its civil society dialogue groups, viewing the former as unjust and the latter as normalization (see e.g. Ashrawi, 1995). Even within the pro-Oslo camp not all supported people-to-people projects. Particularly after the 1996 Netanyahu election, with increased violence, settlement constructions and prospects for real peace waning, fewer and fewer Palestinians felt ready to engage in joint bottom-up peace-building and reconciliation processes with the Israeli side.

The Second Intifada, post-2000

Since the failure of Camp David and the outbreak of the Second Intifada in 2000, the majority of cooperative efforts for peace and coexistence at the grassroots level have stopped. On a material level the developments on the ground – closures, curfews, checkpoints and the construction of the wall dividing the West Bank into several isolated cantons – make meetings almost impossible. Gazans, in any case, are forbidden to leave the Strip, but also for Palestinians in the West Bank, particularly for those who are believed to have links to the resistance, permits to enter Israel or even Jerusalem are very difficult to obtain. This reduces potential participants in dialogue groups to 'the converted' – that is, those who support joint conflict resolution and what remains of the peace process.

As a consequence of such material restrictions, popular opposition to joint peace initiatives grew. In 2000 the Palestinian NGO Network called upon all Palestinian NGOs 'to completely cease all joint projects with Israeli organizations, especially the projects covered under People to People program, Peres Center for Peace, the joint projects program funded by the United States Agency for International Development (USAID), or any other normalization projects' (PNGO, 2000: 27). The breakdown of the talks and outbreak of new violence in

2000 thus brought to the fore what Edward Said (like other critical observers) had warned against earlier when he wrote that '[t]he thought that by working out an arrangement whereby the occupation might continue while at the same time a few Palestinians and Israelis could nevertheless cooperate on a friendly basis, struck me as false and misleading' (Said, 1995: 36).

The Jerusalem Link was among the joint projects that the PNGO blacklisted as a form of normalization. It was, however, not just Palestinian public opinion and material restrictions on the ground, but also internal disagreements between the Palestinian and Israeli women that threatened the joint work of the Link during the early years of the Second Intifada. At a time when their society was suffering from continuous Israeli military aggressions, the Palestinian JCW considered it more urgent to work on intra-Palestinian issues. They thus temporarily froze all joint work with Bat Shalom and shifted their focus to more immediate concerns on the ground, such as the impact that the construction of the wall or house demolitions have on Palestinian women's lives (Interview JCW, 2008).

Donor agendas, however, seemed to be inversely related to such attitudinal and material developments on the ground. For example in 1998, at a time when most Palestinians had turned away from joint projects, the EU institutionalized substantive budget lines for joint Palestinian–Israeli peace-building through its Partnership for Peace Programme.[6] Similarly the first US funds allocated specifically for bottom-up peace-building through the Wye River Memorandum were only released after the Second Intifada began (Herzog and Hai, 2005). The agenda of those peace-building projects that continued after 2000 in an atmosphere of growing violence and opposition to joint encounters displays two major trends.

Feminization of peace-building

First, post-2000 conflict-resolution projects often focus on women as peacemakers. In the light of the very violent and brutal nature of Israeli military oppression and increased militarization on the

Palestinian side (see Johnston and Kuttab, 2001), Palestinian women often are either presented as passive victims of war or their alleged peaceful 'feminine' nature is showcased as a counter-model to such 'masculine' violence. The recent recommendations from the 2005-founded, EU-funded Palestinian–Israeli Peace NGO Forum, an umbrella organization that coordinates various peace initiatives, reflect such feminization of peace-building when calling for the '[c]reation of new Israeli and Palestinian women's groups that would demonstrate together against violence and death, and work on outreach in Israeli and Palestinian societies' (EU, 2007: 8). UNSCR 1325 also encouraged the focus on women as peacemakers. In 2002 Palestinian and Israeli activists Abu-Dayyeh Shamas and Greenblatt called upon the UN Security Council to establish an International Women's Commission to monitor the implementation of the Resolution. The Commission was established in 2005 at an international conference in Turkey convened by UNIFEM and has since been lauded as 'the first-ever global commission working to guarantee women's full participation in formal and informal Israeli–Palestinian peace negotiations' (UN, 2005).

On the ground, however, few ordinary women are aware of the Resolution, although more and more local women's or conflict-resolution organizations have started to add it to their agendas. The JCW, being one of them, focuses on raising women's awareness of 1325 so that they can contribute to its implementation and, more importantly, its adaptation to the specific Palestinian situation. With similar aims the Bethlehem-based conflict resolution NGO Wi'am, together with the Swedish organization Operation 1325, organized a conference on 1325 in 2007. The experience of both Wi'am and JCW was that the majority of Palestinian women with whom they worked found most articles of the Resolution to be inapplicable and not responding to their needs and priorities. The great majority perceived it to be an abstract formula imposed from outside, and stressed the need to adapt it to the specific context of foreign occupation in Palestine (Interview Wi'am, 2007; Interview JCW, 2008). As long as the occupation persists the Palestinian Authority has no means to enforce

1325, let alone guarantee its demands of, for example, providing protection for women. Furthermore, given the fact that Israel ignores other UN Resolutions, NGOs find it very difficult to convince women of the importance and relevance of 1325. If Palestinian women agree to use UN Resolutions at all as a framework for their activism, most would focus on Resolutions such as 194 or 242, which deal with their quest for self-determination, rather than 1325 (Interview JCW, 2008). Whether 1325 will indeed be able to strengthen Palestinian women's peace-building activism thus remains to be seen.

At the same time, however, involving women in peace-building activities and embedding their activism within broader international agendas and frameworks, such as 1325, is without doubt crucial for local actors in their search for financial and ideational support. The international community's focus on civil society rapprochement and on women as peacemakers following the Oslo Accords, the Second Intifada and 1325 not only turned joint peace-building into a business venture (Tamari, 2005/6), but also led to a feminization of this peace-building business.

Intra-Palestinian peace-building and non-violence initiatives

Second, international funding agendas post-2000 show more interest in intra-Palestinian peace-building and non-violence projects. The EU's Partnership for Peace Programme, for example, although preferring joint projects, also supports one-country projects that promote non-violence. Among the EU-funded women's non-violence initiatives is the Israeli NGO Machsom Watch, a women-only organization that stages non-violent protests and reports human rights abuses at checkpoints, and the Bethlehem-based Holy Land Trust, which runs a specific non-violence and conflict-resolution training programme for women aiming at equipping them with theory and praxis of non-violence. The EU has been criticized for supporting non-violence projects. The Israeli side takes issue with the EU's funding of what it perceives as Palestinian resistance designed to 'delegitimize the Jewish state' (G. Steinberg, 2008: 6). At the same time, Palestinians often view non-violence projects, particularly if focused on spreading the concept of non-violence rather than staging proactive non-violent *resistance* protests, as an attempt by Western powers to undermine resistance to the occupation (Interview Mahmoud, 2007;[7] see Allen, 2002).

The Palestinian public's scepticism towards certain forms of peace-building, be it inter- or intra-party, reveals a stark difference between international and local understandings and classifications of peace-building. In the literature and among international actors the terms 'people-to-people', 'conflict resolution' or 'peace-building' are often used interchangeably (with 'people-to-people' referring to joint peace initiatives only). Among Palestinians, however, the terms 'conflict resolution' and 'people-to-people' (which are used in the English original) have a negative connotation and are associated with the foreign-funded NGO peace business. Both terms are used predominantly to refer to those joint conflict-resolution projects that aim at socio-cultural understanding, psychological healing and reconciliation. The term 'non-violence' (or its Arabic equivalent *al-la 'unf*) is used additionally by some to describe NGO peace projects that aim to spread the concept of non-violence within the Palestinian community. Non-violent resistance and anti-occupation protest activism – whether Palestinian-only or joint by Israeli or international solidarity activists – consequently do not come under the umbrella terms of 'conflict resolution' or 'people-to-people', but rather are referred to as non-violent resistance (*al-muqawmah as-silmiyyah*) or popular resistance (*al-muqawmah ash-sha'biyyah*). In short, as one of my interviewees neatly put it: 'here [in the Palestinian–Israeli context] it's not about conflict resolution – we can only resist' (Interview Salwa, 2007).

In the following comparison of organizational forms, aims and strategies of women's post-2000 peace-building I will use 'peace-building' as a generic term covering all forms of civilian-based non-violent peace activism and will differentiate between 'non-violent resistance' and 'conflict resolution'/'people-to-people' according to the Palestinian classification just described.

Organizational forms of women's peace-building

Most joint Palestinian–Israeli women's conflict-resolution projects are carried out by foreign-funded NGOs, while the majority of women's non-violent resistance activities are organized on an ad hoc basis, through political parties or by local popular committees. Joint conflict-resolution projects are sometimes organized by Israeli–Palestinian or Palestinian NGOs, but the majority are carried out by Israeli NGOs which collaborate in joint projects with NGOs from the other side.

The boom in conflict resolution and women's NGOs is part of a general process of NGOization of Palestinian civil society that took place after the Oslo Accords (see Hammami, 1995; Hanafi and Tabar, 2005; Jad, 2004). In this process, the grassroots social movement of the First Intifada became increasingly professionalized and fragmented into smaller NGOs, which often compete for the same funds. It would be incorrect, however, to claim that donors dictate NGO agendas. As one of my interviewees, who works in a women's NGO, explained: 'There is no funder who tells us what we need or don't need, what is allowed and what not. But they propose certain interest issues – and then NGOs decide that this year they should work on that. This makes an organization unprofessional; it makes it look like a supermarket' (Samira, 2007).[8] 'Conflict resolution' and 'gender', being among the interest issues of international funders, are increasingly displayed on the 'supermarket shelves' of NGOs. Together with professionalism and mastery of the English language, they seem to be among the main criteria to attract foreign funding.

The NGOization of Palestinian civil society thus led to the emergence of what has aptly been coined a 'globalized elite': supporters of the peace process, informed by global agendas, mainly urban-based and professionalized (Hanafi and Tabar, 2005: 247–51) and – one might add – concentrated in the West Bank and East Jerusalem. The 'globalized elite', however, is not just globalized because it interacts with global agendas such as Boutros-Ghali's Agenda for Peace (1992), the Beijing Platform (1995) and the UNSCR 1325 (2000), but also because its members participate in global events. International women's peace conferences, such as the 1989 Brussels Conference or the more recent meetings of members of the International Women's Commission with the UN General Assembly or Condoleezza Rice in 2006, provide the space and occasion for the Palestinian 'globalized peace-women elite' to go global. While participants in international women's peace conferences have claimed to speak as 'representative[s] of Palestinian civil society and the women's movement' (Abu-Dayyeh Shamas, 2002: 1), more critical voices have clarified that participants are not locally elected, but rather 'international actors handpicked Palestinian women's representatives to promote peace and mutual understanding' (Jad, 2004: 193). As a result of this selection process, the 'globalized peace-women elite' lacks domestic legitimacy and finds it difficult to mobilize women broadly for peace-building back home.

Women's activism in non-violent resistance, on the other hand, is to a great extent organized through informal networks, political parties or local popular committees. Much non-violent resistance protest is staged on an ad hoc basis and triggered by specific events. In November 2006, for example, women in Beit Hanoun were mobilized by a call from the local Al Quds Radio station to participate in a protest march to the mosque in which resistance fighters were hiding. While the Israeli military claims their snipers killed two female protestors because women were acting as human shields hiding armed men among their crowd (see BBC, 2006), supporters of non-violent resistance have celebrated the Beit Hanoun women's courage, and other Palestinian women have expressed their intention to join non-violent resistance activism, declaring 'It would have been an honor to act as our sisters in Gaza have acted' (cited in Ernshire, 2006).

Non-violent protests against the construction of the wall can also take place on an ad hoc basis, but for the most part they are more systematically organized. Much of this resistance, such as the weekly protests in the West Bank villages Bil'in or Ni'lin in which Palestinian, international and Israeli female activists regularly participate, is coordinated by local popular committees and the Grassroots Palestinian Anti-Apartheid Wall Campaign. This campaign aims to model itself in many ways on the First Intifada grassroots organizations: it works with more than fifty popular committees in local communities threatened by the wall, but also strives to mobilize support for non-violent resistance at the national and global levels. Some of the local popular committees have established special women's branches. In Tulkarm, for example, the Women's Wall Defense Committee was formed in 2003 and has mobilized Palestinian women from different socio-economic backgrounds to participate in anti-wall protests, which were joined by international and Israeli women (Interview Mohammad, 2007; see also IWPS, 2003).

Most NGOs, however, have not taken a leadership role in mobilizing the grassroots for collective resistance, have hardly participated or voiced support for the boycott of Israeli goods, and have not contributed to strengthening local popular committees. As a result, it has rightly been noted that the '[t]he [Second] Intifada exposes a disconnection between NGOs and popular movements in Palestine' (Hanafi and Tabar, 2005: 14). Many of the NGO leaders to whom I spoke agreed with such criticism. For example, one of my interviewees, who leads a women's NGO, told me that 'an NGO should mean working from the grassroots, but we should admit that we know nothing about the grassroots. We are not from our society. We are the elite, influenced and to a great extent directed by the donor agenda' (Interview Jumana, 2008).

The non-support of most NGOs for popular non-violent resistance mostly stems from conditions set down by donors. Since donors do not want to be involved in or be blamed for funding Palestinian resistance activities, they rarely give support to organizations or initiatives that aim to mobilize Palestinians for proactive (non-violent) popular resistance (al-muqawmah ash-sha'biyyah). Instead, and as described above, they prefer to fund non-violence projects – that is, projects that aim at spreading the concept and practice of non-violence (al-la 'unf) within Palestinian society. The great majority of Palestinians, however, feel that such foreign-funded non-violence projects are part of the NGOization of Palestinian civil society and yet another interest issue of donors which local NGOs add to their agendas merely to attract funding. They perceive and reject it as an outside attempt to undermine, commodify and weaken the Palestinian national struggle and popular resistance. Consequently, organizations working to strengthen the Palestinian popular movement have to engage in a constant negotiation process between the discourse and requirements of donors and that of their local Palestinian public. The titles they give to their training packages and projects reflect this balancing act. The Holy Land Trust, for example, titles its women's training session 'training for non-violent popular resistance' (al-muqawmah al-la 'unfiyyah ash-sha'biyyah), reflecting the two conflicting discourses from within and without (Interview Holy Land Trust, 2008).

NGO involvement in gendered peace-building and conflict resolution thus clearly has its risks. Not only have studies shown that '[t]he contribution of Palestinian Third Sector activities to peace-building is minimal and to date is largely insignificant' (Hassassian, 2000: 29), but the process of NGOization also led to the fragmentation of the national movement. Claiming to be apolitical actors, NGOs involved in peace-building risk depoliticizing the national agenda and leaving its leadership to unelected and 'foreign-handpicked' individuals unable to broadly mobilize local peace constituencies. Most of women's non-violent resistance, on the other hand, takes the form of social movement activism, using a much broader notion of civil society which comprises not only NGOs, political parties and other formalized organizations, but also informal associations, the family as well as religious and charity organizations (see Singerman, 2006). Being part of a popular movement, organized mainly through such informal networks and often on an ad hoc basis, women's non-violent resistance activism, in contrast to NGO conflict resolution, is a more collective and inclusive and – at least in its attempts – sustained form of female peace-building.

Aims of women's peace-building

Joint conflict-resolution projects often aim at affecting personal changes at the ideational level, while women engaged in non-violent resistance activism strive for political and material changes on the ground. Additionally – albeit differently – both forms of female agency impact upon processes of social change and women's empowerment. When discussing their rationale for supporting joint conflict resolution women often refer to the phrase 'the personal is political'. Golan and Kamal, evaluating joint Palestinian–Israeli women's people-to-people projects, for example, find that:

> Perhaps the most striking difference is in the presence of emotion and personal accounts in the opening of women's dialogue and even in track two meetings, as distinct from the more confrontational and accusatory openings of men in mixed groups. The clear implication is that 'the personal is political'. (Golan and Kamal, 2005/6: 60)

By stressing that 'the personal is political' they emphasize that the personal and political levels are interlinked and that political change is affected and sustained only if individual people also change. The argument that women are less confrontational, find it easier to reduce stereotypes and thus are more suitable for dialogical conflict resolution projects is widespread (e.g. d'Estrée and Babbitt, 1998; Powers, 2007). Particularly in psychosocial approaches to conflict resolution, which have been on the rise since the 1990s, the feminist expression 'the personal is political' is often used to support the new focus on the (inter)personal level. In order to overcome political oppression people's personal attitudes and behaviours towards the other need to change, and women, it is argued, are particularly strong at making such personal changes.

This, however, is a misinterpretation of the slogan 'the personal is political'. 'The personal is political' was coined by second-wave feminists who wanted to stress that women's so-called personal problems, such as domestic violence or lack of health- and childcare, are in fact not personal but political issues, because they result from broader systemic political injustices. They stressed this interconnection between the personal and the political to substantiate their argument that an individual struggle against seemingly personal, but in fact political, issues will have little impact. What they called for instead was collective political action to address those systemic injustices that trickle down to the very personal level (see e.g. Hanisch 1970). In the interpretation of mainstream women's psychosocial conflict resolution the slogan 'the personal is political' was turned upside down. It was changed from its original meaning – that women's 'personal' problems are produced or at least implicated by broader systemic political structures – to meaning that all political circumstances are the result of personal choices and actions of individuals.

Such a focus on personal behavioural and attitudinal change not only misrepresents the feminist phrase 'the personal is political', but also the Palestinian–Israeli conflict by pathologizing it as an identity-based conflict. The causes of the conflict are reduced to a big misunderstanding between individuals (Lloyd Jones, 2000) and its historical and political roots negated. In short, the prioritizing of personal over political change in women's joint conflict resolution does exactly what the slogan 'the personal is political' was trying to prevent: it detaches individual personal problems from broader material injustices and, as a solution to the conflict, proposes individual agency through dialogue, empathy and understanding rather than collective action. In doing so, it offers little potential of reaching up to effect political changes.

The conditions set down by the Palestinian JCW before re-establishing the Jerusalem Link and restarting the joint projects with its Israeli counterpart Bat Shalom reflect this concern. In order to reject the accusation of normalization and with the aim of reaching up to effect political changes, JCW agreed to cooperate with Bat Shalom only in joint projects which are based on full recognition of their revised principles and are of a strictly political nature (Interview JCW, 2008).

Critics of joint work, however, question whether joint women's conflict-resolution projects, even if politically based, can be effective in bringing about social or political change. Maha Nassar, director of the PFLP-affiliated UPWC, for example, explains:

> Our Union boycotted joint projects from the beginning. For us they are a waste of time and effort and we consider them to be the wrong way of involving women in political activism. Our aim is

to empower women and to give them a stronger political role, but this doesn't mean involving them in the peace negotiations. Political activism means to change laws to be empowered, to share in the decision-making process, etc. – but it has nothing to do with joint projects with Israeli women, because we will never be on an equal footing. (Interview Nassar, 2008)

Nassar's final argument, that dialogical conflict resolution is hardly applicable to a conflict situation like the Palestinian–Israeli one, which is characterized by stark power asymmetries between occupier and occupied, is often mentioned by critics of joint projects (see e.g. Kuttab and Kaufman, 1988). Even those Palestinians who do not categorically oppose all joint projects are careful to stress that dialogue must be seen as a means to an end, not an end in itself. Dialogue, they stress, can serve as a way to mobilize people for collective political action, but reconciliation and healing are post-conflict issues, something that is better left 'as a consequence of concord [rather] than a condition for it' (Tamari, 2004).

The differences between the aims of Palestinian and Israeli peace activism were clearly articulated in a joint (mixed gender) peace-building meeting that I attended in the West Bank in 2007. Discussing their future agenda, one of the Palestinian participants stressed the need to proceed from dialogue to joint advocacy and solidarity activism, which they could, as she proposed, stage at the checkpoints. Israeli participants, however, did not feel ready to participate in such joint protests, wanting first to get to know each other better and hear more personal stories from each participant. When I enquired further about the purpose of their joint meetings, the Israeli coordinator mentioned the need to build trust and raise Israeli awareness about the everyday situation of Palestinians under occupation. The Palestinian coordinator, however, described the meeting as a preparatory stage geared towards joint public anti-occupation activism. In our discussion after the meeting (and once the Israeli participants had left) two female Palestinian participants complained about the Israelis' *haki fadi* (empty talking) and their hesitation to act publicly. The coordinator agreed, quite disillusioned: 'yes – Israelis want to show the world that they want peace, but they don't want to do anything for it in practice' (Interview Mohammad, 2007).

Such criticism of the Israeli peace movement is often expressed by Palestinian peace activists, and most stress the need for action rather than words. As a condition for restarting their work with Bat Shalom, JCW, for example, not only insisted on the political nature of their joint projects, but also stressed that political dialogue needs to be accompanied and followed by joint political protest action (Interview JCW, 2008). Palestinian women's activist and director of the FIDA-affiliated Palestinian Federation of Women's Action, Siham Barghouti, aptly summarized the requirement that she as a Palestinian woman sets for joint projects, when she stated that 'now [after the failure of the peace process and given the new realities since 2000] the question is no longer how do we live together, but rather how do we *struggle* together' (Interview Barghouti, 2008).

Women's non-violent resistance activism reflects such a focus on action rather than words, on struggle rather than coexistence, and also offers a more accurate interpretation of the slogan 'the personal is political'. Stressing that political injustices, like house demolitions or the construction of the wall, have different and often disproportionate consequences for women as opposed to men, Palestinian women not only make but also feel and live the link between the personal and the political every day. Shalhoub-Kevorkian analysing the gender-specific impact of house demolitions, for example, finds that '[f]or Palestinian women, the threat of losing the house/home means an increase in their vulnerability but also increased determination to combat such oppression' (Shalhoub-Kevorkian, 2007: 7). The newly formed women's committees against the wall and my discussions with female non-violent resistance activists confirm Shalhoub-Kevorkian's findings. Karima, a women's activist from Bethlehem in her sixties, when telling me about the various forms of peace and resistance activism she has participated in during her life, concluded our conversation by insisting: 'now you should listen to me, but when you return back home: act! We must resist. We have to damage this wall – to be free as before' (Interview Karima, 2007).

The very direct impact that the occupation has on women's everyday life thus promotes and encourages their participation in resistance and protest activism. Although non-violent resistance is much less frequent now than it used to be in the First Intifada, it is still a broadly accepted form of political activism in Palestinian society and thus one in which many Palestinian women from different social backgrounds, regions and age groups participate. According to UPWC director Maha Nassar:

> Palestinian women usually respond to national issues first, before they respond to gender-related issues. It is easy to get women to the street for a national demonstration. You just say we have a confrontation with the Israeli army in this or that village and most of the women from the village will turn up. (Interview Nassar, 2008)

By striving to mobilize women for collective action on a shared political basis and by targeting the political reality of the occupation directly, female activists and supporters of non-violent resistance aim for political-structural rather than personal-attitudinal change. The fact that their resistance is built on a more apt analysis of the Palestinian–Israeli conflict, of course, does not mean that they will actually effect change at high political level. However, in comparison with joint conflict resolution, women's non-violent resistance activism does not misrepresent the conflict and challenges rather than reinforce the status quo. Joint Palestinian, Israeli and international women's activism, if not similarly based on such a political basis aiming for material structural change but remaining restricted to ideational change at personal level, seems unlikely to be successful or sustainable in bringing about social or political change.

Strategies of women's peace-building

The discourses of peaceful femininities, global sisterhood or motherhood are often mobilized by women to support their peace-building activism. The assertion that women are essentially different from men and, as concerns peace studies, are more tolerant and peaceful and thus more suited to enacting peace is drawn from the theoretical position of difference feminism. As a strategy for women's peace activism difference feminism has been widely debated in feminist literature (see e.g. Cockburn, 2004). It has been criticized for reducing women to nothing but mothers, for assigning them a passive, apolitical role, and thus for reinforcing the status quo of existing patriarchal gender power structures where women are defined in relation to men rather than as political activists in their own right. Given these legitimate criticisms, why then do women who are active in different forms of peace-building and resistance so often tend towards self-essentialization? And does self-essentialization indeed not have any transformative potential? Tracing how women themselves view their role in peace-building, this final section differentiates between women's anti-nationalist, maternal care-based and rights-based discursive peace-building strategies.

Feminist anti-nationalist peace-building strategies

It is often claimed that women are particularly suited to joint conflict-resolution projects because they are more likely to feel empathy and build bridges with representatives of the other side (d'Estrée and Babbitt 1998; Powers, 2007). One of the reasons cited for the alleged success of women's bonding across national divides is the assumption that women share a similar position in patriarchal societies. Golan and Kamal, for example, find that

> Barriers are also further overcome through women's 'shared experience,' of living in patriarchal societies. No matter how different the strata of society or the respective cultures, women, as women, have experienced some form of oppression, gender discrimination and sexist slights. Thus, women have been able to build on a mutual understanding of injustices experienced as women in either society (Golan and Kamal, 2004/5: 60).[9]

The significant majority of the Palestinian women I spoke to, however, were sceptical of such a position and would agree with critical feminist scholars (e.g. Mohanty, 1991) who find that such a notion of global sisterhood forges an unnatural bond between women all over the world on the basis of their common oppression under patriarchy, ignoring not only national, political, ethnic, class and other divides *between* but also *within* different feminist and women's movements. Particularly the applicability of a feminist anti-nationalist stance which deconstructs nationalism as patriarchal and andocentric (e.g. Lentin in Abdo and Lentin, 2002a; Yuval-Davis, 1997) to the Palestinian situation of unrealized self-determination is questioned by many Palestinian activists. Maha Nassar, for example, explains her criticism of global feminist sisterhood bonding thus:

> It is very nasty to bring poor Palestinian women who need food and clothes for their children to meetings with privileged Israeli women just *because both live in a male-dominated society*. This is not a gender perspective. Our gender perspective in the Union is closely related to both the class and national struggle. ... We mobilize women and organise their [social and political] struggle by addressing their practical needs first and by involving them in activities in which we [train them how to] change their practical needs into strategic benefits for them. (Interview Nassar, 2008; emphasis added)

Based on a similar critical view, the Palestinian Campaign for the Academic and Cultural Boycott of Israel, founded in 2004 by Palestinian academics and intellectuals, has developed a toolkit for joint women's dialogue groups. It finds that a majority of the encounters initiated after the 1989 Brussels conference aimed to connect Palestinian and Israeli women on the basis of their shared criticism of male chauvinist nationalism and their feminist awareness that the national boundaries which separate them are to the benefit of men, not women. If a joint women's project is presented as apolitical, strives for feminist goals and to overcome psychological barriers per se (i.e. without linking them to the political situation), the brochure advises Palestinian women activists to boycott the project (PACBI, n.d.).

Given the disproportionate oppression on the political level and the resulting strength of the national unity discourse, a near-universal majority of my interviewees prioritized nationalism and practical gender needs over strategic gender issues and found it difficult to identify with the feminist rejections of all forms of nationalism as male-dominated. Deconstructing nationalism is viewed as an intellectual theoretical exercise and a luxury of those women who live in established nation-states. In their context of unrealized nation-state building most Palestinians perceive the feminist anti-nationalist stance of mainstream conflict-resolution initiatives to be irrelevant at best, but more often they view it as a threat to national unity, something better not to be associated with. While Palestinian women activists are not uncritical of patriarchal positions in the Palestinian national movement and institutions, they generally consider Palestinian nationalism not inherently gender-discriminatory but rather 'a liberatory movement with the potential for opening up a space for social justice and gender issues' (Abdo in Abdo and Lentin, 2002a: 8).[10]

Mother politics: care-based and rights-based peace-building strategies

Palestinian women often stress their nurturing role as mothers to support their political activism. In such mother politics they politicize the domestic sphere by presenting their domestic duties and biological reproductive role as a form of political activism and domesticate the public sphere by basing their political activities and entry into the public sphere on their domestic role as mothers (Peteet, 1991: 175–203). A mother's responsibility to provide her children with a friendly and 'normal' environment is often invoked as a way to prevent further radicalization. Karima, for example, explained to me her reasons for participating in non-violent resistance activism in an area of Bethlehem that has been completely deserted since the construction of the wall, in the following way: 'We came here to plant seeds – seeds of peace. We are mothers, we want our children to come here and meet each other. We want them to be happy also in this place' (Interview Karima, 2007). Women thus stress that as mothers it is their responsibility to take an active political role in the public sphere. As mothers they enjoy a well-established status within Palestinian society. Motherhood – as a subaltern counterpublic (Fraser, 1990) – provides them with a strong platform and leverage for their political activism.

Some joint Palestinian–Israeli women's conflict-resolution groups also work with mother politics by adopting a maternalist care-based conflict-resolution approach, finding that women's experience of mothering entrusts them with more peaceful, relational, nurturing – in short, maternal – qualities.[11] One such organization that relies on the notion of motherhood bonding is the Parents Circle, an EU-funded NGO registered in Israel and the USA. It brings together mothers and fathers from across the Palestinian–Israeli divide who have lost children in the conflict. Talking about her work in the Parents Circle, Peled-Elhanan, an Israeli peace activist whose 13-year-old daughter was killed in a suicide bombing attack, believes that '[m]otherhood, fatherhood and the wish to save the children who are still alive are only the common denominators that overcome nationality and race and religion' (Peled-Elhanan, 2003). Women are brought together in the Parents Circle as mothers, to share their grief, and jointly to find ways to cope with their loss and initiate processes of reconciliation.

While the notion of motherhood as a basis for political activism is accepted in Palestinian society, motherhood bonding across the national divide, just as sisterhood bonding, faces challenges. For example, when I asked Karima if she and the other members in her peace-building group also meet with Israeli mothers, she told me:

> If we have permits, we can go and speak with the [Israeli] ladies, but they can't come here and we can't go there. How can we do negotiations between the two nations while the wall separates us? How can I open my heart to them if all of this is going on? (Interview Karima, 2007)

Her statement points towards the very real material obstacles that hinder joint Israeli–Palestinian peace work, but also highlights the impact that the occupation and the harsh realities on the ground have on her own readiness to engage in a process of bonding with

Israeli women. Stressing the link between the political systemic injustices and their consequences for the personal experience of motherhood (which is seen as very different from that of Israeli mothers), an overwhelming majority of my interviewees rejected a psychosocial focus on reconciliation and maternal caring, criticizing motherhood (just as sisterhood) bonding for merely seeking friendship while ignoring the Palestinians' right to self-determination (see also Farhat-Naser, 2005).

Palestinian women thus support and follow a rights-based strategy of peace-building and often situate this approach within the socially accepted framework of mother politics. Such rights-based mother politics, which mostly finds expression in non-violent resistance activism, is decidedly different from the maternal care-based approach of joint conflict-resolution projects. Al-Shanti, who led the women's march in Beit Hanoun, summarizes rights-based mother politics well when – speaking as 'a mother, sister or wife' – she asserts: 'The women of Palestine will resist this monstrous occupation imposed on us at gunpoint, siege and starvation. Our rights and those of future generations are not open for negotiation' (Al-Shanti, 2006).

There are, however, various pitfalls to the politicization and idealization of women's reproductive role. Assigning women the role of 'mother of the nation' or 'mother of the martyr' can render them pawns to nationalist discourses that deny women's active agency in the national struggle. This question of whether (which forms of) feminism work with (which forms of) nationalism in Palestine has been widely debated (see e.g. Abdo and Lentin, 2002b), and it is true that mother politics can backfire by offering patriarchal nationalist forces a discursive strategy with which they can argue for relegating women to the home, particularly once the 'exceptional' conflict situation is over.

Palestinian women's non-violent resistance activism, however, points to different dynamics. While the more traditional role of women as mothers of martyrs still has some currency, a significant majority of my interviewees who participate in non-violent resistance activism defined themselves as female resistance activists, as political-resistive, rather than passive, caring mothers. They often contrast their very proactive role as resistive activist mothers with what they perceive to be the passive, impotent role of male leaders. Describing the rationale behind her participation in the Beit Hanoun march, Um Ahmed, for example, told the *Guardian* 'It was a way of encouraging women to do something. We did something that the Arab leaders couldn't do' (quoted in McCarthy, 2006). Similarly, Shireen from Tulkarm refugee camp introduced herself to me as a sister of a martyr and resistance activist, but at the same time insisted that 'there is no difference between men and women. Women can even be stronger: in politics and as resistance activists' (Interview Shireen, 2005).

Female resistance activists thus strategically use the essentialist notion of mother/sister/wife, but with a view to furthering their rights-based agenda as Palestinian people. Viewing themselves first as people who have been denied their right to self-determination and only secondly stressing their alleged specific traits as mothers or women, they make a clear distinction between their *aim*, where they see no difference between people, whether men or women, and their *strategy*, where they find the symbolic usage of motherhood, due to its acceptance in Palestinian society, particularly powerful and effective in promoting their (people's) cause.

To sum up, there are various strategies underlying women's peace activism in the Palestinian–Israeli context, which generally tend to essentialize women in one way or another. While a feminist anti-nationalist and maternal care-based approach is often used in mainstream foreign-funded conflict resolution initiatives to establish an (essentialist) sisterhood or motherhood bonding across the national divide, most Palestinian women reject such a prioritization of feminism or gender over political identities and instead use rights-based mother politics to gain a strong, publicly supported platform for their non-violent resistance activism. Such a strategy of women's self-essentializing as political mothers claiming their rights as people through non-violent resistance activism can have transformative potential. Being, first, part of a collective, transformative national movement (rather than an institutionalized nationalism) and, second, a strategic act with which women carefully negotiate and bargain with existing gender norms to open up new spaces for female political agency, non-violent resistance activism promises to be more empowering than joint conflict resolution for Palestinian women activists, both as women and as people.

Conclusion

This chapter has compared the organizational forms, aims and strategies of women's joint conflict-resolution and non-violent resistance activism in Palestine. It has shown that the mainstream international gender and conflict-resolution approach is largely detached from Palestinian women's realities on the ground: it is organized mainly through foreign-funded NGOs with an accompanying risk of fragmentation of the national movement; it strives for reconciliation and attitudinal–behavioural change while neglecting to address the historical and political dimensions of the conflict; and it follows a maternal care-based or feminist anti-nationalist peace-building strategy aiming to bridge the national divide on the basis of a shared gender or feminist rather than political agenda. Stressing this clash between certain feminist and political agendas is not to deny the political nature of (most forms of) feminism. Rather, it stresses that the mainstream joint conflict-resolution approach relies upon this specific anti-nationalist feminist stance prioritizing strategic gender over political interests, precisely because it is not willing to tackle the political nature of the Palestinian–Israeli conflict. Unsurprisingly such a mainstream depoliticized gender and conflict-resolution approach is perceived by a large number of Palestinians as a western agenda aimed at undermining and weakening the unifying political discourse of resistance to the occupation.

Global feminist peace agendas, if not carefully responding to local contexts, can thus exacerbate local fragmentation and end up exercising *power over* rather than giving *power to* local women activists (Jad, 2004). In Palestine the decontextualized mainstream approach risks empowering the few female NGO peace activists who subscribe to its agenda of anti-nationalist or maternal care-based conflict resolution for reconciliation, while delegitimizing the many female activists who, with their rights-based mother politics in non-violent resistance activism, press for structural-political change. To avoid such counterproductive impact any proposed women's peace and solidarity activism needs to be assessed against the specific local material and ideational context. If, as this case study of the Palestinian context has shown, the suggested form of activism does not relate to predominant ideational structures (i.e. existing gender norms and the political culture of resistance) and material realities on the ground (i.e. the occupation), it is likely to have little, or even detrimental, effect on both political (conflict) and social (gender) transformation processes.

Contextualizing female peace-building means, most importantly, repoliticizing it. While conflict-resolution NGOs tend to depoliticize the national movement, Palestinian female non-violent resistance activists take a clear political standpoint: they aim to foster a social-movement, rights-based approach to peace-building, clearly addressing the political realities and calling for an end to the occupation. With their strategically essentialist rights-based mother politics they gradually broaden rather than provocatively challenge local normative gender and political frameworks, and, in so doing, are able to rally more widespread domestic support and open up new channels for female political agency and women's empowerment.

Given this effectiveness of women's self-essentialization as political-resistive mothers, it might be counterproductive for women's solidarity peace initiatives to reject essentialism altogether. A feminist position which insists that mother politics invariably strengthens the status quo of patriarchal power structures – albeit theoretically sound – does not provide women who find themselves caught up in conflict with a promising strategy to mobilize for joint anti-war activism. Similarly, the above-described feminist anti-nationalist approach is hardly applicable to female political agency in national liberatory movements. Such anti-essentialist and anti-nationalist feminist positions lack a clear differentiation between theory and praxis, between the theoretical shortcomings of an essentialist and/or national approach and its effectiveness in strengthening women's struggles in practice.

To conclude, women's transnational anti-war solidarity initiatives promise to be sustainable and successful in bridging national, class, ethnic and other divides only if based on a shared political agenda (additional to but not instead of which they might propose shared gender or feminist goals) and if working with, negotiating and broadening rather than provocatively challenging existing gender and political normative frameworks. In the Palestinian context peace-building solidarity needs to follow the joint political agenda of opposing and resisting the occupation. Based on such a political platform, the strategy that promises to strengthen domestic support and mobilization for specifically *women's* transnational solidarity activism is a strategically essentialist position of political–resistive rather than peaceful–caring women/mothers. Such a contextualized praxis-based approach to gendered peace-building offers more transformative potential than an anti-essentialist postmodern or a depoliticized anti-nationalist theoretical stance. Rather than theory informing praxis, it seems that in conflict situations – in a context where practical and creative solutions are sought urgently – feminist theory can still learn from women's practical everyday struggles on the ground.

Notes

I am grateful to and my doctoral supervisors Prof. Gerd Nonneman and Dr Ruba Salih for their careful reading of earlier drafts of this chapter and for providing insightful and constructive comments. My thanks are also due to the many Palestinian activists who helped me clarify and sharpen my ideas, as well as to Exeter University's Institute of Arab and Islamic Studies for funding my Ph.D. Research.
1. The empirical data for this chapter were collected in July 2005 and from October 2007 to September 2008. I attended various dialogue groups, meetings and conferences on gender and/or peace-building in the region and conducted more than fifty qualitative semi-structured interviews and focus groups with mainly female (but also a few male) activists from various

age groups and socio-economic, religious and political backgrounds in different villages, camps and towns in the West Bank and East Jerusalem.

2. The Union later branched into four factions, which, although each was affiliated with the four major political parties, did not differ much in their agendas (Jad, 1990).

3. By the First Intifada an estimated 10,000 women from towns, villages and camps had joined the four Committees (Abdo, 1994).

4. The Intifada, however, also provided Islamist groups with opportunities to restrict women's freedom in public life. In 1988 Hamas started to attack women who did not wear the hijab (see Hammami, 1990).

5. In 1991 Abed Rabbo split from the Democratic Front for the Liberation of Palestine (DFLP, then renamed from PDFLP) and formed the Palestinian Democratic Union (FIDA), which now is considered among the strongest supporters of joint political dialogue.

6. Before 1998 the EU had supported Palestinian–Israeli peace projects through already existing budget lines.

7. Unless specifically stated all interviewees' names have been changed to preserve anonymity.

8. For a detailed discussion on donor–recipient relations in Palestine see Hanafi and Tabar 2005: 86–251.

9. For a similar position which considers peace-loving femininity the result of women's socialization in patriarchal society, see Brock-Utne, 1989.

10. Abdo (1994) and Jad (2004) propose a similar argument. For a detailed discussion of feminist anti-nationalist stances in women's anti-war movements, see Abdo and Lentin 2002b; Cockburn, 2007: 192–202.

11. For the theoretical position on maternal peace politics, see Ruddick, 1990.

References

Abdo, Nahla (1994) 'Nationalism and Feminism: Palestinian Women and the Intifada – No Going Back?', in Valentine M. Moghadam, ed., *Gender and National Identity: Women and Politics in Muslim Societies*. London: Zed Books.

Abdo, Nahla, and Ronit Lentin (2002a) 'Writing Dislocation, Writing the Self: Bringing (Back) the Political into Gendered Israeli–Palestinian Dialoguing', in Nahla Abdo and Ronit Lentin, eds, *Women and the Politics of Military Confrontation: Palestinian and Israeli Gendered Narratives of Dislocation*. New York and Oxford: Berghahn Books.

Abdo, Nahla, and Ronit Lentin, eds (2002b) *Women and the Politics of Military Confrontation: Palestinian and Israeli Gendered Narratives of Dislocation*. New York, Oxford: Berghahn Books.

Abu-Dayyeh Shamas, Maha (2002) Statement by Maha Abu-Dayyeh Shamas, Security Council Arria Formula Meeting, United Nations, New York, 7 May. www.peacewomen.org/un/sc/is_pal_arria/UNSCStatement-Maha.pdf.

188   WOMEN AND WAR IN THE MIDDLE EAST

Al-Ali, Nadje (2005) 'Reconstructing Gender: Iraqi Women between dictatorship, War, Sanctions and Occupation', *Third World Quarterly* 26(4–5): 739–58.

Al-Shanti, Jameela (2006) 'We Overcame Our Fear', *Guardian*, 9 November. www.guardian.co.uk/commentisfree/2006/nov/09/israel.

Allen, Lori A. (2002) 'Palestinians Debate "Polite" Resistance to Occupation', *Middle East Report* 225: 38–43.

Ashrawi, Hanan (1995) *This Side of Peace: A Personal Account.* New York: Simon & Schuster.

BBC (2006) 'Gaza Women Killed in Mosque Siege', 3 November. http://news.bbc.co.uk/1/hi/world/middle_east/6112386.stm.

Brock-Utne, Birgit (1989) *Feminist Perspectives on Peace and Peace Education.* New York: Pergamon Press.

Cockburn, Cynthia (2004) 'The Continuum of Violence: A Gender Perspective on War and Peace', in Wenona Giles and Jennifer Hyndman, eds, *Sites of Violence: Gender and Conflict Zones.* Los Angeles: University of California Press.

Cockburn, Cynthia (2007), *From Where We Stand: War, Women's Activism and Feminist Analysis.* London: Zed Books.

Cohn, Carol, Helen Kinsella and Sheri Gibbings (2004) 'Women, Peace and Security', *International Feminist Journal of Politics* 6(1): 130–40.

D'Estrée, Pearson T., and Eileen F. Babbitt (1998) 'Women and the Art of Peace-making: Data from Israeli–Palestinian Interactive Problem-Solving Workshops', *Political Psychology* 19(1): 185–209.

Ernshire, Eliza (2006) 'Who Was Perpetrating the Terror? The Women of Beit Hanoun', *Counterpunch*, 7 November. www.counterpunch.org/ernshire11072006.html.

EU (2007) *Europe's Role in the Resolution of the Palestinian–Israeli Conflict – Working Group Recommendations*, International Peace NGO Conference, Montecatini Terme, Florence, 11–13 June. www.peacengo.org/cms/upload/WG%20recommendation1.pdf.

Farhat-Naser, Sumaya (2005) *Verwurzelt im Land der Olivenbäume: Eine Palästinenserin im Streit für den Frieden.* Basle: Lenos Verlag.

Fraser, Nancy (1990) 'Rethinking the Public Sphere: A Contribution to the Critique of Actually Existing Democracy', *Social Text* 25/26: 56–80.

Golan, Galia and Zahira Kamal (2005/6) 'Women's People-to-People Activities: Do We Do It Better?', *Palestine–Israel Journal of Politics, Economics and Culture* 12(4)/13(1): 58–63.

Hammami, Rema (1990) 'Women, the Hijab and the Intifada', *Middle East Report* 30(3): 24–9.

Hammami, Rema (1995) 'NGOs: the Professionalisation of Politics', *Race and Class* 37(2): 51–63.

Hanafi, Sari, and Linda Tabar (2005) *The Emergence of a Palestinian Globalised Elite: Donors, International Organizations and Local NGOs*, Jerusalem: Institute of Jerusalem Studies/Muwatin, The Palestinian Institute for the Study of Democracy.

Hanisch, Carol (1970) 'The Personal Is Political', in Shulamith Firestone and

Anne Koedt, eds, *Notes from the Second Year: Women's Liberation, Major Writings of the Radical Feminists*. New York. With new introduction by Carol Hanisch accessed at http://scholar.alexanderstreet.com/pages/viewpage.action?pageId=2259.

Hassassian, Manuel (2000) 'The Role of Palestinian NGOs in Peace Building and Conflict Resolution', in Sami Adwan and Dan Bar-On, eds, *The Role of Non-Governmental Organisation in Peace-Building Between Palestinians and Israelis*. Beit Jala: PRIME.

Herzog, Shira, and Aviva Hai (2005) *The Power of Possibility: The Role of People-to-People Programs in the Current Israeli–Palestinian Reality*. Bonn: Friedrich Ebert Stiftung, Israel Office.

IPCRI (Israel/Palestine Center for Research and Information) (2002) *YES PM: Years of Experience in Strategies for Peace Making: Looking at Israeli–Palestinian People-to-People Activities, 1993–2000*. Jerusalem: IPCRI.

IWPS (International Women's Peace Service) (2003) 'Palestinian Women Mobilising to Resist Israel's Apartheid Wall', *House Report* 43, 17 September. http://electronicintifada.net/v2/article1938.shtml.

Jad, Islah (1990) 'From Salons to the Popular Committees: Palestinian Women, 1919–1989', in Jamal R. Nassar, and Roger Heacock, eds, *Intifada: Palestine at the Crossroads*. New York: Praeger.

Jad, Islah (2004) *Women at the Crossroads: The Palestinian Women's Movement Between Nationalism, Secularism and Islamism*. Ph.D. thesis, SOAS, University of London.

Johnson, Penny, and Eileen Kuttab (2001) 'Where Have All the Women (and Men) Gone?', *Feminist Review* 69: 21–43.

Kamal, Zahira (1998) 'The Development of the Palestinian Women's Movement in the Occupied Territories: Twenty Years after the Israeli Occupation', in Suha Sabbagh, ed., *Palestinian Women of Gaza and the West Bank*. Indianapolis: Indiana University Press.

Kuttab, Jonathan, and Edy Kaufman (1988) 'An Exchange on Dialogue', *Journal of Palestine Studies* 17(2): 84–108.

Lloyd Jones, Deiniol (2000) 'Mediation, Conflict Resolution and Critical Theory', *Review of International Studies* 26(4): 647–62.

McCarthy, Rory (2006) 'Sisters, Mothers, Martyrs', *Guardian*, 5 December. www.guardian.co.uk/world/2006/dec/05/gender.israel.

Mohanty, Chandra Talpade (1991) 'Under Western Eyes: Feminist Scholarship and Colonial Discourses', in Chandra Talpade Mohanty, Ann Russo and Lourdes Torres, eds, *Third World Women and the Politics of Feminism*. Indianapolis: Indiana University Press.

Nasser-Najjab (2004) *Palestinian–Israeli People-to-People Contact Experience, 1993–2004: An Evaluation*. Ph.D. thesis, University of Exeter.

Oslo II, Israeli–Palestinian Interim Agreement on the West Bank and Gaza Strip (1995). www.jewishvirtuallibrary.org/jsource/Peace/interim.html

PACBI (Palestinian Campaign for the Academic and Cultural Boycott of Israel) (n.d.) *Relations to Israeli Women: Between Normalisation and Peacebuilding* (in Arabic). Ramallah: PACBI. www.pacbi.org/campaign_resources.htm.

Peled-Elhanan, Nurit (2003) 'The Bereaved Parents for Peace', ZNet, 3 January. www.zmag.org/znet/viewArticle/11199.

Peteet, Julie (1991), Gender in Crisis: Women and the Palestinian Resistance Movement. New York: Columbia University Press.

PNGO (Palestinian NGO Network) (2000) 'Announcement Palestinian Non-Governmental Organizations' General Assembly', PNGO Annual Report, Ramallah, 23 October. www.pngo.net/data/files/reports/annual/report2000.pdf.

Powers, Janet M. (2007) Blossoms on the Olive Tree: Israeli and Palestinian Women Working for Peace. Westport CT and London: Praeger.

Ruddick, Sara (1990) Maternal Thinking: Towards a Politics of Peace. London: Women's Press.

Said, Edward W. (1995) 'The Limits to Cooperation', in Edward W. Said, Peace and Its Discontents. New York: Vintage.

Shalhoub-Kevorkian, Nadera (2007) 'House Demolition: A Palestinian Feminist Perspective', in 'Not Only Was The House Lost': A Photo Essay. Jerusalem: ICAHD, JCW, Bat Shalom.

Sharoni, Simona (1995) Gender and the Israeli–Palestinian Conflict: The Politics of Women's Resistance. New York: Syracuse University Press.

Singerman, Diane (2006) 'Restoring the Family to Civil Society: Lessons from Egypt', Journal of Middle East Women's Studies 2(1): 1–32.

Steinberg, Donald (2008) 'Beyond Victimhood: Engaging Women in the Pursuit of Peace', Testimony to the House of Representatives Committee on Foreign Affairs, 15 May. www.crisisgroup.org/home/index.cfm?id=5444andl=1.

Steinberg, Gerald M. (2008) 'Europe's Hidden Hand: EU Funding for Political NGOs in the Arab–Israeli Conflict: Analyzing Processes and Impact', NGO Monitor Monograph Series, Jerusalem: NGO Monitor. www.ngo-monitor.org/data/images/File/NGO_Monitor_EU_Funding_Europes_Hidden_Hand.pdf/.

Tamari, Salim (2004) 'The Case for Geneva', Guardian, 6 January. www.guardian.co.uk/world/2004/jan/06/comment.

Tamari, Salim (2005/6) 'Kissing Cousins: A Note on a Romantic Encounter', Palestine–Israel Journal of Politics, Economics and Culture 12(4)/13(1): 16–18.

UN (2004) Facts and Figures on Women, Peace and Security. New York: UN.

UN (2005) 'Palestinian and Israeli Women Create Global Panel to Work for Just Middle East Peace', UN News Centre, 28 July. www.un.org/apps/news/story.asp?NewsID=15201andCr=middleandCr1=east.

Väyrynen, Tarja (2004) 'Gender and UN Peace Operations: The Confines of Modernity', International Peacekeeping 11(1): 125–42.

Wrege, Henriette (2008) 'Friedensaktivistinnen im Nahostkonflikt: Dialog – Jetzt erst Recht', Qantara, 16 June. www.qantara.de/webcom/show_article.php/_c-736/_nr-3/i.html?PHPSESSID=5.

Yuval-Davis, Nira (1997) Gender and Nation. London: Sage.

Yuval-Davis, Nira, and Floya Anthias (1989) Gender, Nation, State. London: Sage.

PART III

Gender, Citizenship and
Post-conflict Reconstruction

SIX

Fragmented Citizenship:
Communalism, Ethnicity and Gender in Iraq

Martina Kamp

This chapter examines the actions and attitudes of the internal and external actors involved in the constitution-drafting process in 2005, following the fall of the Ba'th regime, and demonstrates how the relationships between state power and the subject are being re-negotiated in a context of internationalized reconstruction processes. I analyse how questions of ethnic autonomy and the role of religious and communal ideologies are intertwined with a redefinition of gender relations.

While many commentators and security policy experts link the communal violence experienced by Iraq to the multi-ethnic and multi-confessional fabric of Iraqi society, research on the history of Iraq undertaken by Hanna Batatu (1982), Marion Farouk-Sluglett and Peter Sluglett (1991), and Charles Tripp (2000) – to name but a few – reveals ample evidence that twentieth-century Iraqi history was shaped by 'strategies of co-operation, subversion and resistance adopted by various Iraqis trying to come to terms with the force the state represented. It has also been a history of the ways the state transformed those who tried to use it' (Tripp, 2000: 1). Although ethnic and religious identities played a role, so did questions of class, rural or urban society, socio-economic background, affiliation to family networks, political association and gender.

Suad Joseph's (2000) and Mounira Charrad's (2001) research on the Middle East and North Africa have underlined how issues of women's rights are tied to questions about the social fabric of the state, and both authors make use of the concept of a *kin contract* to frame citizenship. I also draw on Elizabeth Thompson's (2000) concept of 'colonial citizenship'. Rather than understanding colonial rule as governance of colonizers over subjects, she refers to a kind of *colonial contract*, whereby representatives of colonial powers negotiated with mediating elites on citizenship rights. These citizenship rights, as argued by Carole Pateman in *The Sexual Contract* (1988), are gendered.[1] She challenged the liberal myth that individuals – that is, elite, white European men – give up unrestricted freedom in return for personal security and demonstrated that the state's monopoly on power did not guarantee women freedom from violence in either the private or the public sphere. On the contrary, it is only a recent trend that states prosecute domestic violence and other forms of gender-specific violence. A theoretical framework for analysing citizenship in the Iraqi nation-state, I would suggest, should make use of all these hidden contracts, and illuminate the intersectionality of gender, race, ethnicity, religion and nationality in *citizenship bargains*.

Citizenship is the relationship between the state and the individual; however, it is not an individual phenomenon. People's rights and duties are mediated through their membership in specific communities – for example, ethnic, religious or regional collectivities. Citizenship, as Nira Yuval-Davis points out, can only be analysed as individual and collective phenomena (1997: 91). In citizenship bargains, questions of ethnic autonomy and the role of religious and communal ideologies are intertwined with a redefinition of gender relations. This chapter traces various policies of integration and confrontation of Iraqi state–society relations in the ongoing constitutional debate and legal processes. It takes into account various forms of direct, structural and symbolic violence against women, which dramatically increased after the fall of the Ba'th regime. Gendered violence in this respect is a means to insert power within struggles of constructing Iraqi citizenship since 2003. The chapter is based on a critical re-evaluation of media reports and grey literature from a gendered perspective. Additionally, interviews with Iraqi female politicians and civil society actors were carried out. Drawing on Clifford Geertz's concept of 'thick description' (1997) to understand socio-cultural discourses, I use the materials and sources to develop a multilayered 'historical thick description' for analysing the discourse on the 'new' Iraqi citizenship.

Transition in the shadow of violence and conflict

The overthrow of the Iraqi Ba'th regime by the coalition forces in 2003 ended an extremely repressive rule. It is beyond any shadow of doubt, however, that in matters of security and personal safety Iraqi citizens still have enough reason to be concerned, albeit the former government's firm grip on the state's monopoly of power has ceased to exist. The collapse of the state and the disbandment of most national institutions were followed by a series of misguided administrative decisions by the Coalition Provisional Authority (CPA). It enabled armed groups to seize control and set off a spiral of violence, which has leaked into all spheres of Iraqi society. The assassinations of academics and scientists have shattered the educational system and healthcare institutions. Shortages in the supply of electricity and potable water cause health risks, accelerated by insufficient sewerage systems. Many Iraqis either have left the country, or have moved from the central and southern provinces to the relative stability of the cities under Kurdish control, or from one neighbourhood to another. The displacement of Iraqis, externally and internally, has altered the ways Iraqis have been living together despite their sectarian or ethnic belonging.

While car bombs and attacks on cars are primarily directed against the police forces and politicians cooperating with the new regime, the bombing of mosques and markets mainly targets civilians, as do the widespread kidnappings. While Western media report on foreign hostages and speculate on the political motivations of the abductors, most of the estimated fifty kidnappings a day are criminal, target Iraqis, and go unnoticed. Violence has become a means to make money. The perpetrators may follow the example set by protégés of the former Ba'th regime, especially by 'Uday Hussein, who was never prosecuted for his vast accumulation of capital through smuggling and trafficking. The failure of the police and law enforcement to put a halt to criminal violence adds to the feeling of general vulnerability among Iraqi citizens. It is especially true for women, who also face gender-specific violence such as rape, attacks and killings of unveiled women, whilst the police and law enforcement largely ignore these crimes.

Media and policymakers' focus has largely been on the 'insurgency' against the occupying forces and the Iraqi political elite and, since 2004, communal violence between and among armed groups. Violence against women hardly ever makes the headlines, despite the many attacks on female students, academics, journalists, activists, politicians and sex workers. Only on rare occasions do these incidents make their way into media, such as the rape of women by members of the Iraqi police in February 2007,[2] which immediately was swiftly denounced as another outburst of communal violence.

The outbreak of violence in the public sphere accompanying the invasion of Iraq in 2003, however, has not been without precedent, because it parallels to some extent the situation following the Second Gulf War in the early 1990s, when '[g]angs of demobilized men roamed the streets and many women were raped. War-traumatized conscripts returned home to take out their aggression, frustration, distress and anger on wives, daughters, mothers and sisters' (Omar, 1994: 64). Exposure to violence is gendered: it is linked to complementary role models for men as providers and protectors of the family and women as dependants to be protected. The state assumes a crucial role in developing policies to prevent women's exposure to violence – for example, the prosecution of rape, strategies against domestic violence, funding of women's shelters. In this respect, the former Iraqi state's policy on gender-specific violence may serve as a point of departure for understanding the extensive 'climate of fear' Iraqi women have faced since 2003 (Human Rights Watch, 2003).[3]

In times of conflict, women's lives and bodies are at risk. Not only is violence against women an integral part of war (e.g. amongst others, Seifert, 1995; Lentin, 1997; Goldstein, 2001; Turshen, 2001; Zipfel, 2001)[4] but women are also marked as reproducers of ethnic and/or national collectives and representatives of the nation; thus, violence against women targets the collective of the enemy.[5] Iraq has a history of almost three decades of war, starting with the attack on Iran in 1980, resulting in eight years of warfare; the invasion and occupation of Kuwait in 1990; the military action by the coalition forces in 1991; followed by the uprisings of Iraqi Shi'a and Kurds and their brutal repression by the Iraqi regime, as well as the long-term sanctions regime imposed by the United Nations until spring 2003.[6] My point is not that violence is a characteristic of Iraqis; rather, I want to stress the fact that war has strengthened the notion of the legitimate use of violence. And it is violence exerted by men, who, in turn, are affirming their power to inflict violence (Wobbe, 1994; Sauer, 2002), thereby perpetuating an imbalance of power in gender relations. Cynthia Enloe (1998, 2000), Mary Kaldor (1999) and Karen Hageman (2002), among others, have explored the role of warfare for the evolution of the modern nation-state and illustrated how citizenship rights have been entwined with the capability to bear arms, and the duty to defend the nation.

In the First Gulf War, the soldiers' readiness to sacrifice their lives for the Iraqi nation was prominently displayed in the Iraqi media, especially when the long years of war squashed the Ba'th government's hope for a swift victory over neighbouring Iran, presumed to be weakened by revolutionary turmoil. The image of the 'hero warrior', however, was undermined not only by the losses of war, but also by the gender policy of the state encouraging women to participate in the labour force. Accordingly in the late 1980s, the regime was willing to make a shift in direction and put a halt to its politics of equal rights. The ideal of 'patriotic motherhood' stressed the reproductive role of women.[7] Social, medical and legal measures aimed at increasing the birth rate of Iraqi women by restricting contraceptives and abortion by legal means. Polygamy, which had previously been marked as an anti-modernizing relic, became the state's strategy to cope with the increasing numbers of war widows.[8] Although the former regime was overthrown, these laws are still in effect. Moreover, women are struggling with a wartime economy marked by a severe lack of security and employment. The government does not offer equal opportunities for women in regard to economic support and employment (Zuhur, 2006: 36). Indeed, women's labour force participation has deteriorated.

During the Second Gulf War, women's rights were further restricted. In February 1990, the government abolished the prosecution of murder and acts of violence against women in cases where the female victim was accused of having defied sexual norms, or attempted to avoid enforced marriage (Omar, 1994: 60–71). The immunity from prosecution was in effect not only in central and southern Iraq, but also in the Kurdish provinces, where a de facto state evolved during the 1990s. Although the Kurdish government passed a formal law in 2000 ruling that so-called 'crimes of honour' were illegal, the law was never officially enforced (Mojab, 2002: 1–7). Moreover, Kurdish female politicians and women's organizations raising this issue have come under attack for 'dishonouring' the nation, or are told to hang fire until the national question is settled.[9] In this respect, the Iraqi state's monopoly of power was and still is gendered. When the state tolerates violence by men against their female relatives, it fails to protect the citizenship rights of women.

Shahrzad Mojab (2003) and Nadera Shalhoub-Kevorkian (2002) have criticized the perception of violence against women as a cultural practice innate to 'Middle Easterners'.[10] Referring to the link between nationalist projects and gender constructions, they stress that the legitimacy or illegitimacy of murder and violence against women is a question of gendered socio-political and economic power.[11] The balance of gender power is not fixed and may shift in different directions according to the nature of nationalist projects.

Adam Jones portrays the escalating violence in Iraq 2003 as a result of a 'masculine crisis' caused by 'the inability or threatened inability to conform to masculine role expectations' (2004: 70). Male unemployment rates have grown as high as 70 per cent while prices are rising and many men are not able to earn a basic living for their families. Furthermore, foreign companies and the coalition forces have hired contract workers from Nepal and Bangladesh, thus increasing the feeling of humiliation. The crisis became acute when the soldiers were demobilized; Jones considers that former members of the Iraqi army were the leading figures of the Iraqi insurgency in 2003, while the followers of Muqtada al-Sadr filled his ranks with poor men and male youth. Both groups rely on military means to regain self-esteem and masculine pride (2004: 70–73).[12] Jones stresses the fact that younger male adults are victims of military struggle, because they face a higher risk of being killed, mistreated and imprisoned. When the media published the images of US soldiers torturing Iraqi prisoners, Iraqi men felt all the more powerless and infuriated. Feminist researchers have underlined the interconnection of conflict and crises of masculinity – for example, in Israel, Palestine, and South Africa – which more often than not triggers a vicious circle of (gendered) violence (Klein, 2001; Peteet, 2002; Meintjes et al., 2003).

Although secular in origin, the Ba'th regime made use of an Islamic discourse to legitimize the reconstruction of gender relations. According to a dominant reading of Muslim law, women face restrictions on their freedom of travel and the Iraqi government decreed that women under the age of 45 were forbidden to leave the country unless accompanied by a male relative. This action specifically targeted female cross-border commuters to Jordan, who were accused of engaging in prostitution there (Al-Ali, 2003: 244; Makiya, 1993: 39).[13] The state augmented men's patriarchal privileges because it was forced to renegotiate state–society relations in the context of economic crisis and weakened state power due to the severe sanctions regime imposed by the United Nations. While in the 1970s and early 1980s, oil revenues fuelled the policy of patronage and repression and enabled the state to monopolize Iraqi society, in the 1990s the Ba'th regime was forced into retreat. It turned to sheikhs and leading authorities within kin or neighbourhood networks who were known to tolerate or back the cause of the party – a process that has been termed the 're-tribalization' of Iraqi politics (Jabar, 2000: 28–31). These individuals were included in a restructured system of patronage and rewarded with the distribution of the imports through the 'oil for food' programme of the UN. This was accompanied by an increase in the regime's Islamic rhetoric – the most prominent indicators being the modification of the national flag by adding 'Allahu Akbar' (God is Great), and a backlash against gender equality.

In her analysis of the state, Islam and gender relations, Renate Kreile argues that discourses on gender within political Islam indicate societal upheaval. Accordingly, Kreile identifies gender relations as part and parcel of the bargain to settle power struggles between state and society, a strategy to 'master the crises' (1999: 156–72; 2003: 197–212). This policy has been frequently employed by several political elites, secular or not, to thwart crises of legitimacy. In Iraq, the Ba'th Party used this strategy first to counter criticisms about war losses in the 1980s, and later to oppose the growing unrest directed against the regime in the 1990s, with women's citizenship rights becoming increasingly more restricted over this period. The overthrow of the regime has by no means put an end to this policy, and the reconstruction of gender relations proves to be once again a central means to bargain the multilayered conflicts, which are discernible in the process of drafting a constitution for the 'new' Iraq.

The citizenship bargain: negotiating communalism, ethnicity and gender

The widespread fighting and bombing in Iraq can be neither reduced to the insurrection against US-led coalition forces, nor simplified or generalized as a sectarian civil war. The violence is in part linked to ongoing debates in Iraqi society on de-Ba'thification, compensation and rehabilitation, and also relates to multiple rifts in the social fabric of Iraqi society. These rifts have gained momentum in the process of reconstructing Iraqi citizenship along the lines of ethnic and religious affiliation as outlined in the Iraqi constitution. The political arena can be roughly divided into two major factions – even though they encompass diverse parties and interest groups. On the one side are the secularists, such as the two large Kurdish parties, the Kurdistan Democratic Party (KDP) and the Patriotic Union of Kurdistan (PUK),[14] numerous secular women's movements, the remains and splinter groups of the once-powerful Iraqi Communist Party (ICP) as well as nationalist and authoritarian ex-army officers. On the other side are religious powers and parties. Most religious parties are predominantly Shiʻi, like the al-Daʻwa, a sectarian social reform party founded in the late 1950s as a religious alternative to the ICP, or the Supreme Islamic Iraqi Council (SIIC, formerly known as the Supreme Council for Islamic Revolution in Iraq, or SCIRI) established in exile in Iran. These parties had a prominent role in the former Iraqi opposition; the number of their supporters, however, was unknown, and the Shiʻi population also constituted the majority in secular parties (Fürtig, 2003: 121–45). In southern Iraq, the religious parties were able to fill the power vacuum following the downfall of Saddam Hussein in 2003. Although they were not able to consolidate their grip on power at first, and were defeated by the secular parties in the elections for the city councils in winter and spring 2004 (Buck, 2004), the policies of the US administration boosted their claims of representing the general Shiʻi population. In contrast, the Sunni Muslim Brotherhood did not gain much support throughout the era of post-colonial military regimes. Sunni notables and politicians have also established several parties, albeit with less outspoken religious programmes.

The occupation caused many more cleavages, for example between groups either cooperating with or confronting the US administration in Iraq. Young militant activists like Muqtada al-Sadr have rebelled against the authority of the established quietist Shiʻi clerics in Najaf and Karbala (Buchta, 2004: 29–34; Jabar, 2003: 12–18; Nakash, 2003: 17–26). Moreover, there exist fault lines cutting across these cleavages,

like divergences between repatriated exiles, who have claimed a share
of political and economic power, and the ones who would not or
could not leave and had to suffer from the economic crises and the
thirteen years of the embargo. These multilayered conflicts loom
over the drafting of the new constitution.

The ongoing constitutional debate, which started well before the
current war, draws attention to another highly controversial subject
concerning the fabric of the future state. The Kurdish demand for
a federal state, by which cultural, political and in part economic
rights are guaranteed amounts to a *conditio sine qua non* for the Kurdish
national movement. The ministries of the Kurdish proto-state established in the late 1990s still shape and implement policies rather
autonomously from the central government in Baghdad.[15] In contrast,
most of the Shi'i parties have long opted for a more centralist state
model without any autonomy rights for ethnic and/or sectarian
groups. Equal citizenship seemed to be a strategy to end the history
of discrimination dating back to the Ottoman Empire and British
mandatory colonial rule, which has been reinforced since the 1980s
(Ibrahim, 1997). Many Sunni parties and factions which oppose a
federal system did not engage in the constitution drafting process until
the US administration put pressure on the Kurdish and Shi'i parties to
ensure the participation of all sectarian and ethnic groups (Zubaida,
2005; Ibrahim, 2005; Al-Ali, 2005; Fürtig, 2005). Communal identities
are a characteristic of the heterogeneous Iraqi population.[16] However,
the formation of political interest groups was also an effect of the
state's clientelist policy under the regime of Saddam Hussein.

Although the constitution was approved by the Iraqi parliament
and a referendum in October 2005, the dispute is by no means
settled – as illustrated by the discussions of the Constitutional Review
Committee (CRC) elected by the parliament. Whilst the elections of
December 2005 were widely regarded as a symbol of the successful
political transition in Iraq, mainly because the Sunni population
abandoned their electoral boycott and took part in the voting, there
have continued to be conflicts between sectarian communities, such
as assassinations by Shi'i armed groups, the bombing of mosques,

the sectarian 'cleansing' of neighbourhoods, and so on. For a long time, the US forces in Iraq concentrated on the 'war on terror' and refrained from attempting to control communal violence, whilst the Iraqi security forces – who are said to have been infiltrated by sectarian armed groups – have largely failed to stop this 'communal civil war' (Biddle, 2006).

The violent collapse of the former Yugoslavia, the ongoing civil war in Sri Lanka and the long-time civil war in Lebanon, to name but a few comparable conflicts, have made minority rights – that is, rights of ethnic and/or sectarian groups – an issue for security policy and peace research. Conflict management in post-(civil) war societies deals with reconciliation and the installing of mechanisms to prevent further communal violence. In this respect, constitutional debates have become a key strategy to settle communal conflicts and guarantee minority rights (Eichhorst 2003; Solioz and Vogel, 2004; Erhart, 2004; Eichhorst and Sinjen 2006). The problematic nature of this policy is that it takes ethnic and/or sectarian affiliation as guaranteed and unchangeable – and thereby ignores the extensive body of critical approaches to identity politics.[17] The essentialist perspective on structural categories is a way of reinscribing these identities in the social fabric of the states.

In the December 2005 parliamentary elections, Iraqi voters cast their vote according to communal identity politics: the majority of the Shi'i population decided on the United Iraqi Alliance, an association of twenty political parties dominated by the two big religious parties, al-Da'wa and the Supreme Islamic Iraqi Council. More than 60 per cent of the Iraqi population is Shi'i and the United Iraqi Alliance won the election with around 41 per cent. The Kurdish population, counting for roughly a quarter of the Iraqi population, voted for the Kurdistan Alliance led by the KDP and the PUK. The Kurdistan Alliance got more than 21 per cent of the national vote. The third best result was achieved by the Iraqi Consensus Front, an alliance of three Sunni parties with an outspoken sectarian programme. All secular parties, the non-confessional associations and non-sectarian factions lost ground.[18]

Despite the fact that the Iraqi political system has been shaped considerably by movements such as the reformist Al-Ahali in the 1930s or the powerful Iraqi Communist Party from the 1940s to the late 1970s, at present secular parties bear no significance. Iraqi citizenship and secularism are hardly compatible any more. That raises the question of how the current ruling parties will be able to represent demands for economic development and social reform, and which space in civil society exists for negotiating interests on criteria such as age, sexual orientation or professional association. And last but not least, how can women participate, if citizenship is not only gendered but also constructed along ethnic and/or religious identities?

The case of Iraq since 2003 is a vivid example of the pitfalls of political representation based on ethnic and/or sectarian affiliation. Sherifa Zuhur has underlined the gendered effects of ethnicizing the political system:

> In the sectarian system, women are merely a subcategory of other constituencies; they are female Kurds, Sunnis, Shi'a, or Assyrians. Sectarian interests rather than gender issues take precedence. If a woman's personal or gender-defined interests collide with those of her community, unfortunately, her needs or goals must defer to those of the most dominant bloc representing any particular community, or to a stance adopted by her own religious or ethnic community. (Zuhur, 2006: 10)

The reconstruction of gender relations as an element of the transition process has received rather scant attention by analysts of Iraq. In December 2003, the Iraqi Governing Council decided to curb women's rights and eradicate the Personal Status Law of 1959 and the amendments of 1978 and 1980. In this meeting, the women members of the council were absent, and it was only a small majority who favoured the decision. The result would have resembled the legal practice in the early-twentieth-century Ottoman Empire, when religious authorities administered the law according to religious and customary laws. In contrast to other mandatory states, the Ottoman reforms of the Personal Status Law during World War I had not been enacted in the Iraqi provinces, which were then occupied in part by

British troops. Although several governments made an effort to draft a unified Personal Status Law, it was not enacted until 1959 under the military regime of 'Abd al-Karim Qasim. The law of 1959 bore the signature of the Iraqi Women's League, the women's organization of the ICP, and the later Ba'th governments made only minor changes (Kamp, 2003, 2005). The governing council's decision to repeal the law would have re-established sectarian rule in Iraq, and nullified the women's movement's efforts of more than half a century (Zubaida, 2004). The Coalition Provisional Authority (CPA), however, vetoed the decision, though only after a massive campaign by women's organizations for nearly a month.

Drawing on Thompson's (2000) groundbreaking work on gender relations as a field for contest and compromise in negotiating citizenship, and taking up Kreile's notion of the link between the reconstruction of gender relations and crisis management, the governing council's legal action can be read as a strategy in the citizenship bargain in transitional Iraq. A closer look at the Iraqi opposition in the run-up to the war shows that the cleavages of federalism versus a centralized state were reinforced by the fault-line of secular policies and political Islam. In December 2002, the various factions of the Iraqi opposition participating in the London conference struggled to find a compromise, and in their final declaration they stated that the future Iraq would be a federal state, with Islam its official religion and the source for legislation. While the English translations read Islam as *a* source, the Arabic version of the declaration identifies Islam as *the* source.[19] In a dominant reading of Islam, gender equality may be guaranteed by the state with respect to suffrage and the right to be elected but not Personal Status Laws. On this basis, many majority Muslim states have ratified the Convention on the Elimination of all Forms of Discrimination against Women (CEDAW) with reservations.[20] Apparently, gender inequalities have become a feature of Iraqi democracy despite the protests of secular women's organizations.

Criticisms of the current constitution centre on two issues: first, the centrality of Islamic law, and, second, the vague wording with regard to the Personal Status Law, which might in fact replace the unified set of laws applied since 1959. Article 2 states that 'Islam is the official religion of the state and is a basic source of legislation', and that 'no law can be passed that contradicts the undisputed rules of Islam.'[21] The reference to established rulings of Islam relates simultaneously to its different readings and to the discursive power of interpretation. In *Foreign Affairs*, a journal close to the US administration, Isobel Coleman pointed out that 'the centrality of Islamic law in the document ... does not necessarily mean trouble for Iraqi women. In fact, sharia is open to a wide range of understanding, and across the Islamic world today, progressive Muslims are seeking to reinterpret its rule to accommodate a modern role for women' (Coleman, 2006: 24). While hardly anyone would argue that movements like Islamic feminism and many women religious scholars have contributed tremendously to the *ijtihad* of the Sharia, recent reforms of personal status laws in countries like Malaysia or Morocco are the results of decades of intensive lobbying by women's organizations, and the willingness of politicians and heads of governments to pass laws and implement reforms in spite of opposition, sometimes even violence, by political Islamists and other conservatives (among others, see Endut, 2002; Sadiqi and Ennaji, 2006). Unfortunately, this is not the case in Iraq, where women politicians and activists are under constant threat, and unveiled women, especially at universities, are threatened.

Article 41 of the constitution states that 'Iraqis are free in their adherence to their personal status according to their own religion, sect, belief and choice, and that will be organized by law.' Although this article does not completely abolish the unified Personal Status Law, it re-enacts the Iraqi Governing Council's policy in December 2004. As a consequence, the constitution re-inscribes sectarian identities in the social fabric of the society and it is unclear what happens in the case of mixed marriages – whether pertaining to different sects or faiths.

The promise of an equitable society, though strongly promoted by US-funded Iraqi women's organizations (Zangana, 2005; Al-Ali and Pratt in this volume), has failed in the face of everyday violence and insecurity, paving the way for a remake of the colonial citizenship bargain, in which mediating elites are granted rights on the basis of communal difference at the cost of subordinated groups in Iraqi society (Watenpaugh, 2003). Nadje Al-Ali and Nicola Pratt undertake a critical assessment of the constitutional process and its implication for the personal status laws:

> It is significant that family law has become a main arena in which contestations over the future identity of the Iraqi nation-state occurs. Ba'thist measures sought to dismantle the authority of the male heads of family, clan and tribe over women to replace it with the authority of the state. The new constitution replaces state authority over women with the authority of communal leaders of the different regions – whether Shi'i, Sunni, or Kurd. Family law is one of the mechanisms for consolidating a multi-ethnic and multi-religious state on the basis of (religious-ethnic) difference within the private sphere. By devolving family law to the regions, the state accommodates social and religious differences, while encouraging the loyalty of communal leaders to the state. Family law becomes a part of a 'social contract', trading communal autonomy for women's rights. (Al-Ali and Pratt, 2006: 23)

In the ongoing citizenship bargain, questions of communal belonging, or the 'kin contract', combine with the 'sexual contract' to provide men with a 'patriarchal dividend'.

Both the historical roots of constitutional process under British colonialism and the direct involvement of the US administration in drafting the constitution of the 'new' Iraq invoke the 'colonial contract'. The US administration shows certain ambivalence with regard to gender equality. On the one hand, the CPA vetoed the repeal of the existing Personal Status Law, closely monitored gender equality within the interim constitution and celebrated the fact that one-quarter of the members of the National Assembly should be women (despite being against gender quotas). The share of women parliamentarians was as high as 31 per cent in the January elections of 2005, but dropped in the elections of December 2005 to 19 per cent.[22] Women politicians are becoming marginalized in the ongoing process of ethnicizing politics, and fear being omitted from the bargaining between the male leaders of their respective parties with regard to ministerial portfolios (Naji 2006). Moreover, international human rights organizations and Iraqi women's organizations have criticized the lack of explicit guarantee for gender equality in the law (Woodrow Wilson International Center for Scholars, 2005). In May 2004 the US administration declared that it would accept an Islamic state in Iraq. This declaration was delivered on the occasion of the World Economic Summit in Jordan, when Colin Powell apologized for the cases of torture in Abu-Ghraib.[23] This statement by the USA may be seen as another bargain between the administration and mediating elites in Iraq at the cost of (secular) women.

Conclusion

In 2002 and 2003, women's rights were a key argument for making war on Iraq, building on the successful media discourse about freeing Afghan women from the burqa in the 'war on terror'. Despite the rhetoric of the US administration on women's empowerment (as discussed by Al-Ali and Pratt in this volume) and some notable gains in blocking the repeal of the unified Personal Status Law in late 2003/early 2004 and achieving a quota for women in parliament, nevertheless women have become largely excluded from the political process. This is partly due to violence and threats of violence against women, the poor economic situation, as well as the nature of the emerging political system. In times of war and conflict, gender relations are renegotiated, and they provide the field of compromise between individuals, communities and the state. In post-Ba'th Iraq, the field of contest comprises diverse actors in the local, regional and global arenas, with diverging political and socio-economic interests. Little attention, however, has been paid to the ways in which gender relations are used to negotiate the 'clash of interests'. The constitution allows for altering the Personal Status Law, and the strategies already deployed by the mediating elites give reason to be concerned that conflicts in state–society relations will be settled by bargaining over women's rights.

Although I do not necessarily agree that history teaches us lessons to be learned, a historical approach may underscore what is at stake in reinscribing ethnic and/or sectarian difference into citizenship. Women's activists in Iraq were calling for legal reforms as early as 1923, when the first women's association, Women's Awakening (Nahda al-Nisa') was founded.[24] After Iraq was formally granted independence in 1932, the government undertook several attempts to draw a unified family law aiming to bridge the Sunni–Shi'a divide in legal matters. Although the debate lasted for more than a decade, between 1936 and 1947, the draft was never put into force, although it was backed by the royal family. The old regime's legitimacy deficit was mitigated by a system of patronage among the political elite of the state and the religious and sectarian notables, who had been granted wide autonomy by the British mandatory power. Any attempt to curtail their autonomy bore the risk of jeopardizing the fragile balance of power. Moreover, the bourgeois women's movement was incorporated into the political elite and had little room for manoeuvre in demanding women's rights. It took a revolution and a new regime which was able to count on the widespread support of Iraqi citizens in order to overcome the colonial patron–client system, and the existence of a significant women's movement with women's rights ranking high on its agenda, finally to enact the unified family law of 1959.

This historic example illustrates that it needs a rare interaction of several willing actors and favourable factors to provide the stage on which women can successfully negotiate gender relations in citizenship bargains. Women's rights cannot be achieved through empowerment policies alone. It is necessary to reconstruct civil society in order to address the effects of wars, tyranny, occupation and civil conflict and to end a politics in which crucial questions concerning the future of the nation are 'solved' by bargaining equal rights for communal autonomy.

Notes

1. See also Kandiyoti, 1992.
2. *Al-Hayat*, 23 February 2007; see also Riverbend, 'Baghdad Burning', 20 February 2007, http://riverbedblog.blogspot.com/2007_01_01:riverbend-blog_archive.html; accessed March 2007.
3. See also Abdela, 2005.
4. For further reading, see also the selected bibliography on sexual violence in wars in Mühlhäuser and Schwensen, 2001: 21–32.
5. 'Raping the enemy's women is never only about sex (or "sexual violence" or even "gender violence"), nor only about 'the power that men have over women', as argued, for instance, by Andrea Dworkin ... Nor is wartime rape only about men sullying enemy *men's* property, nor even only about altering, via women's wombs, the composition of the enemy collectivity. There is something larger at stake. *War itself is rape*. Wartime rape is about taking the enemy's territory, as has been made patently obvious in military discourses equating enemy territory with a woman's body in need of (both military and romantic) conquest ... And, although feminist theory and experience tells us that violence committed against women in wartime replicates and continues violence against women in peacetime, in women's homes and families, and on the street ... wartime rape must be ultimately seen also as the rape of the nation' (Lentin, 2002).
6. On the gendered effects of the embargo, see Buck et al., 1998; Al-Ali, 2003; Al-Jawaheri, 2008.
7. On the discourse of the complimentary role models of 'hero warrior' and 'patriotic mother', see Elshtein, 1994.
8. For an extensive discussion on the changing gender policies of the Ba'th regime, see Efrati, 1999; Rohde, 2002; Kamp, 2005.
9. Interview with Nasrin Mustafa Birwari, then minister for reconstruction, and several Kurdish social workers at the conference on 'The Participation of Women in the Reconstruction of Iraq' organized by the Heinrich Böll Foundation, 30 June–1 July 2006, Berlin. According to the statements of two German NGO activists working in Kurdistan–Iraq, the situation did not change until spring 2006, though gendered violence, especially female genital mutilation, seems to have become an issue in government circles.
10. See also Fischer-Tahir, 2000: 170 ff.
11. This is by no means a characteristic of Middle Eastern or Muslim societies. So-called 'passion crimes', the killing of women by former husbands/partners who have claimed that passion has led them to commit irrational acts, have long been reason for lighter sentences in European and American states.
12. See also Medani, 2004.
13. This policy also made it extremely difficult for women to cross borders to seek asylum. Women refugees faced extreme difficulties and were forced to spend more than double the sum men paid to flee the country.

14. Although the two large Kurdish parties have outspoken secular programmes, there exist parties favouring political Islam in Iraqi Kurdistan, such as the Kurdistan Islamic Union, which challenge the secular identity of the Kurdish national movement but support the claim for Kurdish autonomy.

15. The Ministry of Education in Kurdistan, for instance, uses a curriculum developed in the late 1990s and has begun to formulate its own policy on higher education, as a former foreign consultant stated in an interview. The strong Kurdish stance on autonomy fuels debates on partitioning Iraq by referring to the 'artificial identity' of the Iraqi nation as a result of the mandatory system in the aftermath of World War I. Benedict Anderson (1983) and Ernest Gellner (1983) pointed out, however, that all nations are imagined communities, and deconstructed the essentialist notion of nations as 'natural' entities. Although Iraqi history is characterized by many social struggles and (ethnic) civil wars, it fails to support the idea of partitioning. In contrast, political debates throughout the colonial and post-colonial history centred on the different interpretations of Iraqi identity between the poles of Iraqi nationalism and Arab nationalism, while claims for Kurdish autonomy focused to a large extent on minority rights, not on independence see, for instance, Batatu 1982; Farouk-Sluglett and Sluglett 1991; Tripp 2000.

16. See, for example, the home pages of the Assyrian National Movement, www.nineveh.com; the Assyrian Democratic Organization, www.ado-world.org; or the Iraqi Turkoman Front, www.turkmencephesi.org.

17. For an introduction, see Elwert, 1989: 21–60; Heinz, 1993.

18. On the results of the 15 December elections see Independent Electoral Commission of Iraq, www.ieciraq.org/English/Frameset_english.htm; accessed 15 March 2006.

19. See the 'Political Declaration of Iraqi Opposition', Reuters, 17 December 2002, http://aanf.org/midwest/dec2002/auanewswatch03.htm; accessed 28 August 2004; on the Arabic versions see Haidar 2002: 617; Kurdistan-Rundbrief, 2003: 14.

20. For reservations on CEDAW see United Nations, www.un.org/womenwatch/daw/cedaw/reservations-country.htm; accessed 2 June 2006).

21. On the Iraqi constitution see Iraqi Transitional Government, www.iraqi government.org/ index_en.htm; accessed 3 June 2006.

22. The 25 per cent quota for women in the assembly was met by allotting discretionary seats to women on the basis of the proportion of seats won nationally by their party lists.

23. 'US Says Islamic State in Iraq is Acceptable', Straits Times/Agence France Presse/Reuters, 17 May 2004, www.truthout.org/cgi-bin/artman/exec/view.cgi/9/4501; accessed 28 August 2004.

24. In the literature on women's movements in Iraq, the organization is also cited as Women Arise, Women's Awakening Club, Women's Renaissance Club, Club for the Awakening of Women and Elevation of Women.

References

Abdela, Lesley (2005) 'Iraq's War on Women', Open Democracy, 18 July. www. opendemocracy.net/conflict-iraqconflict/women_2681.jsp.

Al-Ali, Nadje (2003) 'Women, Gender Relations, and Sanctions in Iraq', in Shams Inati, ed., Iraq: Its History, People and Politics, pp. 233–46. Amherst: Humanity.

Al-Ali, Nadje, and Nicola Pratt (2006) 'Women in Iraq: Beyond the Rhetoric', Middle East Report 239: 18–23.

Al-Ali, Zaid (2005) 'Iraq: A Constitution to Nowhere', Open Democracy, 22 August, www.opendemocracy.net/debates/article.jsp?id=2anddebateId=114andarticle Id=2925.

Al-Jawaheri, Yasmin H. (2008). Women in Iraq: The Gender Impact of International Sanctions. London, I.B. Tauris.

Amnesty International (2003) 'Climate of Fear: Sexual Violence and Abduction of Women and Girls in Baghdad', 15 July. www.hrw.org/reports/2003/ iraq0703/.

Anderson, Benedict (1983) Imagined Communities: Reflections on the Origins and Spread of Nationalism. London: Verso.

Anthias, Floya, and Nira Yuval Davis (1989) 'Introduction', in Woman – Nation – State, pp. 1–16. London: Macmillan.

Batatu, Hanna (1982) The Old Social Classes and the Revolutionary Movements of Iraq: A Study of Iraq's Old Landed and Commercial Classes and Its Communists, Ba'thists and Free Officers. Princeton: Princeton University Press.

Biddle, Stephen (2006) 'Seeing Baghdad, Thinking Saigon', Foreign Affairs 85(2): 2–14.

Blom, Ida, Karen Hagemann and Catherine Hall, eds (2000) Gendered Nations: Nationalisms and Gender Order in the Long Nineteenth Century. Oxford: Berg.

Blumenthal, Sidney (2006) 'Bush's World of Illusion', Open Democracy, 17 March. www.opendemocracy.net/democracy/illusion_3367.jsp 2.

Buchta, Wilfried (2004) 'Anmerkungen zur al-Sadr-Bewegung', INAMO 10(37): 29–34.

Buck, Christian (2004) 'Wir müssen den Irakern ein wenig trauen', Die Welt, 23 April.

Buck, Lori, Nicole Gallant and Kim Richard Nossal (1998) 'Sanctions as a Gendered Instrument of Statecraft: The Case of Iraq, Review of International Studies 24(1): 69–84.

Charrad, Mounira (2001) States and Women's Rights: The Making of Postcolonial Tunisia, Algeria, and Morocco. Berkeley: University of California Press.

Coleman, Isobel (2006) 'Women, Islam, and the New Iraq', Foreign Affairs 85(1): 24–38.

Cook, Gretchen (2003) 'Role of Women in New Iraq of Concern', Women's News, 22 April.

Dobriansky, Paula J. (2003) 'Women and the Transition to Democracy: Iraq, Afghanistan, Beyond, Remarks at the Heritage Foundation', Washington, 11

April. www.state.gov/g/rls/rm/2003/19583.htm; accessed 24 August 2004.

Efrati, Noga (1999) 'Productive or Reproductive? The Roles of Iraqi Women during the Iraq–Iran War', *Middle Eastern Studies* 35(2): 27–44.

Eichhorst, Kristina (2003) *Der Bürgerkrieg in Sri Lanka. 'Institutional Engineering' als Lösungsansatz für ethnische Konflikte.* Kiel: Universität Kiel.

Eichhorst, Kristina, and Svenja Sinjen (2006) 'Die irakische Verfassung: Ein geeignetes Mittel zur Lösung der ethnischen Konflikteß', *Politische Studien* 5(4).

Elshtein, Jean Bethke (1994) 'Thinking about Women and International Violence', in Peter R. Beckmann and Francine d'Amico, eds, *Women, Gender and World Politics: Perspectives, Policies and Prospects*, pp. 109–18. Westport CT: Greenwood.

Elwert, Georg (1989) 'Nationalismus, Ethnizität und Nativismus – über Wir-Gruppenprozesse', in Volker Lühr, Manfred Schulz and Georg Elwert, eds, *Ethnizität im Wandel.* Saarbrücken: Breitenbach.

Endut, Noraida (2002) 'Muslim Women and the Law on Domestic Violence against Women in Malaysia', paper presented at the conference 'Negotiating Power, Contesting Violence, and Assessing Perpectives for Transcultural Approaches: Gender and Nation State in Muslim Societies', Carl von Ossietzky University Oldenburg, December.

Enloe, Cynthia (1998) 'All the Men Are in the Militias, All the Women Are Victims: The Politics of Masculinity and Femininity in Nationalist Wars', in Lois Ann Lorentzen and Jennifer Turpin, eds, *The Women and War Reader*, pp. 50–62. New York: New York University Press.

Enloe, Cynthia (2000) *Maneuvers: The International Politics of Militarizing Women's Lives.* Berkeley: University of California Press.

Erhart, Hans-Georg (2004) 'Bedrohung Staatszerfall – Antwort Nation-building?', in Christoph Weller et al., eds, *Friedensgutachten*, pp. 52–60. Münster: Lit.

Farouk-Sluglett, Marion, and Peter Sluglett (1991) *Der Irak seit 1958: Von der Revolution zur Diktatur.* Frankfurt: Suhrkamp.

Fischer-Tahir, Andrea (2000) 'Nationalismus und Frauenbewegung in Irakisch-Kurdistan', in Eva Sabelsberg, Siamend Hajo and Carsten Borck, eds, *Kurdische Frauen und das Bild der kurdischen Frau.* Münster: Lit.

Fürtig, Henner (2003) 'Die irakische Opposition zwischen Aufbruch und Resignation', in Kai Hafez and Birgit Schäbler, eds, *Der Irak: Land zwischen Krieg und Frieden*, Heidelberg: Palmyra.

Fürtig, Henner (2005) 'Irak: Verfassungsdebatte und politische Rekonstruktion', paper presented at the 12th Annual Meeting of the German Middle East Studies Association (DAVO), Hamburg, 27–29 October.

Geertz, Clifford (1997) *Dichte Beschreibung: Beiträge zum Verstehen kultureller Systeme.* Frankfurt: Suhrkamp.

Gellner, Ernest (1983) *Nations and Nationalism.* Ithaca: Cornell University Press.

Goldstein, Joshua S. (2001) *War and Gender: How Gender Shapes the War System and Vice Versa.* Cambridge: Cambridge University Press.

Hagemann, Karen (2002) 'Mannlicher Muth und Teutsche Ehre', in *Nation, Militär und*

Geschlecht zur Zeit der Antinapoleonischen Kriege Preußens. Paderborn: Ferdinand Schöningh.

Haidar, Jamal (2002) 'Problems of Representation', *Al-Ahram Weekly*, 25 December: 617. http://weekly.ahram.org.eg/2002/617/fr2.htm; accessed 24 August 2004.

Heinz, Marco (1993) *Ethnizität und ethnische Identität: Eine Begriffsgeschichte.* Bonn: Holos.

Human Rights Watch (2003) 'Climate of Fear: Sexual Violence and Abduction of Women and Girls in Baghdad', 15 July. www.hrw.org/reports/2003/iraq0703; accessed 23 August 2004.

Ibrahim, Ferhad (1997) *Konfessionalismus und Politik in der arabischen Welt: Die Schiiten im Irak.* Münster: Lit.

Ibrahim, Ferhad (2005) 'Iraks Kampf um die Verfassung', *Blätter für deutsche und internationale Politik* 10: 1175–8.

Jabar, Faleh A. (2000) 'Shaykhs and Ideologues: Detribalization and Retribalization in Iraq, 1968–1998', *Middle East Report* 215: 28–31.

Jabar, Faleh A. (2003) 'The Worldly Roots of Religiosity in Post-Saddam Iraq', *Middle East Report* 227: 12–18.

Jones, Adam (2004) 'Humiliation and Masculine Crisis in Iraq', *Al-Raida* 21 (104/5): 70–73.

Joseph, Suad (2000) 'Gendering Citizenship in the Middle East', in S. Joseph, ed., *Gender and Citizenship in the Middle East*, pp. 3–30. Syracuse: Syracuse University Press.

Kaldor, Mary (1999) *New and Old Wars: Organized Violence in a Global Era.* Cambridge: Polity Press.

Kamp, Martina (2003) 'Organizing Ideologies of Gender, Class and Ethnicity: The Pre-revolutionary Women's Movements in Iraq', in Sherifa Zuhur, ed., *Women and Gender in the Middle East and Islamic World Today.* Berkeley: University of California Press; University of California International and Area Studies.

Kamp, Martina (2005) 'Geschlecht, Kolonialismus, Nation: Patriarchale Nachkriegsordnung(en) im Irak', in Karen Hagemann, Jennifer Davy and Ute Kätzel, eds, *Frieden, Gewalt, Geschlecht: Friedens- und Konfliktforschung als Geschlechterforschung*, pp. 293–314. Essen: Klartext.

Kandiyoti, Deniz (1992) 'Women, Islam and the State: A Comparative Approach', in Juan R.I. Cole, ed., *Comparing Muslim Societies: Knowledge and the State in a World Civilization*, pp. 237–60. Ann Arbor: University of Michigan Press.

Klein, Uta (2001) *Militär und Geschlecht in Israel.* Frankfurt: Campus.

Kreile, Renate (1999) 'Der Krise, Herr' werden – Geschlechterpolitik und gesellschaftliche Transformationsprozesse im Vorderen Orient', in Peter Pawelka und Hans-Georg Wehling, eds, *Der Vordere Orient an der Schwelle zum 21. Jahrhundert*, pp. 156–72. Opladen: Westdeutscher Verlag.

Kreile, Renate (2003) 'Politischer Islam, Geschlechterverhältnisse und Staat im Vorderen Orient', *Feministische Studien* 21 (2): 197–212.

Kurdistan-Rundbrief (2003) 'Die Sharia als Grundlage eines neuen Irak? Ein Kommentar', Kurdistan-Rundbrief 16: 1.

Lentin, Ronit (2002) 'The Feminisation of Catastrophe', paper presented at the Centre for Interdisciplinary Research on Women and Gender, Carl von Ossietzky University Oldenburg, 24 June.

Lentin, Ronit, ed. (1997) Gender and Catastrophe. London: Zed Books.

Makiya, Kanan (1993) Cruelty and Silence: War, Tyranny, Uprising, and the Arab World. New York: Norton.

Medani, Khalid Mustapha (2004) 'State Building in Reverse. The Neo-liberal "Reconstruction" of Iraq', Middle East Report 232.

Meintjes, Sheila, Anu Pillay and Meredith Turshen, eds (2003) The Aftermath: Women in Post-conflict Transformation. London: Zed Books.

Mojab, Shahrzad (2002) '"Honour Killing": Culture, Politics and Theory', Middle East Women's Studies Review 17(1/2): 1–7.

Mojab, Shahrzad (2003) 'Kurdish Women in the Zone of Genocide and Gendercide', Al-Raida 21(103): 20–25.

Mühlhäuser, Regina, and Ingwer Schwensen (2001), 'Sexuelle Gewalt in Kriegen: Auswahlbibliographie', Mittelweg 36(5): 21–32.

Naji, Zainab (2006) 'Female Politicians Fear Exclusion', Iraq Crisis Report, 26 April: 174. Institute for War and Peace Reporting, www.iwpr.net/?p=icrands =fando=261359andapc_state= eniicr9f23e89676c01a91c8f8c822fa473985.

Nakash, Yitzhak (2003) 'The Shi'ites and the Future of Iraq', Foreign Affairs 82(4): 17–26.

Omar, Suha (1994) 'Honour, Shame and Dictatorship', in F. Hazelton, ed., Iraq since the Gulf War: Prospects for Democracy. London: Zed Books.

Pateman, Carol (1998) The Sexual Contract. Stanford: Stanford University Press.

Peteet, Julie (2002) 'Male Gender and Rituals of Resistance in the Palestinian Intifada: A Cultural Politics of Violence', in Catherine Besteman, ed., Violence: A Reader. London: Palgrave.

Reuter (2002) 'Political Declaration of Iraqi Opposition', 17 December. http://aanf. org/midwest/dec2002/auanewswatch03.htm; accessed 28 August 2004.

Rohde, Achim (2002) 'When the Land is Feminine, War is Love, and the Nation is a Family: Iraqi Gender Policies during the Iran–Iraq War', paper presented at the conference 'Negotiating Power, Contesting Violence, and Assessing Perspectives for Transcultural Approaches: Gender and Nation State in Muslim Societies', Carl von Ossietzky University Oldenburg, December.

Sadiqi, Fatima and Moha Ennaji (2006) 'The Feminization of Public Space: Women's Activism, the Family Law, and Social Change in Morocco', Journal of Middle East Women's Studies 2(2): 86–114.

Sauer, Birgit (2002) 'Geschlechtsspezifische Gewaltmäßigkeit rechtsstaatlicher Arrangements und wohlfahrtsstaatlicher Institutionalisierungen: Überlegungen zu einer geschlechtersensiblen politikwissenschaftlichen Perspektive', in Regina-Maria Dackweiler and Reinhild Schäfer, eds, Gewaltverhältnisse: Feministische Perspektiven auf Geschlecht und Gewalt, pp. 81–106. Frankfurt: Campus.

Seifert, Ruth (1995) 'Der weibliche Körper als Symbol und Zeichen: Geschlech-tsspezifische Gewalt und die kulturelle Konstruktion des Krieges', in Andreas Gestrich, ed., *Gewalt im Krieg: Ausübung, Erfahrung und Verweigerung von Gewalt in Kriegen des 20. Jahrhunderts*, pp. 13–33. Münster: Lit.

Shalhoub-Kevorkian, Nadera (2002) 'Reexamining Femicide: Breaking the Silence and Crossing "Scientific" Borders', *Signs: Journal of Women in Culture and Society* 28(2): 581–608.

Solioz, Christopher, and Tobias K. Vogel, eds (2004) *Dayton and Beyond: Perspectives on the Future of Bosnia and Herzegovina*. Baden-Baden: Nomos.

Straits Times/Agency France Presse/Reuters (2004) 'US Says Islamic State in Iraq is Acceptable', 17 May 2004. www.truthout.org/cgi-bin/artman/exec/view. cgi/9/4501; accessed 28 August 2004.

Thompson, Elizabeth (2000) *Colonial Citizens: Republican Rights, Paternal Privilege, and Gender in French Syria and Lebanon*. New York: University of Columbia Press.

Tripp, Charles (2000) *A History of Iraq*. Cambridge: Cambridge University Press.

Turshen, Meredeth (2001) 'The Political Economy of Rape: An Analysis of Systematic Rape and Sexual Abuse of Women during Armed Conflict in Africa', in Caroline O.N. Moser and Fiona C. Clark, eds, *Victims, Perpetrators or Actors? Gender, Armed Conflict and Political Violence*, pp. 55–68. London: Zed Books.

United Nations, 'Declarations, Reservations and Objections to CEDAW', www. un.org/womenwatch/daw/cedaw/reservations-country.htm.

United Nations Development Fund for Women/UNIFEM, ed. (2004) 'Gender Profile of the Conflict in Iraq', 28 August. www.womenwarpeace.org/iraq/iraq.htm.

Watenpaugh, Keith D. (2003) 'The Guiding Principles and the US "Mandate" for Iraq: 20th Century Colonialism and America's New Empire', *Logos* 2(1): 26–37.

Wobbe, Theresa Wobbe (1994) 'Die Grenzen der Gemeinschaft und die Grenzen des Geschlechts', in T. Wobbe and Gesa Lindemann, eds, *Denkachsen: Zur theoretischen und institutionellen Rede vom Geschlecht*, pp. 177–207. Frankfurt: Suhrkamp.

Woodrow Wilson International Center for Scholars, ed. (2005) *Building a New Iraq: Ensuring Women's Rights*. Washington DC: Woodrow Wilson Center.

Yuval-Davis, Nira (1997) *Gender and Nation*. London: Sage.

Zangana, Haifa (2005) 'Colonial Feminists from Washington to Baghdad: Women for a Free Iraq as a Case Study', *Al-Raida* 22(109–110): 30–40.

Zipfel, Gaby (2001) '"Blood, Sperm and Tears": Sexuelle Gewalt in Kriegen', *Mittelweg* 36(5): 3–20.

Zubaida, Sami (2004) 'The Next Iraqi State: Secular or Religious?', *Open Democracy*, 13 February. www.opendemocracy.net/debates/article-2-73-1737.jsp.

Zubaida, Sami (2005) 'Iraq's Constitution on the Edge', *Open Democracy*, 22 August. www.opendemocracy.net/conflict-iraq/deadline_2771.jsp.

Zuhur, Sherifa (2006) *Iraq, Women's Empowerment, and Public Policy*. Carlisle: Strategic Studies Institute of the US Army War College.

SEVEN

Gendered Palestinian Citizenship:
Women, Legal Pluralism and Post-conflict Aid

Riina Isotalo

The contours of Palestinian citizenship have been researched from legal and gender approaches (inter alia Johnson and Hammami 1999, Jad et al., 2000; Jad, 2004; Khalil, 2006, 2007; Welchman, 2000). Studies have identified a persistent male bias in national discourses and documents, commented on the conditions established by laws granting and passing down citizenship, as well as analysed social context and political issues around reforming the personal status legislation during the transitional period. Some analyses have predicted that Palestinian citizenship will be decoupled from residency (Khalil, 2007), suggesting an 'extraterritorial' (Basch et al., 1994) state form in the future. The present chapter joins the debate on Palestinian citizenship by bringing together a transnational approach, gender and 'substantive citizenship' in the non-sovereign self-governing territories.[1]

Polity in the Palestinian context is to a great extent transnational. I have found it useful to apply the recent scholarship on gender and citizenship, particularly in developing and post-colonial countries, and Glick Schiller's (2005) insights on 'transborder citizenship'.

Framing my discussion in these terms stems from the absence of a sovereign Palestinian state, as well as the distinction between formal and substantive citizenship. Formal citizenship can be understood as the relationship between the state and the citizen, whereas substantive citizenship is that which goes beyond the confines of formal politics and law to encompass the economic, social and political relationship between social groups and power structures that mediate the standing of individuals in the polity (Mukhopadhyay, 2007: 6).

Although it is necessary to elaborate on some elements of formal citizenship, the focus of my discussion is on substantive citizenship. I look at two interrelated issues: first, the relationships among gender, aid and post-conflict in Palestine; and second, border-crossing practices that are more typical for women than for men. Such physical, social, political and economic practices are indicative of gender-specific social and political membership in the national community. These issues bring together several legal and normative domains.

My argumentation follows the lines of Jad et al. (2000), who suggest that women's citizenship in the transitional period has been framed primarily in terms of their roles as reproducers. I argue that at the core of women's citizenship, which is understood as 'modes of incorporating individuals within a framework of social and political community' (Charrad, 2007: 94), are Palestinian women's roles in practices related to *getting there* (either to WBGS, East Jerusalem or the State of Israel), *staying there* and *maintaining connectivity* between and among groupings that wish to maintain 'closeness' (*qaraba*)[2] across borders. Many substantive citizenship practices in the non-sovereign self-governance areas in parts of the West Bank and the Gaza Strip (hereafter WBGS) are embedded in collective rather than individual membership in the polity. One must nevertheless pay attention to intersectionality as it is understood in recent research on feminist theory: women are not categorically disadvantaged in the drafting of the contents of Palestinian citizenship.

Although women's connective practices oppose Israeli occupation and Palestinians' enforced dispersal, I am not willing to equate them with resistance. Citizenship is formed in the relationships among agency, personhood and rights. The term 'everyday resistance' (Taraki, 2006) that has been used in recent scholarship to describe Palestinians' practices that in my view fall into the category of substantive citizenship indicates such individual agency and capacity, which the social structures that forge citizenship-related practices in the WBGS and East Jerusalem do not grant to everyone. Because these practices draw from customs and traditions, they are constituted in hierarchical structures that subordinate women and juniors. Thus, my second argument is that although informal practices that keep up the Palestinian community can be interpreted as active citizenship, women's active social and political citizenship is not always empowering or an indication of a democratic or inclusive citizenship regime.

Palestinian state-building is fundamentally shaped by different forms of mobility and dispersal: more than half the households in the WBGS have relatives who live abroad (PCBS, 1997; cf. Hilal, 2006: 201). Estimations based on kinship do not reveal all personal ties between Palestinians abroad and the WBGS. Some forms of mobility have been initiated by force and others by choice, which means that Palestinian communities abroad are heterogeneous. Because the massive refugee problem remains unresolved, Palestinian transnationalism has been discussed much more in terms of displacement than multi-placement. However, both displacement and multi-placement are indispensable concepts needed to comprehend the dynamics of transborder citizenship. The questions of cohesion and dispersion among the Palestinians are reflected in substantive citizenship. When citizenship practices are examined in the context of transnationality and legal pluralism, they illustrate tension between a collectivist idea of citizenship (Galloway, 2000), which emphasizes the role of citizenship as a tool for promoting social cohesion and preserving common traditions, and the existence of differentiated transnational social fields among the Palestinians.

Connective practices, women's memberships and structural marginalization

In this section I will look at some of the ways Palestinian women are incorporated into the framework of social and political community. According to Charrad (2007: 94) and Mukhopadyay (2007: 7), the modes of incorporation are at the heart of citizenship. In the present discussion, social and political communities are divided by the Israeli–Palestinian conflict and by multiple borders. Consequently, citizenship practices may be formed around the goal of maintaining connections – that is, community – across borders or alternatively around marking boundaries. Women's contributions are essential in the maintenance of community but are rarely regarded as substantive citizenship. Rather, their activities are seen as inseparable from their reproductive roles and are not necessarily regarded from a citizenship perspective as deserving of recognition for women qua citizens. Fifteen years after the establishment of the Palestinian Authority, Palestine seems to be in an indefinite period of transition towards statehood. Consequently, substantive citizenship practices remain normatively organized around national liberation and resistance, and consequently the male political subject is privileged.

Recent scholarship has called into question the myth of the eternal elasticity of the Palestinian family as a shock absorber. Kuttab (2006: 235–7) argues that women are often the main agents in family-based economic survival strategies, but they also bear the brunt: their mental and physical tolerance sets the limits of 'resistance economy' at the household level. Because a household rather than an individual has been called the basic unit of Palestinian society (Heiberg et al., 1993), Kuttab's argument raises questions about how Palestinian legal pluralism – which implies contesting views whether an individual or a collective is the subject of law – shapes women's agency and its relationship to personhood and rights. I have chosen to build my analysis in this section around 'Salwa'[3] and her family. Her 'case' shows that despite the central societal and political role of gender relations in conflict-related lifestyles, women's citizenship practices are at the margins of the conflict and are regarded as marginal to it: they gain little attention outside the context of personal status legislation, the women's movement or the household-economy approach.

Lisa Taraki (2006: xix) notes the immense amounts of time and energy that Palestinian women invest in visiting lawyers, attending trials and keeping in regular contact with sons and husbands in prison while catering to their needs for basic supplies and food. Such practices are more typical for women than for men, illustrating the significance of gender as an organizing principle for the polity and substantive citizenship. Salwa's family is a case in point of the deep impact political activism has on a household and family dynamics. From the perspective of the legal foundations of Palestinian women's social membership, what is relevant in this particular case are Israeli Nationality Law, Entry into Israel Law (Temporary Order), security reasons, family unification policy and Israeli recognition of human rights standards. The last is the basis of Palestinians' appeals in the Israeli High Court. Laws and place of residence have a diversifying effect in terms of different Palestinian groupings: for women living in the non-sovereign autonomous areas, the particular laws mentioned above may have no relevance at all.[4] The influence of laws in the questions of cohesion and dispersion underlines the relevance of intersectionality when women's rights in conflict situations are considered. The legal foundations for Palestinian women's social and political membership vary from one context to another, around which accrues the practical importance of informal norms that evolve from kin-based structures.

Salwa[5] and her children live in the small village of Issaywia in East Jerusalem. Palestinian Jerusalemites are a numerically marginal group whose legal and political status is anomalous. On the one hand, they are liminally positioned in relation to the Palestinian political community and resistance to the occupation. On the other hand, daily encounters with Israeli society constantly remind Palestinian Jerusalemites of unequal power relations and their inferior status.

Salwa's husband died of cancer in 2005 when he was 34 years old. Nidal was from a nearby village, Anata, considered a part of the West Bank. The couple met in Ashkelon prison (in Israel) where Nidal was incarcerated at the same time as Salwa's father, whom she visited every week. None of their three children has a birth certificate because Israeli authorities claim the centre of family life was in the West Bank during the time of the children's birth. In the course of the years Salwa has showed Israeli authorities the documents of the family-owned building, her electricity and gas bills, as well as the receipts for her and the children's daily expenses to prove that they have lived in Jerusalem. In spite of the fact that the children do not exist officially, they enjoy Israeli health insurance, which Salwa pays for on a yearly basis. She is able to do this because, in *de facto* terms, officials know that her children were born in Jerusalem: Israel has illegally[6] annexed East Jerusalem. In Israel a mother must show her identity papers in order to check the child out of the hospital after giving birth, which means that children are registered in hospitals.

Israeli authorities' disbelief is based on their assumption of Palestinian patrilineality and patrilocality – that the woman follows the man in marriage. In essence, at both policy and practical levels, Israeli authorities operate homogenizing stereotypes regarding gender relations among the Palestinians; moreover, the idea of group citizenship, rather than of an individual citizen, is deeply rooted in Israeli–Palestinian relations. Officials' denial of birth certificates is also tied to Israeli national policy to 'Judaize' (a term coined by Oren Yiftachel, inter alia, 2005) Jerusalem by way of settlements and revocation of Palestinians' residency rights. These grounds for exclusion relate directly to gender, social and political citizenship. Salwa was born in Jerusalem, her family resides there and her narratives indicate that she considers it her right to remain a Jerusalemite regardless of whom she married. She also regards it as nationally and politically vital to sustain connections across the Israeli-imposed borders among the Palestinians.[7] Salwa hopes that her children will eventually receive birth certificates through an order from the Israeli High Court, where she has filed a case on humanitarian – that is, rights-based – grounds. Different courts are thus arenas in which substantive citizenship is forged both in positive and in negative terms: women may or may not become visible as individuals on rights-based or other legal grounds. Although Salwa's economic resources are relatively meagre and the lawyers' fees are expensive, she feels that she has no choice: legal procedures in the Israeli court system are the last resort in her efforts to make her children visible. She has had a lawyer for seven years.

Individual but gendered agency comes into play in Salwa's choice to marry a West Banker and remain a Jerusalemite. During the marriage, her husband could not move to Jerusalem for two reasons. First, as an ex-prisoner, he was considered a security threat by Israel and his entry was banned on the basis of the Entry into Israel Temporary Order. During his illness he was recurrently denied entry at checkpoints on his way to treatments. Second, as the only son of the family, he had caretaking responsibilities towards his mother and unmarried sisters. Thus, family life was conducted in two places: Salwa and the children lived three days a week in Anata and the rest of the week in Issaywia.

The discontents of Salwa's status as a Palestinian Jerusalemite[8] cannot be separated from her social and political membership of the Palestinian nation, Palestinian state-building in the WBGS, and gender. She belongs to a family of active Fateh members in which male family members have spent long periods in prison. Also Salwa supports Fateh and is involved in its activities, which revolve around national liberation. Salwa's father was jailed in Israeli prisons for thirteen years because of his political activism, and consequently her mother knows the whole country because she visited him everywhere. The last time he was jailed was in 1994, just after the signing of the Oslo Accords.[9] Currently, Salwa's younger brother Amjad is in Ansar prison (called Ktziot in Hebrew), but Salwa does not visit him: 'I can't see him in prison, I just can't. He's more to me than a brother, he's like my son.' Instead, their mother travels every week to a prison that is located in the middle of a desert close to the Egyptian border.

Three sisters and their parents live in a small block of flats that is surrounded by their relatives' houses. In the absence of any males except the elderly father, women of the family have pooled their resources. Amjad's wife Maysoon and her son (whose father has been in prison for his entire lifetime) moved to Salwa's parents' apartment after Amjad's imprisonment. Salwa's mother, her youngest sister and Maysoon take care of Salwa's three children and Maysoon's child while Salwa works. Most meals are cooked and eaten together.

Maysoon and Amjad are first cousins. Maysoon has American citizenship and her parents live in the USA. She is petrified that the Israeli authorities may revoke her residency right, using a combination of security reasons and her American citizenship as a justification. Israel allows dual citizenship,[10] but does not always recognize it in the case of Palestinian Jerusalemites, whose residency permits can be revoked for a number of reasons: more than three years' consecutive absence, alleged living in the WBGS and security.

Sustaining (even creating) family relations and maintaining connections across borders by establishing marriages and visiting fathers, brothers and husbands in prison are essential components of women's social and political citizenship in this family. The institution of marriage is a central instrument of social and national cohesion. In Salwa's family, the cross-cousin marriage that is favoured by Palestinians maintains family connections between United States and Israel/Palestine. Yet being married to Amjad has placed Maysoon under fear of expulsion and caused circumstantial patrilocality and deepened intra-familial dependency.

The above examples illustrate how Palestinians' efforts to maintain presence and connectivity in the WBGS, East Jerusalem and Israel at the collective level sometimes contribute to women's exclusion and structural discrimination at a personal level. The relationship between kinship structure and gender is essential in maintaining access to and from the Occupied Palestinian Territories and to East Jerusalem and Israel through transborder citizenship practices. Citizenship can be understood as the 'legal foundation of social membership' (Jad, 2004: 2). The direct influence of Israeli laws and national policies as well as international laws in Salwa's daily life and her efforts to claim rights and recognition for her children through legal channels make void some of the assumptions regarding the public–private dichotomy and the allegedly distant relation between women and the state in the Middle East. In her case, 'private life' – marriage and establishing a family – is regulated by different sets of laws as much as any aspect of political activity. Moreover, assumptions regarding gender roles, such as patrilocality, are used to marginalize her politically and ethnically. Paradoxically, 'personal issues' are where the 'red line' is drawn in intra-Palestinian discussions of women and legislation. As will be discussed in the following sections, the last bastion of 'authenticity' in the era of legal globalization and donor-driven legal reform, 'personal issues' remain regulated mainly by religious law and informal norms and traditions.

Gender conventions and post-conflict

The Palestinian economy is one of the most donor-driven economies in the world, which is why international development thinking is part of the transnational framework of Palestinian citizenship. Thus, a thread running throughout this chapter is the reflection on donor approaches to gender in post-conflict situations that takes its empirical cue from the relationships among women's rights, legal pluralism and gender in 'post-conflict' Palestine.

The international donor community defined Palestine as a post-conflict site for peace-building and reconstruction in the early 1990s. From the vantage point of 2009, Palestine cannot be described as 'post-conflict' at either a practical or a political level. Palestine is a case that shows how difficult it is to define 'post-conflict' situations clearly. In many countries emerging from war, overt armed conflict may come to an end while low-level violence continues for many years, involving former factions, demobilized combatants, bandits and militias (Barakat, 2004: 8). Protracted low-intensity conflicts have a tendency to escalate cyclically in the absence of a mutually satisfactory political resolution to the conflict's 'root causes', particularly in the absence of powerful custodians of peace. The Israeli–Palestinian conflict can be characterized as a protracted low-intensity conflict that features occupation, settler-colonial movement and the largest population displacement problem in the world.

Neither the Madrid peace conference in 1991 nor the Declaration of Principles (hereafter DoP) in 1993 made reference to gender. Neither did the memoranda, blueprints and roadmaps that followed. Moreover, not only the Israeli–Palestinian peace process but the great majority of peace negotiations are gender-blind. This fact illustrates the lack of political weight given in 'high politics' – that is, security and economics – to 'gender mainstreaming' and 'gender sensitivity', which have become a part of donor-driven agendas for conflict management and peace-building from 'human security' and 'civilian crisis management' points of view. The international experience with gender mainstreaming has not been entirely positive: according to many analysts, its failure stems from its depoliticization, which means that it has moved from being a process of transformation to an end in itself pursued with solely instrumentalist intent (Mukhopadhyay, 2007: 4).

Yet gender is a central factor in defining societal development alternatives in post-colonial and post-conflict transitions, as well as in state-building efforts, for instance, in democratization and legal reforms. The alleged failure of gender mainstreaming makes it even more important to examine the place of gender in post-conflict political transitions and social transformations. Although gender sensitivity is missing from most peace agreements, gender issues can – at least rhetorically – be used by donors as a justification for transnational interventions and allocation or withdrawal of inter-national assistance.[11]

Contemporary humanitarian aid and development assistance draw on humanitarian principles, and their approach to gender is based on human rights. A rights-based approach to gender originates from Western liberalism and relies on supranational legal frameworks, mainly human rights conventions such as CEDAW[12] (Goetz, 2007: 13) and, in the context of war, UN Security Council Resolution 1325 that mandates gender mainstreaming in peace and security.[13]

The international human rights regime is known in Palestine, but the relationship between human rights discourse and the issue of women's rights as human rights is not straightforward. For Palestinians, the concept of human rights is mainly clustered around those rights violated within the framework of military occupation and repression of the national struggle for independence. Four conceptions of rights around which human rights talk is selectively focused emerge from Smith Polfus's (2006: 138–45) analysis: the right to self-determination, issues related to personal liberty, the right to freedom of movement and the right to non-violation of private property. In relation to these rights conceptions, the effects of the occupation are seen as affecting men directly and women mainly indirectly – 'as apolitical attachments to political men' (144). Therefore, according to Smith Polfus, the concept of human rights in the Palestinian context refers mainly to men, whilst women's rights are perceived to be a social issue rather than a question of human rights.

It is crucial for the present discussion that since the 1990s, the international aid regime has tied security and development tightly together (Duffield, 2001; Kaldor, 2007). This association stems from liberal peace theory and the changed nature of wars. At its core are assumptions about the pacifying effects of democracy and development. Drawing on the work of Immanuel Kant, the 'liberal peace thesis' states that democracies do not go to war with one another. Thus in the Palestinian case, the rationale of the donor community is based on this thesis: building a democratic state would buttress the peace between Israel and the PLO as well as promote domestic peace (Turner, 2006: 740–41).

In principle, the only basis for humanitarian aid is need, and the aid is intended to be strictly impartial, whereas (for example the EU's) development assistance criteria are based on needs plus performance. However, because of the prevalence of the 'liberal peace thesis' in policy documents of the UN, the international financial institutions and Western governments (Turner, 2006: 742), humanitarian aid is increasingly politicized. Contemporary humanitarian aid, even in acute war situations, not to mention post-conflict reconstruction programmes, is 'radically developmental' (Duffield, 2001). One of the implications of human security policy is combining humanitarian and development assistance (Kaldor, 2007: 193). This is important for an analysis of the place of gender in post-conflict transitions and has deep significance for the forging of post-conflict citizenship. According to Duffield (2001), such aid is intended to effect a complete turnover in society's values and behavioural patterns towards democracy in order to make it a partner in liberal peace. However, I argue, assistance to post-conflict societies involves striking paradoxes when it comes to gender rights. While politicized humanitarian aid and development assistance claim commitment to human rights and gender justice, as a result of multi-level aid and, even more importantly, heavy emphasis on security, donors simultaneously support mechanisms that sideline women. Informal justice systems and faith-based peace-building where women are not allowed to participate can be mentioned as cases in point about such mechanisms and structures.

Moreover, in the current neoliberal era, development assistance is essentially targeted towards individuals: it has a self-help component built into it. This means that aid creates new subjectivities that relate to resources. Simultaneously, post-conflict reconstruction programmes rely heavily on institution-building, which indicates legal globalization and the transnationalization of certain legal models, frameworks and ideas. Civil society, namely NGOs, has a number of roles to play on both sending and receiving ends: international intergovernmental organizations such as the UN have subcontracted large amounts of post-conflict assistance to Northern NGOs, while Southern, 'local' NGOs are important aid recipients alongside the embryonic state structures.

In the contemporary era of multi-level aid, many stakeholders have started to look at legal pluralism in positive terms, particularly when it comes to 'alternative conflict resolution' mechanisms. In essence, these mechanisms are informal justice systems, upon which I elaborate in the Palestinian context later. ACR has gained much positive attention in recent donor-initiated peace-building efforts (for example, in Somalia). Suffice it to say that these trends have conundrums for women's rights and citizenship in post-conflict transitions, because so-called alternative conflict-resolution mechanisms are often tied to justice systems that are embedded in group membership and the collective subject of law. Moreover, the favouring of ACR is parallel to the rise in forging crisis management and initiating peace processes in terms of religion, either in an inter-faith or in an intra-faith basis.

Post-conflict transitions involve much claim-making and resource competition. The universalist rights-based ideology is sometimes applied by donors as part of post-conflict reconstruction programmes in a top-down vein or in combination with military missions or peacekeeping forces. That is why some stakeholders (not only Islamists and religious conservatives) claim that a rights-based approach to gender is imperialistic, using this argumentation against women's rights activists, often associating them with 'Westernized elites'. Rights-based approaches have also been criticized by some feminist philosophers for falsifying the position of the socially weak, who are in no position to make claims or ensure that more powerful actors meet their obligations. For this reason it is often in the interests of economically and socially vulnerable women to invest in traditional connections and relations (Goetz, 2007: 13). This criticism of the rights-based approach ignores the fact that the socially vulnerable cannot ensure that their entitlements are met any more effectively in reciprocal moral economies.

The DoP and the rights-based approach that characterizes post-conflict reconstruction assistance were at odds as regards rights and law. The Oslo Agreements avoided rights-based discourse altogether: they did not mention national rights and avoided frameworks of international law, universal rights and principles of equality (human rights discourse) in order to conclude a series of transitional agreements. The Oslo Accords also accepted the limitations to the powers of the legislative authority of the Palestinian Legislative Council as decided by the Israeli military governor (Khalil, 2007: 34). The Israeli occupation has been characterized as a legalistic occupation

(Kelly, 2006), in that Israel has used law as a tool to consolidate its occupation – for example, to expropriate lands, imprison activists, and so on. The Palestinian judiciary has been subject to the Israeli military commander and the occupier has changed existing laws through military orders (see also Birzeit University Institute of Law, 2006: 4). Yet legal reform, institution-building, good governance and democracy are central to the international aid community's approach towards Palestinian state-building. This overarching paradox boils down to gender issues as a combination of depoliticization of gender mainstreaming and a rights-based approach to gender among the donors.

Gender, aid and non-liberal processes

The Palestinian Authority (hereafter PA) has been accused of corruption, nepotism and serious assaults on human rights. It was obvious from the outset of the interim period that combining the safeguarding of Israel's security – which was the main task the PA was assigned in the DoP – with good governance and democracy was no easy task. The interim quasi-state has recurrently been characterized as neo-patrimonial. International critics – that is to say, human rights organizations and donors – have shown more understanding towards these faults than have the local opposition, including both the secular NGO movement and the Islamist movement (inter alia Hanafi and Tabar, 2005).

In the first Palestinian presidential elections held in January 1996, independent candidate Sameeha Khalil gained 13 per cent of the votes (PSR, 1996). She was not a wife, widow or daughter of a famous political personality, which has been women's traditional avenue to a political career in many Asian countries. Sameeha Khalil was not a party politician, but a nationalist and the founder and director of Inash el Usra organization for women. Who voted for her? According to a joke that circulated at that time, residents of Hebron (which is known for its social conservatism) cast their votes for her: 'Who is this woman who dares to challenge Abu Ammar? Let us cross her name out on the first round!' This 'daring woman' was considered old-fashioned in terms of gender-earmarked NGO funding, while both rights-based and security-focused peace-building approaches turned a blind eye to Yasser Arafat's legitimization and mobilization of hierarchical kinship-based structures.[14]

During an era when the international community allocated generous funds to Palestinian women's organizations, Khalil's NGO[15] was somewhat marginalized in terms of funding. Hanafi and Tabar (2005) assert that Western donor funding of Palestinian women's organizations was at that time dominated by an approach that differentiated between women's practical and strategic needs, favouring the latter.[16] That is why Khalil's income-generating organization (although it fits well into the self-help component of the neoliberal aid paradigm) was considered 'traditional', as a synonym for 'backward': it was seen as focusing on women's practical needs, instead of their strategic needs in comparison to more advocacy-oriented and gender awareness-raising organizations (Hanafi and Tabar, 2005: 91–115).[17]

Relationships between Khalil's presidential candidacy, the allegedly conservative gender conventions of her organization and the then current donor agenda for women's organizations shed light on the complications of supporting women in post-conflict transformations. Emphasising the role of and assistance to a 'globalized NGO elite' – that is, non-governmental organizations that have managed to create good relations with Northern NGOs – gender-aware development agencies can unintentionally contribute to privatization and professionalism of gender and competition among the women's movement over gender-earmarked donor resources. An aid regime that endeavours to change values, attitudes and behavioural patterns but is simultaneously security-centred may overlook women's political agency that is embedded in 'traditional' gender conventions but challenges those non-liberal political processes that characterize post-conflict transformations, as did Khalil's presidential candidacy.

Thus, gender as a cross-cutting attribute of citizenship practices in transitional periods is situational and strategically tied to the specific social and political context. Sometimes, exercises such as the Palestinian Model Parliament: Women and Legislation forum in the West Bank and the Gaza Strip in 1998, intended to promote gender equality, have in retrospect proved to be counterproductive for drafting a more inclusive citizenship for women (Jad, 2004; for a detailed analysis from the perspective of personal status legislation and for a literature review, see Welchman, 2000: 360–72). However, the Model Parliament was an important effort to open up a social debate. This exercise made visible exactly at which point Islamists, some important interlocutors of Islamic jurisprudence and social conservatives drew the line in social issues:[18] that is, the personal status law and who is 'legitimately' allowed to debate its drafting, codifying and application (Jad, 2004; Welchman, 2000; Jad et al., 2000).[19]

Gender issues were disputed in ways that are usual for post-conflict transitions in general rather than being specifically Palestinian: many stakeholders insisted on either keeping personal status matters 'private' or officially tying those matters to cultural and religious norms. This can be related to two issues. The first is the gradual revival of religion as a social force in Palestinian society and the fact that customary law and religion are connected and partially overlapping. The second issue is strategic. According to the Birzeit Law Institute study of informal conflict-resolution systems (2006a), many members of the Palestinian Legislative Council were elected on a clan basis, which President Yasser Arafat revived by giving official acknowledgement to kinship-based social organizations. As Mukhopadhyayi (2007: 15) reminds us in her discussion on gender justice, citizenship and development, traditional communities remain the prime sites in which rules are formulated and rights legitimized.

Drafting citizenship in conflict

Legal experts point out that conformity with international standards on the issues of citizenship presumes accountability and statehood (Khalil, 2006, 2007). Yet, one of the first measures that the PA carried out after the establishment of the non-sovereign self-government was to issue 'passports',[20] which manifests the importance that is attached to citizenship and mobility by a population, half of which is *de jure* stateless. In this section I review briefly recent scholarship by Asem Khalil and other Palestinian legal scholars in order to illustrate my premiss that drafting Palestinian citizenship is inseparable from transnationality.

Palestinian legislation (including Sharia legislation) is undergoing reform that is national in aspiration but thoroughly transnational in character. Laws that touch directly upon citizenship of the future Palestinian state are the Draft Citizenship Law in 1995 that was never adopted, the Basic Law for the Palestinian Authority in 2002, and the Draft Constitution 2001–2003. Although the Basic Law and the Draft Constitution recognize the principle of equality and non-discrimination (Birzeit University Institute of Law, 2006b) and the constitutional process is formally committed to equality and democracy, Sharia remains one of the legal sources (Welchman, 2000: 353–7; Khalil, 2006, 2007). Thus, the contours of future Personal Status Law will be important for the contents of formal *and* substantial citizenship.[21] However, from the perspective of women's rights it is important to note that each law that the Palestinian Legislative Council passes, whether economic, social or political, constructs the citizenship.

Defining citizenship of the future Palestinian state is overshadowed by the fact that every nation-state is exclusive. Because of the refugee problem, exclusion is the most painful undercurrent of the entire state-building project. Palestinian formal citizenship-making may also tell us something more general about transnational nation-state projects and citizenship forms in post-conflict situations that involve large and protracted population displacements. The PA is not a legal subject in the face of international legislation, and for this reason it is not capable of signing treaties. In other words, the PA does not have rights in the international community. Instead, the Palestine Liberation Organization (PLO) as 'the sole representative of the Palestinian people' has a legal character under international law and is the only authority able to sign 'treaties' 'on behalf of the PA'

(Khalil, 2006, 2007). Moreover, instead of the Palestinian Basic Law, agreements with Israel are the highest law of the land. Palestinian self-government enjoys a special status under international law: it is presumed to move towards statehood and may thus be described as a nascent state (Khalil, 2006, 2007).

The Palestinian Legislative Council[22] has three major areas of legal activity: the unification of legal systems of the Gaza Strip and the West Bank, considered as one jurisdiction; the 'purification' of the existing legislation from imposed 'colonial' provisions; and the creation of new laws and institutions. According to Birzeit University legal researchers, these objectives are directly linked to state-building and decolonization efforts (Birzeit University Institute of Law, 2006b: 5).

The contours of Palestinian state citizenship have been partly sketched in the Basic Law, in the Draft Constitution and by the Interior Ministry of the Palestinian Authority in a Draft Citizenship Law in 1995 that was never passed. The Basic Law (hereafter BL) is intended to regulate the relations between the powers in the PA during the transitional period. It was approved by the PLC and its implementation would be applicable in autonomous territories. It is intended to be replaced eventually by the constitution. It is significant for the dynamics of transborder citizenship that the BL's concept of the Palestinian nation and Palestinian people is not coherent. Usually, the BL refers to all Palestinians and sometimes only to WBGS and East Jerusalem (Khalil, 2007: 15). Thus, the BL has not formalized the separation between Palestinian nationality and citizenship (Jad, 2004: 6). Instead, it left the definition of citizenship to future legislation (Khalil, 2007: 16).

The former president the late Yasser Arafat appointed a special constitutional committee that prepared three drafts on 14 February 2001, 9 February 2003 and 14 May 2003. The Draft Constitution refers to Palestinians living in the WBGS and/or those who will enjoy citizenship in the future state of Palestine as the 'Palestinian people'. It also sketches some features of state-level transnationality: 'According to the Draft Constitution, the Palestinian state would incorporate the

PLO and the PA. Palestinian nationals who are not citizens will be represented by 150 members of the Advisory Council and their duties will be specified in the constitution' (Khalil, 2007: 16).

The Draft Constitution prevents Palestinians (and their descendents) who had been living within the 1948 territories but who left or were forced to leave from obtaining Palestinian citizenship automatically. In other words, mostly stateless refugees would not have the right to obtain Palestinian citizenship automatically under the Draft Constitution (Khalil, 2007: 40–41). This exclusion may be generally illustrative of the characteristics of citizenship in state formations that emerge in a post-conflict situation. I will return to this point later on. The relations between the WBGS and the diaspora may be redefined in future because the constitution needs to be approved by popular approval directly or through the people's representatives (PLC). There is always a chance that the constitution may not be accepted and that there may be a new draft (Khalil, 2007: 17).

The PA Interior Ministry drafted a Citizenship Law in 1995, but the law was never adopted. In the view of Palestinian commentators, the timing was too early and the citizenship, including institutionalizing the relationships between the Palestinian state and the diaspora, should not be codified within the given limitations.[23] Anes Kasem, former chairperson of the PLC Legal Committee, pointed out that in the Draft Citizenship Law, as in most Arab states, citizenship was understood as a gift from the government rather than as an individual right (Khalil, 2007: 40). His interpretation corresponds to my observations on political returnees' insights. For many Palestinians, the right of return has taken on the characteristics of a reward. Several people who had returned to the WBGS on political grounds explained to me in different ways how they had earned their return, which was given to them (by the embryonic state) as a reward.

Especially relevant from a gender point of view is the definition and passing down of citizenship. The first constitution draft made distinctions of gender and generations. Transferring citizenship from father to son – a definition that excluded Palestinian women's children and Palestinian men's daughters from citizenship – was applied only to Arabs who lived in Palestine before May 1948. After that date, sons and daughters of Palestinian men and women were considered Israeli or Palestinian citizens according to their place of birth (Khalil, 2007: 41).

Post-conflict legal pluralism and the subject of law: towards which citizenship model?

In January 2006, the Islamic Resistance Movement Hamas won a majority of seats in the Palestinian Legislative Council elections. The international community boycotted the Hamas-led government, halting assistance and freezing funds. However, the donor community emphasized its willingness to continue supporting 'the suffering Palestinian people', who, according to this line of argument, did not overlap with the Hamas voters. Executive power was eventually removed from the elected government and a Fateh-led government cabinet appointed. This contributed to an armed conflict between Fateh and Hamas, and consequently the Gaza Strip and the West Bank are governed by competing parties. The former is controlled by the Hamas movement and the latter is governed by a 'caretaker' government and different PA security forces.

Political divisions between geographical entities and a condition that borders on anarchy despite the existence of governmental infrastructure characterize many post-conflict transformations. It should not be assumed that there exists a national consensus on a vision for the nation's future reconstruction and its development priorities in social transformations that take place in the aftermath of conflict. Despite the emergence of fairly free and heterogeneous media in the self-governance era and the pluralism of political movements (Brown, 2005), the enduring conflict has meant that in Palestine there has been no neutral political space for debate to enable such a vision to emerge.

Palestinian state-building in the West Bank, East Jerusalem and the Gaza Strip is marked by legal pluralism, weak central governance and 'gradual sovereignty' (Ong 1999), indicating that residents are divided into several categories with respect to their rights to reside, move and participate in political processes. As a result of the Oslo Accords, the West Bank and Gaza Strip are divided into areas A, B and C. Self-governing cantons are separated from each other physically. In November 2007 I asked many people, 'Who is running the West Bank?' A common response was 'Nobody'. Yet my interlocutors believed that the PA will remain a fact on the ground and that marginalization of the PLO is still under way. Palestinian anthropologist Sharif Kanaana characterized the PA as a 'contractor state', an expression that points to the oligarchic transnational elements of Palestinian state-building as well as the technocratic caretaker government. In other words, the PA acts like a private contractor, whom Israel and the international community have contracted as a distributor. This has been a recurrent criticism among Palestinian laypeople since the late 1990s, and it reflects both the disadvantages that are specific to the Palestinian experience and the transnational dimensions common to post-conflict state-formation projects where international assistance and asymmetrical power relations play a role. Also outside the Palestinian context, a 'contractor-state' can typify security-centred aid to post-conflict transitional societies.

According to Mukhopadhyay (2007: 6), a key dilemma in the idea and practice of citizenship is the way in which citizenship, as a relationship between the state and the individual, is in reality a relationship between the state and groupings representing particular identities. These identities may be based on religion and/or on kinship groupings, tribe, ethnicity and other formations. Mukhopadhyay's argument could be extended to the Palestinian national project by relating it to interests and antagonisms: groupings do not only 'represent' particular identities. Palestinians in different groups also experience particular antagonisms in their relation to the conflict between Israel and the Palestinians as well as to the Palestinian state-building efforts.

Some groupings fall into bifurcations: refugees and non-refugees, West Bankers and Gaza Strip residents, townspeople and rural dwellers, Muslims and Christians, Palestinians in the WBGS and in the state of Israel. Jerusalemites are a particular group by reason of their anomalous legal status. Although categories are relevant in certain practical senses, the groupings overlap, and their boundaries are porous and open to exchange. Across the physical and political borders dividing the WBGS, East Jerusalem and Israel, Palestinians share traditions of belonging such as kinship-based social organization. The social structure has made a deep imprint on how political membership is distributed. Mounira Charrad (2007) argues that in societies of the MENA region, the incorporation of individuals into the political community and the state comes about via their belonging to kinship-based formations.

Palestinian legal pluralism consists of customary law, religious (mainly Sharia) law,[24] Israeli military orders, British Mandate law remnants, Jordanian laws from the period of Jordanian rule over the West Bank, and Egyptian laws from the period of Egyptian rule over the Gaza Strip (Birzeit University Institute of Law, 2006b: 4). This legal morass is applied in three judicial systems, which ideologically partially overlap. First, there is the formal court justice system, nizami, that applies the state law (kanun) in the spheres of civil and criminal legislation; second, there is the informal justice system that is based on regional and local customary law ('urf) and mediation (sulh); and third, Islamic law is applied in Sharia courts in matters of personal status. Judicial systems are partially divided on gender, both ideologically and practically.

Women can act as judges and lawyers in nizami courts and they can file cases. Of 116 judges, 11 (9 per cent) are female, whereas the percentage of female prosecutors is 12 per cent (ESCWA, 2005: 21). Without commenting on the contents and sources of the state laws,[25] the subject of civil law (and military orders) is an allegedly gender-neutral individual, which indicates an unmediated relation between a citizen and the state.[26] The 'state' legislation (kanun) that is applied in the formal court justice system (nizami) is not unified, owing to historical reasons and the prolonged Israeli occupation. The formal (civil and religious) judiciary is currently undergoing a reform that intends to unify legislation applied in the West Bank and the Gaza Strip. This is considered to be an important component of the state-building project. One aim of the legal reform is to change negative attitudes towards the state civil law, which stems from Palestinian history under different rulers.

Immediately after the occupation of the WBGS, Israel set up an infrastructure of military laws and courts. As a protest, West Bank lawyers initiated a strike that lasted until the 1980s. Consequently, informal justice was sometimes the only available alternative. Moreover, recourse to alternative systems to resolve disputes is socially encouraged as part of the resistance to occupation (Birzeit University Institute of Law, 2006b: 5). People still avoid civil courts for many reasons:[27] long delays in procedures 'kill' cases in comparison to the speedy proceedings of informal islah and sulh mechanisms. Moreover, a common perception is that going to an official court is expensive because of the lawyers' and the courts' fees (Birzeit University Institute of Law, 2006a).

In the informal justice systems all actors are men. Women cannot represent their cases or be present in central rites and procedures. They are represented by a male guardian, who stands for the family group. Thus, the subject of informal law is in essence collective instead of individual. It is embedded in kinship-based structures and sanctions; enforcement mechanisms and rulings are collective (Birzeit University Institute of Law, 2006a). This legal tradition is constituted in mediation and the established convention that both parties eventually accept the ruling that usually includes financial compensation, but might involve, for example, temporary expulsion from one's town or village (Birzeit University Institute of Law, 2006a). To make a rough generalization deduced from some insights from the early anthropology of conflict reconciliation (Gluckman 1973, 1977; cf. Bose, 2005), 'alternative conflict resolution mechanisms' and customary law are embedded in reciprocal kinship-based moral economies. Information from a recent study of Palestinian informal conflict resolution mechanisms (Birzeit University Institute of Law, 2006a) suggests that they are used by and large to maintain social order, which indicates that the rulings often take the side of the stronger party.

In Sharia courts, women can act as judges and file their cases in courts. However, there are only two female judges within the Sharia court system. Nahda Sh'hada (2005), in her study on Sharia courts in the Gaza Strip, emphasizes that judges are members of their communities. Informal justice (customary law) and Sharia as it is practised in Palestinian Sharia courts share this insight; customs are one of the sources of Islamic jurisprudence. In Gaza, Sharia court judges rule relatively often on women's benefits in individual cases – women are considered the weaker party. However, rulings never challenge gender ideology that is constituted in hierarchy and complementary roles rather than in equality between women and men (Sh'hada, 2005). In 'women-friendly' decisions it is problematic that Sharia courts are lacking effective enforcement mechanisms (Sh'hada, 2005). Islamic jurisprudence, fiqh (also outside the scope of personal status legislation), is gendered, and consequently, the subject of law is explicitly gendered. In practices such as male guardianship the relation between female subject and the law is explicitly mediated.[28] This accumulates the structurally mediated relationship between a gendered citizen and the state. Sharia court rulings, however, are individual.

These legal systems are based on different ideologies as regards the subject of law – that is, citizenship. However, Lynn Welchman's (2000) study of Sharia courts in the West Bank concludes, in a chapter on future personal status legislation, that customary rules frequently constitute a stronger controlling force than formal 'law', particularly in matters involving women and the family. Moreover, in a recent Birzeit University study of informal justice (2006a), several interviewees who are involved in these mechanisms characterized Palestinian society as 'tribal' and mentioned that informal conflict-resolution mechanisms are often used in gender-related cases, for example those relating to inheritance and 'honour'. The reports of the Gaza-based Palestinian Center for Human Rights verify this trend. Thus, customs and traditions create a social fabric that ties together and interweaves all judicial traditions. Islam is another interweaving moral discourse: all systems are partially constituted in religious norms and sometimes codified by religious persons.[29] Elements that are common to all judicial traditions indicate mediated citizenship that is based on hierarchical gender conventions and/or group membership.

The PA has utilized a kinship-based social structure that all Palestinians recognize, independent of their position towards it, together with an informal justice system, using both in ways that seriously undermine embryonic independent judicial power. Political parties that fight over other issues are uniform in their attitude towards the informal judiciary, which is treated either neutrally or positively. Both Fateh and Hamas rely on its procedures (Birzeit University Institute of Law, 2006a: 143). Why does a kinship system persist as a basis for mobilization and incorporation? Why do actors support the informal judicial system despite legal globalization and general rights consciousness? After all, human rights discourse is known among the Palestinians, and there are several Palestinian human rights NGOs. Moreover, the Basic Law and the Draft Constitution mention democracy, equality and non-discrimination.[30]

Several reasons can be identified. To begin with, as Lisa Hajjar (2005: 6) points out, international humanitarian laws (upon which a rights-based approach to gender draws) were not formulated to address a situation resulting from decades of military rule. Moreover, international human rights conventions, democracy and transnational interventions did not result in peace accords. Palestinians appealed to human rights and international law in several arenas without concrete outcomes. The donor community first activated the international human rights regime in a Palestinian political context concretely in a post-conflict framework, which was a result of peace accords that avoided a rights-based discourse.

Moreover, as mentioned earlier, the legalistic Israeli occupation has used laws mainly against the Palestinians. The Palestinians' steadfastness ideology was embedded and was made possible by a kinship-based moral economy of reciprocity in which family has been the central locus of the welfare contract. Such moral economies are not uniquely Palestinian, but typical of survival strategies in poor, developing countries. It has also been acknowledged that laws and citizenship have a limited capacity as tools for social change in the conflict circumstances that post-conflict stages often entail (Jad, 2004; Birzeit University Institute of Law, 2006b). Keeping in mind the characteristics of 'post-conflict' as elaborated at the outset, it is not surprising that a kinship-based social structure remains a meaningful reference, although its material and practical importance varies a great deal.

Development thinking and 'legal globalization', which indicates transnationalization of legal models, frameworks and ideas (Dezalay and Garth, 2002; Merry, 2006) are brought together in post-conflict state-building projects. One prominent manifestation of 'legal global-ization' is the human rights regime and its filtering of the issues of gender, development, peace and security through certain frameworks and instruments. The WBGS is undergoing legal reform partly as a result of international pressure, partly in response to internal requests since the late 1990s by laypeople, politicians, human rights activists and secular[31] and Islamist women activists alike.

Legal reform is seen by the donors as a step towards 'good governance' and 'democracy', concepts that remain at the centre of the international aid regime. Transnational interventions such as internationally driven post-conflict reconstruction programmes invade local or regionally specific legal spaces and rely on the as-sumption of law as a tool for social change and peace-building. Local lawmakers would sometimes like to codify norms that are based on a gender hierarchy, for example, to tie state legislation formally to Islamic Sharia and maintain informal judicial systems. Often such mechanisms respond to their electoral basis – that is to say, clans or other kinship groups. As mentioned earlier, members of PA bodies, including individual Legislative Council members, have revived kinship-based structures by acknowledging them officially. Numerous members of the PA security forces and also PLC members support and are actively involved in informal dispute-resolution mechanisms that are often used in gender-related cases, for example those relating to inheritance and 'honour' (Birzeit University Institute of Law, 2006a).

International human rights conventions and Western legal traditions have influenced the Palestinian constitutional process (Khalil, 2006) and continue to shape legal reform. The priority order of legal reform is partially imposed by international donors. Nevertheless, every new law (for example the election law, labour law or public retirement law) is seen through a prism of citizenship and followed by a burst of citizenship debate.[32] Thus, Palestinians could be characterized as a nation that is still in the process of deciding the norms by which it wishes to be governed.

Post-conflict legal reforms are meeting points of different normative and political agendas, and thus forums where women's citizenship is pulled in many directions. Increasingly, international post-conflict reconstruction and peace-building agendas take a positive attitude towards 'alternative', traditional conflict-resolution mechanisms and sometimes promote them (for example, in Guatemala, South Africa and, most recently, Somalia). Some feminist strategies for inclusive citizenship recommend 'positive engagement with legal pluralism' (Goetz, 2007: 19). Their emphasis is on identifying and building on those aspects of customary law and practice that accord women rights over resources. Goetz (2007: 19) promotes 'interpreting customary law in the light of human rights norms'. The Palestinian situation demonstrates that the relationships among rights-based approaches, legal pluralism, gender and citizenship are problematic and complex and provoke many questions regarding how to promote and protect women's rights in post-conflict social transformations.

Developmentalizing the diaspora – indications for gendered citizenship?

Nina Glick Schiller (2005) defines transborder citizens as people who live their lives across the borders of two or more nation-states, participating in the normative regime, the legal and institutional systems and the political practices of these various states. As do all citizens, she continues, they claim rights and privileges from the government, but transborder citizens make claims and act on a relationship vis-à-vis more than one government and political entities other than governments. These characteristics were a part of Salwa's citizenship practices, as discussed above. Glick Schiller's account must also be considered from a reverse angle, since transnational nation-states make claims on their transborder citizens (see, for example, Vertovec, 2004). Moreover, it is not unusual that 'extraterritorial nation-states' (Basch et al., 1994) expect different things from transborder citizens who live in different places. Palestinian evidence suggests that such claims are initiated before citizenship is formally drafted and before the state project is completed in terms of sovereignty. Consider an example from 1999, when a high-ranking PA civil servant, a returnee himself, sketched the relationship between the state-project and the diaspora:

> Our philosophy in the PLO, in the PA and here in the Department is to encourage investments but not permanent return. Be good Latins first but do not forget about Palestine … return [from Latin American countries] has nothing in common with refugees or return from the Arab countries. It's not about quantity, it's about quality. Fifty returns [from the Arab world] and each establishes a kiosk, one comes [from Latin America] and invests US$5 million.[33]

The above citation reflects 'an embryonic developmental characteristic of the emerging state' (Khan, 2004: 7): economic nationalism that tries to engage expatriate capitalists who could be potential development partners of the state. In order to shed light on the relationships among conflict, diaspora, social transformation and gender, it is important to examine whether Palestinian transnational social fields privilege different gender conventions and how such conventions are forged into a state-level transnationality. Because an overwhelming majority of expatriate capitalists are men, Palestinian economic nationalism is a male business, despite the fact that Palestinian mobility is by and large organized by kin and simultaneous lifestyles rely on women's contributions as well as men's.

Furthermore, the above citation illustrates mechanisms that are typical of state-level transnational practices related to development and security: several states of the global South, as well as international financial institutions such as the World Bank and the IMF, are trying to connect migrants to development.[34] In return for their investments, migrant-sending countries acknowledge migrants' contributions symbolically and politically without necessarily encouraging them to return permanently. The gender implications of these mechanisms vary according to context. The above citation refers to Palestinians in Latin America. Palestinian migration to South and Central America is rather different in terms of departure, social and political citizenship in destination countries, and lifestyle in comparison to the Arab world, for example, or some European countries.

Finally, the earlier quotation shows that institutionalizing the Palestinian transborder citizenship was under way at political and developmental levels, although the drafting of Citizenship Law was halted due to the limitations imposed by the political framings. The fact that a 'philosophy' that categorized the diaspora hierarchically in relation to development and return was enacted at the ministerial level suggests that the lines between formal and substantive citizenship are blurred in a transnational context. Where are socially vulnerable groups situated in the processes of drafting citizenship through 'developmental characteristics' – that is, the developmental potential of different diaspora groups? Many refugees do not have a state citizenship. Is hierarchical or gradual citizenship a characteristic of new state formations that emerge in post-conflict circumstances?

Conclusion

Gender is at the crux of post-conflict social transformations because codified gender relations and the formal subject of law are measures of either the endurance of traditional connections or the recognition of changes that every conflict causes in the relationships between women and men in a society. Post-conflict social transformations involve much claim-making and resource competition. The Palestinian experience suggests that, from the viewpoint of women's rights, it can be counterproductive if donors apply a rights-based approach only selectively and on conditions of security.

Three issues are particularly important. First, it is problematic to apply a rights-based agenda to gender successfully in conflicts that are lacking a rights-based political resolution. Such inconsistency may end up strengthening unequal gender relations.[35] Second, it is difficult and somewhat artificial to separate 'women's strategic needs' from their practical needs in post-conflict transitional situations. Third, given the premiss of this chapter, namely that post-conflict state-building projects are transnational enterprises, it is particularly important that the donor community considers carefully its attitude towards post-conflict legal pluralism. Even feminist strategies for inclusive citizenship increasingly suggest 'a positive engagement with legal pluralism', indicating that they be read through human rights conventions (Goetz, 2007). But how to combine human rights, equal rights for women and legal pluralism in a situation in which informal legal traditions do not allow women a presence in their procedures and where their rulings are collective? Formally recognizing or encouraging 'alternative dispute resolution mechanisms' may have negative consequences for women's citizenship rights in situations in which traditional structures are already vitally important instruments in maintaining communality in a setting that is physically divided by the conflict. Supporting legal structures constituted in group membership instead of in human rights may curtail women's rights both qua citizens and qua women.

From the vantage point of 2009, Palestinian transborder citizenship lacks coherence, reflecting its constitution in extreme legal pluralism and differentiated transnational social fields. This state of affairs raises several questions regarding women's rights and emphasizes the need to bring the notion of intersectionality into the discussions about women, war and reconstruction. Looking at the gender contours of transborder citizenship has shown that development thinking, legal globalization and culturally constructed social norms are involved in the forging of transborder citizenship in a post-conflict situation.

There is a need for further research on post-conflict transitions that take the complex gender–conflict–development–politics nexus seriously. The goal of gender equality is central to development thinking and to the modalities that are applied in post-conflict state-building aid. However, legal pluralism is a fact on the ground and involves processes that may promote community cohesion but that work against gender equality. In order to gain understanding of this subject area, it is not sufficient simply to analyse legal systems or citizenship as autonomous institutions (as legal scholars tend to do) or to limit attention to specific problems (as is characteristic of development thinking or human rights organizations). Finally, the focus on gender in post-conflict citizenship issues should not be limited to personal status legislation, the women's movement or the family.

Notes

1. Stemming from a wide analytical framework, my discussion is based on written and ethnographic data that are by no means representative. Ethnographic material for this discussion was collected in the WBGS and Israel during more than two years of fieldwork between 1996 and 2003, and again in November 2007.

2. For analyses of this term among the Palestinians, see Moors 1999; and in the transnational context Isotalo, 2005.

3. All family members' names have been changed in order to respect their privacy.

4. Yet family unification policies bring together different groupings' kin-based border crossing.

5. Discussions with Salwa, her children, siblings and parents at her home, workplace and political activities took place in November 2007.

6. In terms of international law.

7. These aspirations were illustrated, for example, in her contribution to invite politicians from Ramallah to Jerusalem.

8. In terms of formal state citizenship, this is an anomalous legal category that parallels statelessness.

9. When I commented on timing, Salwa reminded me that not only suspected members or supporters of the Islamist movement, but also many Fateh activists were imprisoned because of Israeli demands during that time. I was reminded of this fact also by Hamas supporters in interviews in 1997.

10. Maysoon's case is not that of dual citizenship: she has American citizenship and the right to reside in Jerusalem, which she obtained through marriage

via family unification. Most Palestinian Jerusalemites do not have Israeli citizenship. Instead, they have a permanent residency right and either Jordanian citizenship or a Jordanian travel document. Those who do not have a Jordanian citizenship are *de jure* stateless.

11. For example, gender equality is one of the goals of Finnish foreign policy and development cooperation through gender mainstreaming as a cross-cutting theme. See Ministry for Foreign Affairs of Finland, 2003. Moreover, several countries have UNSCR 1325 National Action Plans.

12. The Convention on the Elimination of All Forms of Discrimination Against Women, adopted in 1979 by the UN General Assembly, is often described as an international bill of rights for women.

13. United Nations Security Council Resolution 1325 was passed unanimously on 31 October 2000. It is the first resolution ever passed by the Security Council that specifically addresses the impact of war on women and women's contributions to conflict resolution and sustainable peace. See http://peacewomen.org/un/sc/1325.html.

14 One of Arafat's first presidential measures was to establish the Tribal Affairs Department through Presidential Decree no. 161 for the year 1994. This is considered the reconsolidation of the role of the informal justice system; Birzeit University Institute of Law, 2006a: 37. International attention was focused on the relationship between the Authority and the Islamist opposition movement and, to an extent, accusations of corruption in the PA.

15. In this organization women are taught sewing and hairdressing in order to learn professions that they can practise, even at home. Moreover, the organization's Inash el Usra College has programmes in Nursing and Secretarial and Medical Records. Traditional embroidery and food (the organization has a small food-processing factory) are sold and the organization runs a kindergarten. Inash el Usra also sponsors the university education of several young women. Society of Inash el Usra, 2007.

16 Recent discussions of gender and development suggest that it is very difficult to differentiate between and prioritize women's practical and strategic needs.

17. Also interviews with the author at Inash el Usra, February 1999.

18 Johnson and Hammami (1999) point out that in Palestine 'social issue' is a political term that refers primarily to gender issues and their conflicts.

19. This is also useful in identifying who is considered the Palestinian *ulama*.

20. In de facto terms the PA-issued 'passport' is a travel document, and exit and entry to the WBGS are strictly controlled by Israeli rules and regulations, which indeed remain the highest laws in the land.

21. Excellent analyses of interim personal status legislation, Sharia courts and gender in Palestine are in Sh'hada, 2005; Welchman, 2000.

22. The Legislative Council is the Palestinian elected parliament. Elections were last held in January 2006, when the Islamist Hamas movement won the majority of seats.

23. Author's interview with Reem Al-Botmeh, 19 November 2007, Birzeit University Institute of Law.

24. The Ottoman-introduced Mejelle system, a sectarian religious court system, prevails in the West Bank and Gaza Strip. Different Christian minorities have their own religious courts for matters of personal status.

25. The sources and principles of state legislation are heterogeneous and, to an extent, contradictory.

26. There are some exceptions, for example the requirement for a male guardian's approval when a woman applies for a passport. This practice is not valid any more.

27. Tobias Kelly's study (2006) presents an alternative view that underlines Palestinians' legal rights consciousness. According to him, West Bank Palestinians have considerable readiness to make claims through Israeli as well as Palestinian civil courts and to use them. He points out that in the beginning of the millennium there was an abundance of legal-aid NGOs in Ramallah, which helped Palestinians to seek their rights through the formal justice system.

28. The practice of male guardian is common to customary law and Islamic jurisprudence.

29. Thus, 'Islamist' is first and foremost a political term as regards legal reform.

30. Non-discrimination relates directly to gender equality.

31. The women's movement in Palestine used to be connected to political parties, whereas in the post-Oslo era it is to a large extent affiliated with secular NGOs. This does not mean that women activists are not religious. Thus, in this context the term 'secular' is primarily political – some women's organizations are affiliated with the Islamist movement.

32. Author's interviews with Reem Al-Botmeh, 19 November 2007, and Kamal Shafei, 20 November 2007, Birzeit University Institute of Law.

33. Interview with the author, Ministry of Planning and International Co-operation, 1 February 1999 and 7 February 1999.

34. For example, Mexico, the Philippines, India, Turkey, etc.

35. The contemporary Palestinian women's movement can be regarded as a social movement with a gender justice agenda.

References

Barakat, Sultan (2004) 'Setting the Scene for Afganistan's Reconstruction: the Challenges and Critical Dilemmas', in S. Barakat, ed., *Reconstructing War-Torn Societies: Afganistan*. London: Palgrave Macmillan.

Basch, Linda, Nina Glick Schiller and Cristina Szanton Blanc (1994) *Nations Unbound: Transnational Projects, Postcolonial Predicaments and Deterritorialized Nation-States*. Amsterdam: Gordon & Breach.

Birzeit University Institute of Law (2006a) *Informal Justice: Rule of Law and Dispute Resolution in Palestine. National Report of Field Research Results.* Birzeit, West Bank.

Birzeit University Institute of Law (2006b) *Legal Reform and the Process of De-colonization and State-Building in Palestine.* Project Document, not published.

Bose, Pradip P. (2005) 'Anthropology of Reconciliation: A Case for Legal Pluralism', in Samir D. Kumar, ed., *Peace Processes and Peace Accords.* New Delhi: Sage.

Brown, Nathan (2005) *Evaluating Palestinian Reform.* Democracy and Rule of Law Project, Carnegie Papers, Middle East Series, no. 59, June.

Charrad, Mounira (2007) Unequal Citizenship: Issues of Gender Justice in the Middle East and North Africa', in M. Mukhopadhyay and N. Singh, eds, *Gender Justice, Citizenship and Development.* New Delhi and Ottawa: Zubaan and IDRC.

Dezalay, Yves, and Bryant Garth, eds (2002) *Global Prescriptions: The Production, Exportation and Importation of a New Legal Orthodoxy.* Ann Arbor: University of Michigan Press.

Duffield, Mark (2001) *Global Governance and the New Wars.* London: Zed Books.

Galloway, Donald (2000) The Dilemmas of Canadian Citizenship Law', in Alexander Alenikoff and Douglas Klusmayer, eds, *From Migrants to Citizens: Membership in a Changing World.* Washington DC: Brookings Institution Press.

Glick Schiller, Nina (2005) 'Transborder Citizenship: An Outcome of Legal Pluralism within Transnational Social Fields', in Franz Bender Beckman and Keebit Bender Beckman, eds, *Mobile People, Mobile Law: Expanding Legal Relations in a Contracting World.* London: Ashgate.

Gluckman, Max (1973) *Custom and Conflict in Africa.* Oxford: Oxford University Press.

Gluckman, Max (1977) *Politics, Law and Ritual in Tribal Society.* Oxford: Oxford University Press.

Goetz, Anne Marie (2007) 'Gender Justice, Citizenship and Entitlements: Core Concepts, Central Debates and New Directions for Research', in M. Mukhopadhyay and N. Singh, eds, *Gender Justice, Citizenship and Development.* New Delhi and Ottawa: Zubaan and IDRC.

Hajjar, Lisa (2005) *Courting Conflict: The Israeli Military Court System in the West Bank and Gaza.* Berkeley: University of California Press.

Hanafi, Sari (2003) 'The Broken Boundaries of Statehood and Citizenship', *Borderlands* 2(3).

Hanafi, Sari, and Tabar, Linda (2005) *The Emergence of a Palestinian Globalized Elite: Donors, International Organizations and Local NGOs.* Jerusalem and Muwatin: Institute of Jerusalem Studies and Palestinian Institute for the Study of Democracy.

Heiberg, Marianne, and Geir Ovensen, eds (1993) *Palestinian Society in Gaza, West Bank, and Arab Jerusalem: A Survey of Living Conditions.* Fafo Report 151. Oslo: Fafo Institute for Applied International Studies.

Hilal, Jamil (2006) 'Emigration, Conservatism, and Class Formation in West

Bank and Gaza Strip Communities', in Lisa Taraki, ed., *Living Palestine: Family Survival, Resistance, and Mobility Under Occupation*. Syracuse NY: Syracuse University Press.

Isotalo, Riina (2005) *Many Routes to Palestine. The Palestinian Return, Forged Transnationalism and Gender*. Helsinki: Interkont Books.

Jad, Islah (2004) *Citizenship under a Prolonged Occupation: The Case of Palestine*. Berkeley CA: Berkeley Electronic Press.

Jad, Islah, Penny Johnson and Rita Giacaman (2000) 'Transit Citizens: Gender and Citizenship under the Palestinian Authority', in Joseph, Suad, ed., *Gender and Citizenship in the Middle East*. Syracuse NY: Syracuse University Press.

Johnson, Penny (2004) 'Agents for Reform: the Women's Movement, Social Politics and Family Law Reform', in Lynn Welchman, ed., *Women's Rights and Islamic Family Law: Perspectives for Reform*. London: Zed Books.

Johnson, Penny, and Rema Hammami (1999) 'Equality with a Difference: Gender and Citizenship in Transitional Palestine', *Social Politics*, Fall: 314–43.

Kaldor, Mary (2007) *Human Security: Reflections on Globalization and Intervention*. Cambridge: Polity Press.

Kelly, Tobias (2006) *Law, Violence and Sovereignty among West Bank Palestinians*. Cambridge: Cambridge University Press.

Khalil, Asem (2006) *The Enactment of Constituent Power in the Arab World: The Palestinian Case*. Basle: Helbing and Lichtenhahn.

Khalil, Asem (2007) *Palestinian Nationality and Citizenship: Current Challenges and Future Perspectives*. EUI: RSCAS.

Khan, Mushtaq (2004) 'Introduction: State Formation in Palestine', in Mushtaq Khan, George Giacaman and Inge Amundsen, eds, *State Formation in Palestine: Viability and Governance During a Social Transformation*. London: Routledge.

Kumar, Samir D., ed. (2005) *Peace Processes and Peace Accords*. New Delhi: Sage.

Kuttab, Eileen (2006) The Paradox of Women's Work: Coping, Crisis, and Family Survival', in Lisa Taraki, ed., *Living Palestine: Family Survival, Resistance, and Mobility Under Occupation*. Syracuse NY: Syracuse University Press.

Merry, Sally E. (2006) 'Anthropology and International Law', *Annual Review of Anthropology* 35: 99–116.

Ministry for Foreign Affairs of Finland (2003) *Strategy and Action Plan for Promoting Gender Equality in Finland's Policy for Developing Countries 2003–2007*. Helsinki.

Moors, Annelies (1999) *Women, Property, and Islam: Palestinian Experiences 1920–1990*. Cambridge: Cambridge University Press.

Mukhopadhyay, Maitrayee (2007) 'Gender Justice, Citizenship and Development: An Introduction', in M. Mukhopadhyay and N. Singh, eds, *Gender Justice, Citizenship and Development*. New Delhi and Ottawa: Zubaan and IDRC.

Mukhopadhyay, M., and N. Singh, eds (2007) *Gender Justice, Citizenship and Development*. New Delhi and Ottawa: Zubaan and IDRC.

Ong, Aihwa (1999) *Flexible Citizenship: The Cultural Logics of Transnationality*. Durham NC and London: Duke University Press.

PCBS (Palestinian Central Bureau of Statistics) (1997) *Demographic Survey of the*

West Bank and Gaza Strip: Final Results. Ramallah: Palestinian Central Bureau of Statistics.

PSR (Palestinian Center for Policy and Survey Research) (1996) *Palestinian Elections: Election-Day Survey*, 20 January. www.pcpsr.org/survey/polls/2008/p28e.html; accessed 15 January 2008.

Polfus, Turid Smith (2006) *Lobbying for Women's Rights in Palestine. The Strategies of the Palestinian Women's Movement 1994–2000*. Dissertation, University of Oslo.

Sh'hada, Nahda (2005) *Justice without Drama*. Maastricht: Shaker Publications.

Society of Inash el Usra (2007) *Four Decades of Service*. El-Bireh.

Taraki, Lisa (2006) 'Introduction', in Lisa Taraki, ed., *Living Palestine: Family Survival, Resistance, and Mobility Under Occupation*. Syracuse NY: Syracuse University Press.

Turner, Mandy (2006) 'Building Democracy in Palestine: Liberal Peace Theory and the Election of Hamas', *Democratization* 13(5), December: 739–55.

United Nations Economic and Social Commission for Western Asia (2005) *Social and Economic Situation of Palestinian Women 1990–2004*, UN doc. E/ESCWA/WOM/2005/Technical Paper 1, 3 June.

Vertovec, Steven (2004) 'Migrant Transnationalism and Modes of Transformation', *International Migration Review* 38(3), Fall: 970–1001.

Welchman, Lynn (2000) *Beyond the Code: Muslim Family Law and the Shar'i Judiciary in the Palestinian West Bank*. The Hague: Kluwer Law International.

Yiftachel, Oren, and Arnon Ghanem (2005) 'Understanding Ethnocratic Regimes: The Politics of Seizing Contested Territories', *Political Geography* 23(4): 647–76.

CONCLUSION

Gendering War and Transnationalism
in the Middle East

Nadje Al-Ali and Nicola Pratt

At the time of writing this last chapter, we had long stopped using
the terms 'post-conflict', 'reconstruction', not to mention 'peace',
when thinking and writing about the Occupied Palestinian Territories
and Iraq. Both countries are still in the midst of acute conflicts
and extensive and interlinked violence on many different levels:
violence by occupation forces, political violence, sectarian violence
and gender-based violence. Meanwhile, both Palestinians and Iraqis
continue to experience severe hardships and harsh living conditions.
Despite some of the similarities and links between the occupation
of and conflicts in Palestine and Iraq, the contributions in this
volume also point to significant differences in terms of historical
and political contexts, particularly in terms of the way gender and
(trans)nationalism intersect and interact.

In this final chapter, we aim to highlight some of the main points
and arguments raised in the various chapters, point to both similarities and differences between the Iraqi and Palestinian situations, and
try to address some of the wider issues and possible future research
agendas when thinking about women, war and transnationalism in

the Middle East. In light of the preceding chapters and the main findings of our contributors, we reflect on the set of questions that we initially posed with regard to the links between gender and transnationalism in contexts of conflict, conflict resolution and peace-building. Finally, we raise some methodological and political issues that have emerged in the context of our respective research projects and writing.

Transnational interventions and gender

The contributors here have all discussed different types of trans-national interventions by different actors in the context of Palestine and Iraq. These have included the European Mediterranean Partner-ship and EU Partnership for Peace Programme funding of civil society organizations and the international donor community's support for legal reform and constitution drafting as a means of peace-building and conflict resolution, but also the US invasion and occupation of Iraq and the ongoing Israeli occupation of Palestine. The outcome of these interventions is, for the most part, not positive with regards to ensuring women's rights and enabling women's involvement in 'post'-conflict reconstruction processes – despite a stated commitment to 'empower' women. The interventions considered here, at their best, are irrelevant to improving women's situation; for example, the EU Partnership for Peace Programme, which funds 'people-to-people' conflict resolution in a context in which there is limited political movement towards a just solution to the Israel–Palestine conflict or the Euro-Med Partnership that has been slow to mainstream gender into sectors beyond the economic and social spheres. At their most dangerous, transnational interventions empower actors and/or strengthen structures that undermine women's empowerment and women's rights, largely due to strategic security concerns.

In the Iraqi context, we see that the US invasion and occupation of Iraq have weakened the central state, strengthened ethnic/sectarian leaders and opened the way for the growth of the informalization of the economy and increasing inequality with regard to gender roles and relations. This has led to a *de jure* reversal in women's citizenship rights and a *de facto* deterioration in women's situation. Simultaneously, US funding of women's NGOs threatens to fragment and weaken the women's movement at a time in which women's collective agency for the sake of protecting their rights is more critical than ever.

In the Palestinian case, we see that ongoing Israeli occupation and international pressure on the Palestinian Authority (PA) to meet Israeli security demands severely limit the PA's administrative capacity to establish institutions that may guarantee women's rights, human rights and the rule of law, as well as reinforcing the significance of kin-based structures that marginalize women. It should come as no surprise that Palestinian women's grassroots activism is concerned to resist Israeli occupation, the single most important source of their deteriorating situation, rather than engage in building bridges with Israeli women activists on the basis of 'shared' gender interests.

Many of the authors here concur that the negative impact of transnational interventions is directly linked to the spread of neoliberalism – as both a practice, in terms of free-market reforms, and an ideology that valorizes the market as a route to development, peace and good governance. As V. Spike Peterson notes in her chapter, neoliberalism is 'promoted primarily by geopolitical elites in the interest of powerful states and the inter- and transnational institutions they effectively control'. Donor agencies, whether governmental, inter-governmental or multilateral, are involved in promoting neoliberalism through their policy prescriptions, their attempts to fashion new subjectivities and to create a new (trans-national) class of individuals embedded within the successful growth of neoliberal capitalism, as several of the chapters here illustrate. In both Palestine and Iraq, war and occupation represent opportunities for the spread of neoliberalism in the name of peace-building, conflict resolution and 'post'-conflict resolution. Yet, simultaneously, the restructuring of institutions, the economy and social relations creates new actors and new competition for resources, prestige and power, thereby contributing to further fuelling conflict, as Roland

Paris also argues with regard to UN peacekeeping operations in other parts of the world (Paris, 2004).

Shahrzad Mojab argues that local NGOs, often entirely supported by Western funding, have become a significant conduit for neo-liberalism. Yet, as Isis Nusair demonstrates, women's NGOs in the Arab world have also been crucial in pushing forward reforms of women's rights. In addition to local NGOs, and as other chapters here discuss, transnational networks include Western governments, Western aid agencies, Western-based NGOs and contractors, UN agencies, Iraqi and Palestinian official bodies and diaspora activists, as well as 'conflict entrepreneurs, war profiteers, traffickers, money launderers, and those who produce and/or transport trafficked goods' and who operate across borders (V. Spike Peterson in this volume). What emerges from the cases examined here is that transnational political fields are hierarchical and reflect global power inequalities. More powerful actors are able to co-opt less powerful actors in ways that strengthen neoliberalism and US global hegemony. Yet, particularly in a context of armed conflict and occupation, where national state institutions are weakened, transnational networks also provide resources, such as donor funding, that may be otherwise unavailable, thereby increasing the agency of less powerful actors, such as women's groups.

In some cases, resources gained through transnational networks may be used to resist neoliberalism and/or the occupation that accompanies it. Resistance also impacts upon gender relations. Resist-ance may take the form of non-violent activism, as Sophie Richter-Devroe describes in the Palestinian case, and thereby create new opportunities for women's agency and possibilities for women to challenge existing gender inequalities. Opposition to occupation may also take the form of armed resistance. In the Palestinian and Iraqi cases, women have joined armed militias and been part of military operations, thereby directly challenging the restriction of women's roles to the domestic sphere. However, as V. Spike Peterson discusses, the creation of 'combat economies' that finance resistance to oc-cupation often heavily overlap with criminal economies (smuggling of oil, for example) that are based on undermining someone else's ability to cope with the challenges of living in a conflict zone (such as rising fuel prices). It is usually women who bear the burden of household coping, and therefore there is an indirect link between women's deteriorating situation under occupation and the financing of resistance to occupation.

In addition to the socio-economic impacts of resistance to occupation, the greater threat to women's situation is often related to the ideological dimensions of resistance. This may take a variety of forms. In the case of Palestine, resistance is national – even if there are divisions between the secular-oriented Fateh and Islamist Hamas. In the case of Iraq, resistance is fragmented along geographical, sectarian and ethnic lines. In the Palestinian case, the growing Islamization of society that has accompanied the increasing political power of Hamas has resulted in the spread of particular notions of gender roles that certainly run counter to ideas of gender equality promoted by secular-oriented Palestinians. However, in the Iraqi case, not only are secularists in a small minority; the absence of a national resistance movement increases the pressure on women to conform to the conservative notions of gender roles and relations that mark boundaries between different sect-based or ethnic-based spheres of authority, as well as between the resisters and the occupiers, as described by Martina Kamp and ourselves in this volume. For example, in Basra the Mahdi Army has harassed women in public for not wearing the headscarf, for driving, as well as for going out to work. This is quite different from the experience of Palestinian women, who have managed to carve out a significant space for public activism in the name of nation-building and national resistance to Israeli occupation.

Implications of 'gender mainstreaming'

As Isis Nusair discusses in her chapter, gender mainstreaming in the context of conflict, post-conflict reconstruction and peace-building aims at transforming gender relations in ways that empower women as a means of building peaceful societies. These assumptions certainly underpin the funding of 'people-to-people' conflict resolution in the Palestinian case and women's political participation in the Iraqi case. As we mention in the Introduction, these assumptions are based on numerous feminist writings that posit a link between militarization, violence and masculinities. However, explicitly promoting gender equality through gender mainstreaming as a key to peace-building is brought into serious question in the chapters here. Sophie Richter-Devroe demonstrates that the types of dialogue activities funded by foreign donors and aimed at empowering women are perceived by the majority of Palestinians as irrelevant to supporting national resistance against Israeli occupation – the perceived major source of the conflict. In Iraq, funding for activities promoting women's political participation and lobbying of the constitutional drafting committee has categorically failed to bring an end to the conflict (let alone a protection of women's rights). Indeed, elections and constitution drafting have increased conflict and helped to fuel violence.

In other words, 'gender mainstreaming', as currently interpreted and practised by transnational and international actors, largely fails to address the causes of war and occupation, which include US empire-building, global energy demands, the strategic security interests of the West, the competition for political power and/or aspirations for nation-statehood. Indeed, neoliberal and neoconservative interpretations of gender mainstreaming as a part of conflict resolution and peace-building may operate to distract certain people from focusing on the political, economic and military interests that fuel the continuation of conflict. On the other hand, foreign attention to gender issues in the context of occupation may simply fuel a backlash against women's rights. In both scenarios, the promotion of gender mainstreaming by international donors may contribute to hardening perceptions of national and religious divisions in conflict situations, as gender is reproduced as a marker of difference.

Whilst women play a key role in (re)building their communities after conflict, and notions of femininity and masculinity are implicated in the mobilization for and sustenance of war and armed

conflict, gender cannot be considered in isolation from other structures of inequality that give rise to conflict and must be addressed as
part of resolving conflict. Despite several decades of feminist thinking
about intersectionality (as we briefly discussed in the Introduction),
gender mainstreaming as implemented by various donor agencies
continues to focus on adding 'women's bodies' in the public sphere
or on addressing legislation, policies and/or measures that directly
impact upon women as women. As Riina Isotalo argues in relation
to the impact of legal pluralism on women's situation in Palestine,
'the focus on gender in post-conflict citizenship issues should not be
limited to personal status legislation, the women's movement or the
family'. Rather, it should include consideration of a whole range of
institutions and processes (many of which are transnational in nature
and/or responses to occupation) that impact upon gender relations
and notions of femininity and masculinity. Martina Kamp's chapter
draws attention to the intersectionality of gender and communal
identities in defining (albeit not guaranteeing) a 'post'-conflict settlement in Iraq that is supported by the USA and its allies.

The above discussion implies the significance of gender in forging
alliances transnationally between different actors in the context
of war and conflict. The US invasion and occupation of Iraq, the
creation of combat and criminal economies, the resolution of the
Israel–Palestine conflict are not only transnational enterprises facilitated through transnational networks. They also assume particular
notions of femininity and masculinity and of gender relations.

In the case of Palestine, Riina Isotalo demonstrates how Palestinian
institution-building is dependent upon the construction of transnational social fields in which male members of the diaspora are
privileged over female. In the case of Iraq, Shahrzad Mojab describes
the alliance between the US administration and Kurdish women's
NGOs, and we discuss the alliance forged between the USA and
Iraqi women activists in the diaspora, based on the symbol of the
Iraqi woman as victim of Saddam Hussein. Simultaneously, the USA
has built alliances with Iraqi (male) political leaders on the basis of
ceding to them authority over gender relations – despite the lack of

influence granted to these leaders in other areas (Al-Ali and Pratt, 2009). As Martina Kamp demonstrates, the negotiation of women's rights in the constitution of 2005 constitutes a gendered colonial bargain in which Iraqi 'mediating elites' define their power in relation to domestic constituencies, as well as to the US administration.

Transnational feminism

In a context in which gender is instrumentalized by those actors who are implicated in war and occupation and where the international promotion of gender mainstreaming may intensify rather than ameliorate gender inequalities, what role can feminist/women's solidarity movements play and what sort of transnational feminist politics should be constructed in contexts of 'post'-conflict in order to support women's empowerment and peace-building?

We suggest that it is necessary to differentiate analytically between transnational feminist networks and campaigns that are *transnational in method* by virtue of their spanning borders and nation-states in terms of membership, networking, communication (especially the Internet) and lobbying, but not necessarily rooted in post-colonial, anti-imperialist and global justice approaches.

In other words, certain feminist organizations that are transnational in their method are not necessarily transnational in their politics, working with neocolonial, capitalist and militaristic government agendas. Some transnational feminist organizations, campaigns and networks might even reproduce certain structural inequalities pertaining to capitalist exploitation, colonial domination or racial inequalities while championing the cause of women's rights. This is evident, for example, in both the Iraqi and the Palestinian contexts, where feminist activists and gender-mainstreaming experts fail to recognize the intersectionality of structural oppressions and the diversity of women's experiences and subjectivities.

On the other hand, we can point to an emerging self-conscious transnational feminism that pays attention to intersections among nationality, race, gender, sexuality and other marks of difference in perpetuating economic exploitation, imperialism and neocolonialism. Self-proclaimed transnational feminist activists and organizations tend to pursue anti-capitalist, anti-imperialist, anti-militarist and anti-racist positions, whilst paying attention to the ways in which gender is inscribed in relations of power. Here, one can speak of feminist campaigns that are *transnational in content and practices*. Below is an excerpt from a statement by a group of self-proclaimed US-based transnational feminist theorists in response to the so-called war on terror, which encapsulates the intersectional analysis described above:

> First and foremost, we need to analyze the thoroughly gendered and racialized effects of nationalism, and to identify what kinds of inclusions and exclusions are being enacted in the name of [US] patriotism [and that] play a central role in mobilization for war. We see that instead of a necessary historical, material, and geopolitical analysis of 9–11, the emerging nationalist discourses consist of misleading and highly sentimentalized narratives that, among other things, reinscribe compulsory heterosexuality and the rigidly dichotomized gender roles upon which it is based.... These include the masculine citizen-soldier, the patriotic wife and mother, the breadwinning father who is head of household, and the properly reproductive family. We also observe how this drama is racialized. Most media representations in the US have focused exclusively on losses suffered by white, middle-class heterosexual families even though those who died or were injured include many people of different races, classes, sexualities, and religions and of at least 90 different nationalities. Thus, an analysis that elucidates the repressive effects of nationalist discourses is necessary for building a world that fosters peace as well as social and economic justice. (Bacchetta et al., 2001)

The involvement of diasporas in transnational networks with regard to countries in conflict complicates the picture even further and raises a number of issues in relation to transnational politics. On the one hand, diaspora activists may provide important bridges between activists in the North and those in the South. They are able to mobilize necessary resources to send back to their countries of origin, in order to contribute to their rebuilding. On the other hand, the desire of diaspora activists to participate in the nation from outside, through involvement in international political advocacy, as well as social welfare and development projects within their countries of origin, may be perceived as an attempt to capitalize on their diasporic positions to create new hierarchies of power within those countries. This is often perceived to be at the expense of those who 'stayed behind' and who may have suffered persecution and deprivation, losing loved ones, their livelihoods and their health.

Moreover, women from the diaspora are often even more vulnerable to feelings of resentment or active discrediting on the part of local actors. As women, they may be seen as 'instruments' of foreign powers, double agents, or traitors to their 'authentic' cultural roots. This trend has been particularly evident in the Iraqi context where the diaspora has played a disproportionate role in the new Iraqi leadership, supported by the USA, and where US-based Iraqi women have benefited from US funding to establish NGOs within Iraq. Simultaneously, the political involvement of diaspora women might provoke resentment among local women's rights activists who perceive them as patronizing and part of a 'Western ploy' (as our chapter illustrates). Meanwhile, the politics of diaspora mobilization, often focused on the rebuilding of the nation, may be diametrically opposed to transnational feminist politics, which seeks to highlight the ways in which national and state processes involve the construction of hierarchies of power and oppression. This is obvious in the Iraqi Kurdish but also in the Palestinian situation, where nationalist politics and sentiments play an important role among women's rights activists. However, as Sophie Richter-Devroe argues, transnational feminism should support Palestinian women's struggle for self-determination if it is to have any relevance to women there.

The feminist conundrum

The tension between an anti-national, feminist approach that fails to address the significance of the nation-state for securing women's rights and human rights, on the one hand, and a feminist politics embedded within nationalist movements that fails to address the subordination of women within nationalist projects, on the other hand, is not easily resolved by transnational feminism and an intersectional analysis. This is particularly the case in contexts of war and occupation where it may be difficult and dangerous to conduct a full assessment of the structures of power emerging and evolving.

Isis Nusair stresses in her chapter, building on the earlier works of feminist scholars such as Cockburn (1998, 2004, 2007) and Enloe (2000, 2004, 2005), that sustainable peace in the Middle East, as in regions elsewhere around the world, requires a transformation of gender roles, including a focus on women's political rights and participation, property rights, non-discrimination in employment, and the right to freedom from violence as well as addressing the gender-specific traumas of conflict. At the same time, transnational peace and gender mainstreaming initiatives are bound to be viewed with suspicion if they fail to be truly intersectional, which, in the context of Palestine and Iraq, means also a condemnation of and struggle against the occupation. Moreover, gender mainstreaming, as Nusair argues, can all too easily turn into cosmetic changes which fail to address the underlying structures and processes of inequality and social injustice.

In the context of the so-called war on terror, the appropriation by Western governments and international agencies of a terminology previously used by transnational feminists has not only led to a backlash against women's rights and feminists within the Middle East, but has also resulted in a distorted interpretation as neoliberal and neoconservative agendas converge. As our work on Iraq has shown, gender mainstreaming and women's empowerment in the context of the Iraqi occupation have in practice a conservative, depoliticized and largely cosmetic approach, focusing on democracy training and income-generating projects.

Sophie Richter-Devroe's contribution focusing on Palestine leaves us in no doubt that transnational feminist as well as peace initiatives will be viewed with suspicion and continue to fail as long as the Israeli occupation of Palestine continues. UN resolution 1325 cannot be used effectively as a political tool by either the Palestinian authorities or Palestinian women's rights activists as long as UN resolutions pertaining to occupation, settlements and compensation are not addressed by the Israeli government. Richter-Devroe argues that most Palestinian men and women alike view feminist anti-nationalist politics and attitudes as antithetical to their cause. Yet, Shahrzad Mojab argues convincingly, referring to the Iraqi Kurdish context, that nationalism stands in the way of transformative gender politics and hinders a feminist analysis of and struggle against gender-based violence and inequalities.

The complex and vexed relationship between gender and transnationalism in the context of war and conflict, international peace initiatives, political transition, development programmes and diaspora mobilization is inextricably linked to the troubled relationship between gender and nationalism. The question as to whether nationalism and feminism are compatible or mutually exclusive has been a source of contestations and tensions among feminist scholars. What emerges in the various chapters focusing on Palestine and Iraq is that we need to pay careful attention to the specific historical context and current constellation of political and social forces when we analyse a particular nationalism.

First of all, we have to distinguish between different forms of nationalism, whether exclusive, expansive, driven by xenophobia and racism, or those related to liberation struggles. But we also have to examine carefully the specific form and underlying ideology of resistance movements in the contexts of invasions, imperialist encroachment and military occupations. Second, the tensions between gender, nationalism and transnationalism cannot be resolved per se, and also require not only an intersectional but an in-depth empirical approach to grasp the full complexity and nuances of a specific context. We, as feminists, are challenged to examine carefully and assess the form and content of the respective national struggle, the specific transnational interventions and activities, and also, significantly, the various ways resistance is articulated and expressed. Depending on the ideological undercurrents and the context of nationalism and transnationalism, political and social spaces can either open up or close down for women, and gender ideologies and relations can be redressed in terms of both progressive and regressive attitudes and policies.

Gendering war and conflict

The contributions in this volume build on feminist scholarship which recognizes that a gendered analysis – similar to gender mainstreaming – should not simply be equated with 'add women and stir'. Instead, a gendered analysis involves an integration of gender conceptually – and in practice – on both state and non-state levels. Rather than looking at the 'feminine' and 'masculine' as states of being, we suggest it is important to explore processes of feminization and masculinization as both relational and dynamic. As the various contributors have shown in the contexts of Palestine and Iraq, processes related to gender identifications and gender relations are affected by and, in turn, impact upon the development of conflict, the militarization of society, surges in violence (including gender-specific violence such as harassment, verbal and physical abuse, and rape), invasions, open warfare, war economies, occupations, migration, internal displacement, settling in another country, peace-building, subsiding of conflicts and, potentially, post-conflict (re)construction.

Gendering war also involves more than paying attention to instances of gender-specific violence, as often tends to be the case. In our work on Iraq (Al-Ali, 2007; Al-Ali and Pratt, 2009) we have attempted to demonstrate the continuum of violence by exploring the historical development of the Iraqi state, its prevailing gender ideologies and policies during years of state violence, the militarization of society, the increasing glorification of a militarized masculinity, the links between violence sponsored by state and non-state actors, and the ways in which patriarchal authoritarianism has pervaded all aspects of the political system and society. We have also explored the attempts by women to resist, accommodate or support different moments of violence. In this volume, we have focused on diaspora mobilization of Iraqi women and the role of transnational feminism in campaigning for women's rights while either promoting the invasion or calling for an end to the occupation. We have also explored how the failure of a gendered approach to political transition has not only led to a conservative shift in gender ideologies and relations but has also fed into communal and sectarian sentiments and conflicts.

While international relations (IR) remains largely gender-blind – despite the many and excellent critiques by feminist IR scholars – feminist sociologists and anthropologists have managed to put 'gender as a structural feature' more firmly on the agenda. Whether in terms of explicit patriarchal relations and ideologies, social and cultural norms, constructions of identities, family relationships and dynamics, social institutions, labour market participation, political decision-making processes, social movements and migration, sociologists and anthropologists have generally become more conscious of and have taken a greater interest in the different experiences of men and women. Nevertheless, in many studies, especially with respect to the Middle East, gender continues to refer merely to an exploration of the ways women are affected by and impact upon various developments and processes. And within Middle East Studies, women and gender studies continue to be ghettoized, as evident in international conferences and major publications.

However, we are increasingly witnessing an emergence of a new scholarship on the region that combines historically grounded and in-depth empirical insights with an awareness of and engagement with debates within gender studies and feminist scholarship. Much work remains to be done to unearth the gendered dimensions of violence, conflict, wars and occupations in the region, both historically and in the contemporary context. We must reveal further insights into the various ways global capital is linked with existing and emerging war economies, and how these war economies have aggravated patterns of gender inequality and gender-based violence, as well as contributing to the erosion of local livelihoods and the criminalization of the economy, as V. Spike Peterson outlines in this volume.

Furthermore, gendered analyses of conflict in the Middle East need to pay greater attention to the social, economic and political position of women *and* men before and during conflict, and, where and when possible, in the transition to post-conflict. To this end, we have to explore more carefully what happens to men and masculinities before, during and after conflict. There have been many good reasons for our focus on women over the past decades, given the virtual invisibility and absence of women in earlier scholarship. However, it is high time that scholars on the Middle East looked more systematically and critically at the category 'men' and studied the relational dimension of gender in greater detail. How are hegemonic and subordinate masculinities (Connell, 1995) constructed, resisted and subverted? What is the relationship between long-term foreign occupation, the militarization of societies, such as Iraq and Palestine, and prevailing notions of men and masculinities? What are the parameters and channels for contesting hegemonic masculinities? What are the historical and contemporary circumstances in which men are more willing and able to negotiate new forms of gender relations and are more open to agendas of social justice and equality?

Methodological and political considerations

Conducting research on the gendered and transnational dimensions of conflict and war raises a series of methodological and political issues. In terms of theoretical frameworks and tools, any research within this framework would have to be inter- and multidisciplinary. Depending on the specific topic, relevant disciplines might include anthropology, sociology, political science, international relations, migration/refugee/diaspora studies and the emerging disciplines of war and peace studies. Within these various disciplines, it is predominantly feminist scholarship that offers useful and appropriate concepts and tools when trying to discuss the interrelationships between gender and transnationalism in the context of conflict, war, post-conflict reconstruction, conflict-resolution and peace-building.

As has been repeatedly the case, feminist scholars are challenged not only to work across disciplines and be aware of the theoretical debates and developments in various relevant disciplines, but also to engage with their own specific discipline, avoiding the ghettoization that is part of all of our work. Can we as feminist scholars make an impact on 'mainstream scholarship' without losing our feminist edge, vision and politics? Are we eternally damned to make up 'ladies' panels', as we are sometimes called in the context of international conferences or, alternatively, become token women to avoid accusations of being gender-blind?

Rather than victimizing ourselves, we need to look for creative ways of engaging with the situation. Strengthening our networks with like-minded feminist scholars is a good first step. As our scholarship and our networks grow, it becomes increasingly difficult for 'mainstream' scholars to ignore us. Our academic networks may parallel the transnational networks that we study. For those of us who are both academics and activists there might be overlapping networks and alliances, but also potential tensions. How does our positionality as academics, as 'experts', impact on our alliances in terms of power relationships and decision-making processes? Our intellectual involvement might discredit our roles as activists and vice versa. We might, however, also gain a certain level of prestige and power from our double act. We have discussed the opportunities and problems of being activist academics elsewhere (Al-Ali and Pratt, 2006), but any researcher exploring issues related to gender, conflict, post-conflict reconstruction and peace-building cannot help but be political (even if not in the activist sense) in approach to, and writing and presentation of, findings. The specific politics that informs research on gender is obviously wide-ranging and might include anti-militarist, pacifist, anti-imperialist, anti-capitalist but also (neo)liberal orientations.

In terms of political alliances and strategies for transnational feminism, the question of how to protect human rights and women's rights at the local level while avoiding a backlash against women's rights is a core dilemma. How do we avoid being instrumentalized by imperialist and neoliberal governments and institutions? How do we maintain a balance between recognition of and respect for cultural specificity without falling into the pitfalls of cultural relativism and liberal multiculturalism? How do we avoid naive universalism and humanism while holding on to universal declarations and principles of human and women's rights?

These questions are of course not new and have been globally addressed by feminist activists and scholars for decades. This book is a product of our own and our contributors' thinking through and engaging with these issues with regard to the specific empirical realities of the contemporary Iraqi and Palestinian situations. We urge other scholars to investigate these and similar issues in the context of war, post-conflict reconstruction and peace-building in other areas, in order to deepen our understanding of the intersections of gender and transnationalism and their implications for women and for men.

References

Al-Ali Nadje (2007) Iraqi Women: Untold Stories from 1948 to the Present. London: Zed Books.

Al-Ali, Nadje, and Nicola Pratt (2006) 'Researching Women in Post-invasion Iraq: Negotiating "Truths" and Deconstructing Dominant Discourses', Bulletin of the Royal Institute for Inter-faith Studies 8(1/2): 1–22.

Al-Ali, Nadje, and Nicola Pratt (2009) What Kind of Liberation? Women and the Occupation of Iraq. Berkeley: University of California Press.

Bacchetta, Paola, Tina Campt, Inderpal Grewal, Caren Kaplan, Minoo Moallem and Jennifer Terry (2001) 'Transnational Feminist Practices against War', October. www.geocities.com/carenkaplan03/transnationalstatement.html.

Cockburn, Cynthia (1998) The Space between Us: Negotiating Gender and National Identities in Conflict. London: Zed Books.

Cockburn, Cynthia (2004) 'The Continuum of Violence: A Gender Perspective on War and Peace', in Wenona Giles and Jennifer Hyndman, eds, Sites of Violence: Gender and Conflict Zones, pp. 24–44. Berkeley: University of California Press.

Cockburn, Cynthia (2007) From Where We Stand: War, Women's Activism and Feminist Analysis. London: Zed Books.

Connell, Robert (1995) Masculinities. Cambridge: Polity Press.

Enloe, Cynthia (2000) Maneuvers: The International Politics of Militarizing Women's Lives. Berkeley: University of California Press.

Enloe, Cynthia (2004) The Curious Feminist: Searching for Women in a New Age of Empire. Berkeley: University of California Press.

Enloe, Cynthia (2005) 'What if Patriarchy is "the Big Picture"? An Afterword', in Dyan Mazurana, Angela Raven-Roberts and Jane Parpart, eds, Gender, Conflict and Peacekeeping, pp. 280–84. Lanham MD: Rowman & Littlefield.

Paris, Roland (2004). At War's End: Building Peace after Civil Conflict. Cambridge, Cambridge University Press.

About the Contributors

Nadje Al-Ali is Reader in Gender Studies and Chair of the Centre for Gender Studies, at the School of Oriental and African Studies (SOAS), University of London. Her main research interests revolve around gender theory; feminist activism; women and gender in the Middle East; transnational migration and diaspora mobilization; war, conflict and reconstruction. Her publications include *Iraqi Women: Untold Stories from 1948 to the Present* (2007); *New Approaches to Migration* (ed., 2002); *Secularism, Gender and the State in the Middle East* (2000) and *Gender Writing – Writing Gender* (1994), as well as numerous book chapters and journal articles. Her most recent book (co-authored with Nicola Pratt) is entitled *What Kind of Liberation? Women and the Occupation of Iraq* (2009). She is also a founding member of Act Together: Women's Action for Iraq (www. acttogether.org) and a member of Women in Black UK.

Riina Isotalo is Researcher in Gender Studies in Law, University of Helsinki. Her publications include articles and book chapters on return migration, identity politics and post-conflict processes, as well as gender, politics and transnational mobility. Riina's research interests include security and transnational mobility and the intersections of gender and violence in conflict-management practices.

Martina Kamp is a research fellow at the Institute for Social Sciences at the Carl von Ossietzki University, Oldenburg, and a member of the research group 'Migration and Gender' within the Institute. She has been researching and writing on the history of the Iraqi feminist movement.

Shahrzad Mojab is Professor at the Department of Adult Education and Counselling Psychology, University of Toronto (OISE/UT). Her areas of research and teaching are: educational policy studies; gender, state, diaspora and transnationality; women, war, militarization and violence; women, war and learning; and feminism, anti-racism, and colonialism and imperialism. She has published extensively on such topics as 'Islamic Feminism'; feminism and nationalism; education, state and ideology; women's NGOs, transnationalism, and diaspora; feminism, fundamentalism and imperialism. She is the editor of *Women of a Non States Nation: The Kurds*, co-editor of *Of Property and Propriety: The Role of Gender and Class in Imperialism and Nationalism*, and of *Violence in the Name of Honour: Theoretical and Political Challenges*. She is currently conducting research on war, diaspora and learning; women political prisoners in the Middle East; war and transnational women's organizations; and civic education curricula as experienced by immigrant youth from war zones.

Isis Nusair is Assistant Professor of Women's Studies and International Studies at Denison University, Ohio. She teaches courses on transnational feminism; feminism in the Middle East and North Africa; and gender, war and conflict. Isis previously served as a researcher on women's human rights in the Middle East and North Africa at the Women's Rights Division of Human Rights Watch, and at the Euro-Mediterranean Human Rights Network. She is the co-editor with Rhoda Kanaaneh of an anthology on Palestinians in Israel (forthcoming from SUNY Press). Her other publications include 'Orientalism and the Politics of Torture at Abu Ghraib'.

V. Spike Peterson is a Professor in the Department of Political Science at the University of Arizona, with affiliations in Gender and Women's Studies, Institute for LGBT Studies, and International Studies. She is also an Associate Fellow of the Gender Institute at the London School of Economics. Her most recent book, *A Critical Rewriting of Global Political Economy: Reproductive, Productive and Virtual Economies* (2003), examines intersections of ethnicity/race, class, gender/sexualities and national hierarchies in the context of neoliberal globalization. She edited *Gendered States: Feminist (Re)visions of International Relations Theory* (1992) and co-authored (with Anne Sisson Runyan) *Global Gender Issues in the New Millennium* (2010). Her current research focuses on informalization, intersectionality and global insecurities.

Nicola Pratt is Associate Professor in the International Politics of the Middle East, University of Warwick. She teaches and researches on Middle East politics and feminist international relations. She is author of *Democracy and Authoritarianism in the Arab World* (2007), as well as other articles and book chapters on civil society, democratization and human rights in the Arab world. With Nadje Al-Ali, she is co-author of *What Kind of Liberation? Women and the Occupation of Iraq* (2009). She is currently conducting research and writing on gendering security in the Arab world. Nicola is an active member of the Stop the War Coalition and Women's International League for Peace and Freedom.

Sophie Richter-Devroe is a Ph.D. student at the Institute of Arabic and Islamic Studies, Exeter University. Besides a general research interest in women's activism in the Arab world and Iran, her Ph.D. research focuses on gender and conflict transformation in the Palestinian Occupied Territories, looking at both women's integration in Track II dialogue-based conflict-resolution programmes and their participation in various forms of formal and informal resistance activism. Sophie has studied Arabic and Persian to an advanced level. Her publications include translations and reviews of Arabic literary work as well as academic publications on Palestinian and Iranian women's activism.

Index